Stop The Train! I Want To Get On

Rediscovering New Zealand Railway Journeys
Graham Hutchins

EasyRead Large

Copyright Page from the Original Book

First published 2014

Exisle Publishing Limited,
P.O. Box 60-490, Titirangi, Auckland 0642, New Zealand.
'Moonrising', Narone Creek Road, Wollombi, NSW 2325, Australia.
www.exislepublishing.com

National Library of New Zealand Cataloguing-in-Publication Data

Hutchins, Graham.
Stop the train! I want to get on : rediscovering New Zealand railway
journeys / Graham Hutchins.
Includes bibliographical references.
ISBN 978-1-77559-139-9
1. Hutchins, Graham—Travel—New Zealand. 2. Railroad travel—
New Zealand—Anecdotes. 3. New Zealand—Description and travel.
I. Title.
385.0993—dc 23

ePub ISBN 978-1-77559-188-7
Version 1.0

Text design and production by IslandBridge
Cover design by Dexter Fry

TABLE OF CONTENTS

Also by Graham Hutchins and published by Exisle:

Last Train to Paradise
Great New Zealand Railway Journeys
It's Just a Game
Once Upon a Cowpat
Eight Days a Week

Acknowledgements

I wish to credit the assistance of Hamilton City Libraries in research matters and to thank the following people who contributed material to this book: J.D. Fitzgerald, Perry Rice, Keith Rimmer, D.R. Simpson and Russell Young.

The assistance of D.R. Simpson, J.D. Fitzgerald, K.B. Ward, J.A.T. Terry, Terry Bishop and Russell Young in providing photographs is also gratefully acknowledged.

Introduction

Trains were always there. Growing up in Te Kuiti in the 1950s and 1960s – the golden weather days, fading somewhat as the '60s advanced – you accepted trains and the railways as an integral, intermingling force. In the less complicated years of boyhood they had a decided romantic presence. In the mounting complexity of teenage years when romance took on a more personalised character, the good old trains still steamed – or dieseled – their way through our small-town lives.

Friday night in Te Kuiti circa 1963–64. Late afternoon, after school – and the action had already started. Pat and I were thumbing through the glossies at the stationery shop. *Popular Mechanics, Playdate* (a photo of the ugly Rolling Stones, Sandy Edmondes in tight-fitting vinyl). The stationer was edging closer as it became obvious we weren't paying customers. 'Just looking thanks.'

'Well go look elsewhere.'

We did.

The goods express roared north. Pat and I were joined by Sam, whose asthma was playing up as the oil smoke from the KA-hauled express wafted over the main street. Lawrence and his crowd of thugs confronted us outside the billiards saloon. 'We'll beat you bastards tomorrow,' Bug Thomas, their mouthpiece, reckoned. Tomorrow – who cared? We'd beat the bastards at Rugby Park. We had the fitness. Apart from Sam.

Image A

Te Kuiti railway yards and station, 1963. Engine KA 953 and train 403 are about to head south. The station and main street, where we spent a lot of our youthful time, are off to the right.

The five o'clock siren sounded. A diesel-driven southern goods ghosted in. Phil, who had joined us outside the record shop, reckoned he was getting peckish. The AB shunter in the yard made quite a commotion as it shunted that which the diesel-driven goods had bequeathed. Night was falling and the job had to be done. And Phil's father, the AB driver, had to get to the club before the six o'clock swill was over.

Friday night was heating up. Karen B and her friend Alison walked past in matching sweaters. Hoped they were going to the movies, as we were. Another diesel, one we didn't recognise in the half light, barked as it slid down the Waitete Embankment. 'Still like steam best,' said Russ, who had latched on outside Jerry's milk bar.

Tom played the jukebox, number 23D. 'Last train to San Fernando' by Johnny Duncan. Then Tom joined us as we went into Brown's and ordered our fish and chips. 'What's on at the movies, boys?' Mr Brown asked. According to Pat it was a double feature – a western followed by a black-and-white murder. Suddenly, unscheduled, a speeding JA-hauled goods train headed south.

'Late freight,' said Mr Brown, before ducking away to begin our fry up. Melanie Hayward, looking like Rita Hayworth, came into the fish and chip shop. Me, Pat, Sam, Phil, Russ and Tom said nothing. I think she smiled at me but she was probably drunk. Phil reckoned she was always drunk.

We wandered over to the station in good time to set up on the platform seats before the express came in. Don joined us, after helping his parents stack tins of corned beef at their grocery. Melanie Hayward clicked her way down the platform in her stilettos and fur coat. *God she looked like Rita Hayworth.* Similar name too, Don pointed out. Had he been reading my thoughts? The station porter, Harry, glowered at us as we put away a total of 7s 6d worth of fish and chips and a few sausages. He didn't like the notion of us vagrants eating in a public place – his station – as the express came in. Not a good look.

The express was running ten minutes late. 'Hope you fellas have finished your meal by then.' Harry threw the words over his shoulder, not really sure if he had the legal right to move us on.

The express usually arrived at 7.40 and the movies started at eight. Tom did the maths: 7.50 it would be, and after ogling the passengers, particularly the pretty ones, as they either made for the refreshment rooms or sat, expressionless in their carriage seat, it would take a bit of a sprint to catch the first spool of Jack Palance, the varmint and Randolph Scott, the sheriff, deciding on the best time for the former to get out of town. Sundown probably. You could rack that up based on experience. Coincidentally, the sun had just gone down in Te Kuiti.

Doug the drunk lurched out of the shadows as the express slowed beyond the Ward Street signal box. It was a KA tonight. The most powerful steam engine. Tom was hoping for a JA, his sleek favourite. The last of the chips were quaffed and the wrappings wedged behind the seat, just as Lawrence and his monkeys loomed out of the shadows and the express, with its brightly lit carriages eased and squealed to a stop.

At exactly 7.51 a black shadow covered those passengers who hightailed it to the refreshment rooms. Melanie Hayward, as cool as you like, waited patiently until it was safe to climb aboard. God knows where she was going but you wished you knew. Harry the porter jumped around like a jumping jack as luggage and baggage – is there a difference – was taken down or loaded up.

It was now 7.58 and we had to go. The KA was rejoining the express after topping up with water. Melanie Hayward was on board – in a sleeper, if you could believe Tom, and you couldn't always. Everyone in Te Kuiti knew what happened in the sleeper cars.

Image B

A restored JA engine in 2008. It used to be
Tom's favourite but it was mine too. This one
is out of the Steam Incorporated stable.

'Not a lot of sleeping,' Pat yelled as we ran
from the station.

The double feature ground on. Some of us
slept through the last half hour. Then it was
time to return to the station, after a pie at the
pie cart, to wait for the Limited. It was on time,
and much to Tom's delight, had two JAs at its
head – a long Friday-night train. Most of the
passengers were already asleep.

We walked home in those days. No one
owned cars, and besides, the streets were safe.
One by one my friends fell away as we passed
their houses. I was always the last one home.
Mum used to leave the sun-room door unlocked

and I was able to flop into bed fully clothed, full of fish and chips, pies and the haunting image of Melanie Hayward as she boarded the express, which would now be well south of Taumarunui.

As I drifted off to sleep to the sound of 'House of the Rising Sun' by the Animals, the piercing sound of the late Limited echoed down the valley and up into our privileged recesses on the hill overlooking the town. Soon I was dreaming of beating Old Boys and Lawrence and Bug and the rest of those losers. Meanwhile the chuffs of steam trains continued to sound like the bark of disobedient dogs left tethered, punctuating our days and nights.

You'd have to be deaf and blind not to at least notice trains if you grew up in Te Kuiti. Some took them for granted. Perhaps they were sound sleepers, but for many of us the noisy steam and diesel beasts enterered into our subconscious at night, interrupting or even complementing dreams. Unbelievably, for some people trains were just noisy encumbrances, something you had to bear if you lived in a railway town. For others trains became an interest, before developing into a passion and sometimes curdling into an obsession. Often it depended on family influences.

One of the great thrills of my boyhood occurred when Dad, home on time for once, shared the evening meal with the rest of the family and then, still slightly tipsy from a truncated session at the 6 o'clock swill, piled us kids into the car and we went train chasing. The 7.30 Auckland to Wellington Express specifically, which climbed the Waitete Bank out of Te Kuiti, rounded a bend, went under the railway bridge and opened out along the limestone ridge towards the Waitete Viaduct.

Dad put his foot to the floor and we were in good time to take up position on the bridge before the engine blasted its hot smoke up through the bridge slats. My sisters always screamed. Dad always gave me a wink. Not sure why.

As the shadows stretched across the broken hills, it was back into the Citroen for the hair-raising ride towards the Waitete Viaduct reserve where we stumbled out of the car again and looked skyward. On a clear evening stars were already pulsing. Perhaps a half moon was up. The silence was intense, until you heard the express hammering, as gradual and inevitable as the drawing in of night. You sensed a slight vibration of the land, but that was probably just the tremble of boyish excitement. Then a long, mournful whistle blast really did break the silence and seconds later the express roared onto the viaduct.

When I first saw the phenomenon at a very young age, I thought the steam engine was on fire. Which it was – technically – as the firebox flared. My dad patted me on the head when I expressed my concern, which meant in an immediate postwar way, that everything was alright. Steam, smoke and other strange vapours emanated from the KA or JA, usually the latter. To a very young kid it would have looked like a dragon on the run with fire licking from its tongue of a firebox. It was nothing to laugh at in the very early days, although I remember my older sister laughing at me as I looked up in horror at the moving volcano.

Then came the carriages. At this early stage of night – 8pm – all the lights were blazing in the small, moving town on wheels. We waved up but the perfect strangers at the windows couldn't have seen us, down in the gathering gloom, a million kilometres from nowhere, south of Te Kuiti where the expresses plunged into the black wilderness renowned for its lack of light.

We grew up before we really had a chance to explore that black wilderness for ourselves. Leaving town for the big smoke dragged us in other directions. The hum and clatter of the city replaced the chortling, snuffling steam engines. Sirens and screeching tyres took over from the honks of diesels and steady roar of steel on steel, as long trains approached the Te Kuiti marshalling yards. The big city was about cars, buses and bikes – until the latter got nicked. Life was now in earnest. There was no time to sit on the station platform and contemplate the destination point of the express and limited, or new-fangled railcar. We had

made it to our first destination point and perhaps as a consequence, trains receded down the tracks of immediate memory.
Image C

Revisiting the past, the 'Centennial Steam Special' of 1985 resembles a double-headed express from childhood days as it crosses the Waitete Viaduct.

True, we occasionally returned home on the afternoon express, although we were more inclined to keep our hand in with the '60s symbol of youthful freedom, hitchhiking. Soon enough someone bought a car and it was just so much more convenient to chuck a guitar and three months' worth of dirty washing in the boot and hit the road. Three months' dirty washing on the express would be viewed dimly.

Then, out of the blue, I was invited to a function in Dargaville, up in Northland. I had no wheels and buses didn't seem to connect at a sensible hour. Someone suggested I could get there by train – or trains. The Northland railcar could get me as far as Waiotira Junction, where a Dargaville branch line train would take me the rest of the way.

Something stirred in my brain: the dormant passion for railways. On a whim I tried something I'd never done before. I caught the suburban train back to my digs in Mt Eden. It was a purely romantic gesture. By the time I'd clambered down to the Beach Road Station I'd lost fifteen minutes. By the time I walked from Mt Eden Station up to our flat, another twenty minutes were gobbled up. I eventually went back to the mundane, but more convenient number ten bus. Still, the notion of train travel to Dargaville was alluring.

I guess we were insular as we grew up in our railway town. Trains only made sense if they went north and south on the main trunk. That we were familiar with. During the process of leaving home and becoming an Aucklander, typically it was the 5am Limited that carried us north at a time of great dislocation and uncertainty. Becoming an anonymous student at Auckland University was about as unsettling as living in 20-odd flats and boarding arrangements in 18 months. Both were headspinning.

Now, as the Northland railcar headed west on the first leg of the trip to Dargaville, my head started to clear. It suddenly dawned on me that this wasn't the main trunk – the umbilicus that once connected us with Te Kuiti. As we left the city behind I felt the tension ease. I entered an odd, reflective state as farms and estuaries provided a welcome alternative to the teeming city streets, crowded buses and lecture halls. Somewhere along a different line I reconnected with myself – and the railways. And not just the familiar services plying the main trunk, which now seemed to belong to an earlier life.

It was like finding an old friend, one who had severed the cord and struck out for other corners of the country. The railways. I'd forgotten how grounding they could be. Auckland, the sterile city, seemed a long way down the track as the Northland railcar skirted estuaries and sought out rural pockets, as the grumpy guard checked my ticket in an oddly reassuring manner. It was nice to reconnect with a familiar response.

'You'll have to change at Waiotira if you want to get to Dargaville.'

I knew. I nodded, feeling at home in a familiar Fiat railcar going somewhere I'd never been before. It was liberating.

At Waiotira Junction – a station, a house and little else – I climbed down from the railcar. Two middle-aged women did the same, talking as they alighted. The sense of rail adventure intensified. I'd never changed trains at a junction before, and certainly not at one where native birds responded to the honk of the departing railcar and smoke from chimneys looped and swooped above the adjoining platform. Here a strange train made up of a D-something diesel, an empty LA wagon, a wooden carriage and express-size guard's van waited to connect with the west-coast town of Dargaville. The diesel may have been a De – I could recall seeing a similar engine flitting around the Te Kuiti yards in the dying days of small-town habitation, where such upheaving moments were attended by distraction and dislocation, as if you knew it made sense to actively work on distancing yourself from the town it was no longer cool to hold in awe.

After the congestion of city buses and cities in general, the sense of space on the mixed connecting train to Dargaville continued my therapy. The carriage was of the type I'd travelled on to Taumarunui to watch the rep rugby side beat Thames Valley 21-6 and brought back fond memories. The only other passengers were the two women who had much to talk about as the train went through a tunnel or two on its 48kph westward journey to Dargaville.

Image D

Diesel traction has taken over as the Auckland to Wellington Express waits at Hamilton. For us the loss of steam was not a big distraction.

The train swayed through swamps and flax groves. A huge river appeared in the distance. The two women kept talking. The guard welcomed me aboard with a half smile.

A year later, when I finally made the commitment to seek out every possible train journey in New Zealand, it was the twostep trip from Auckland to Dargaville which acted as the blueprint. I was back in Te Kuiti working in a bank, one of those transitory jobs which fitted the bill and back pocket, while other decisions were made. I had been working in the old home town for about a year when my employer drew to my attention that I was due ten days' annual leave. Furthermore, if the leave wasn't taken within the next month, it would be forfeited.

A month. The middle of winter. Surf 's up? Hardly. Back then very few people went on holiday at that time of year. It was still the heyday of the sacred two-weeker at the beach at Christmas. During my lunch hour I wandered along the local railway station platform, where the nostalgic recollections of the boyhood omnipotence of trains returned. Paint was beginning to peel here and there, and there was certainly less hustle and bustle compared with the heyday of rail in the golden years.

I shared my cheese and onion sandwich with a pigeon before getting up from the station seat that used to vibrate with half-a-dozen fish and chip-eating teenagers waiting for refreshment room stampedes. Out of the corner of my eye I saw a poster instructing whomever took the time to ponder it to *See Wairarapa by train.*

I hadn't joined the late '60s pilgrimage to England, nor had I fetched up on a cruise ship heading for Sydney. Even more intrepid '60s savants had headed out on the road to Mandalay, the Himalayas, Nepal, to find the meaning of life. Often all they found were swollen bellies, diarrhoea and disappointment. All I had was the *See Wairarapa by train* poster. And ten days.

Initially my first rail odyssey around New Zealand, utilising the endangered annual leave, struck me as being a see-your-own-country-firstelimination process. Instead, what I found changed the reference points completely. It was like travelling to another New Zealand. Another country. At the same time, my dormant passion for the railways came bursting back, unbridled, like the early years of main trunk travel.

It suddenly seemed the natural thing to do. Jump on a train and see the country. Not that I hadn't seen a fair bit of it and not that I hadn't jumped on a train before. Even when steam was phased out and diesel traction took over, the omnipotence of the railways didn't diminish for many years. The loss of the monstrous, fire-breathing KAs and JAs at the head of expresses and limiteds could have been terminal, but for me there was something beguiling about diesel-hauled passenger trains.

It wasn't just the business of arriving at your destination with white shirt unbesmirched by engine soot from the steam engines; nor was it the deeper sleep afforded the townsfolk at night now that the blustering, choking, belching, noisome coal and oil burners had been pensioned off to the branch lines. It was the sense of modernity. Something less wild and chaotic. Steam engines, after all, were basically fire on wheels as they blustered along, and although they were almost human as a consequence, the quieter, enclosed, no-frills diesel smacked of greater efficiencies. And just as the old-world engine drivers were often as cantankerous as the steam engines they bullied through our valley, diesel drivers seemed more couth and clean cut – even debonair.

As kids we didn't mourn the passing of steam as I now know we should have done. Yes, the diesels were modern, cool – just as motor cars were becoming more streamlined – and attractive. What we didn't realise was that those same cool new cars would spell the demise of the dominance of railways within a short space of time. Besides, the railways now boasted railcars – the new, swish alternative to the old engine-hauled expresses and limiteds. Over the years we learned railcars were nothing new, but what *was* significant about them was the way the Fiats in particular took over from the old conventional passenger trains without missing a beat.

Image E

The changing of the guard. A Fiat railcar and an ancient AB steam engine represent the new and the old, at Ruakura.

And did we, in Te Kuiti at the age of ten, appreciate the fact that because railcars were now the most prevalent form of rail passenger transport, representing, as they did, a reaction to the diminution of rail passenger numbers, concern ourselves with the steady erosion of rail's transport dominance? We did not. The new shiny red Fiats were neat. They went like the clappers. They bucked and swayed a bit but that was because they were quicker off the mark than ponderous old KAs and JAs. In rugby terms, they were like first five-eighths as opposed to tight forwards.

During our later travels it occurred to us that in some cases we were heading for the end of the line, seeing angles and perspectives of New Zealand no road could show you. It may have been just as wondrous if we'd bashed around in an old Volkswagen, but train travel offered the unique advantages of travelling companions, a laid back, hands-off-the-steering-wheel vista, and a smorgasbord of scenery and experiences. Occasionally you might come across a situation where the trains didn't go there anymore, and you felt a unique privilege in being able to say you had been amongst the last passengers to travel on the line. It became a talking point.

The recent history of New Zealand rail is inevitably about closure, adaptation, rationalisation and sometimes resurgence. Sometimes the less you have, the more you appreciate it. It's not hard to imagine inhabitants of France and Germany, where trains have always been thick on the ground, puzzling at New Zealand train enthusiasts. Why go glassy-eyed and all train-spotty just because a modest diesel pulling a sad handful of carriages carrying a wedge of uninterested passengers disappears into the distance? Because it's one of the few trains to make an appearance along this stretch in a New Zealand which fell in love with the motor car about the same time it developed a sneer for trains in general.

After rediscovering the railways I undertook at least three rail odysseys in an attempt to cover as many New Zealand services as I could. Sometimes I struck out alone, on other occasions my mate Russell, or wife Jenny, tagged along. Once or twice a veritable team joined in, some of whom were keen to learn just what it was that attracted us to the railways.

Image F

Graham Hutchins snapped in Alexandra prior to travelling on the Central Otago railcar. Was it a case of seeing your own country first, or travelling on as many trains as possible before services were cancelled?

We covered a good part of the country on those odysseys of the late 1960s, early 1970s and mid-1970s. Many of those journeys are included in this collection. We didn't go to sleep on New Zealand railways a second time. Beyond those odysseys train travel became a regular means of getting from A to B, or simply a pleasurable experience in itself, right up to recent times. These latter journeys make up the balance of the stories.

Some people take to the bottle, others go shopping. I jump on a train, if I can find one, and wait for the swish and sway to take me away. Away from the down times. For me the diversion comes as much from the rhythm as from the passing landscapes seen through the train window. Spare me the dangerous thrust of rail-less motor cars, lacking a divining rod. But an hour on the train to Wairarapa or the Northern Explorer and the stress soon dissipates.

1

The Moonlight Express

Night trains and The Northerner

Image 1

Having made it to the break of day, another night train – the Wellington–Auckland Limited express – ghosts through Pokeno with engines JA 1284 and 1285. The sophistication of Auckland is just up the line.

I had never seen anything like it – and I was terrified. The steam engine was alive. Fit to burst. Its headlight blinded. Its fire-box flared. You could feel the blast of heat as it passed by at 96kph. The engine's whistle split the night – a night that had been silent and still, with just a few bugs buzzing around street lights and the odd dog barking.

The night train – in this case the 229 Limited between Auckland and Wellington – made its presence felt along the length of its route. Cities, small towns like ours, and isolated reaches were not immune to its sudden intrusion.

It was midnight or thereabouts and we were late getting back from the beach. Dad's car blew a gasket outside the Coroglen Tavern and it took him quite a while to drum up a mechanic. He had to do a lot of negotiating while standing at the bar and he must have been really thirsty. I lost count of the number of glasses of beer he drank.

That's why Dad and I were late getting back to town. Mum and the girls were already home, having got a ride, and were no doubt sleeping soundly – not having the worry of blown gaskets and night trains, like me and Dad. We stopped for the train at the north level crossing. The lights were flashing. Then a light started pulsing on Dad's dashboard. 'Dash,' he yelled – or it could have been something stronger – but I now realised why they called it the dashboard. So we climbed out in the swirling fog to check something under the bonnet. The gasket probably. Then the train went past and changed my life.

I got to bed at 12.30, but at 2am I was still awake, thinking about what Dad said was the 229 Limited. I couldn't believe a man-made object could produce so much energy and sheer presence. The phenomenon known as the night train had made itself known to me.

Like night trains everywhere, the New Zealand version had an ambience that was accepted as an integral part of the rail travel landscape. They had their own mystique and atmosphere – secretive and confined, often carrying perfect strangers into dark recesses of the land. Here passengers slept the night away or conjured up notions of nocturnal liaisons, or formed fleeting and sometimes shady dealings among 'people of the night'. Debauchery in compartments or under cover of open carriage darkness sometimes occurred, but above-board social interaction usually led to friendships being made and stories shared.

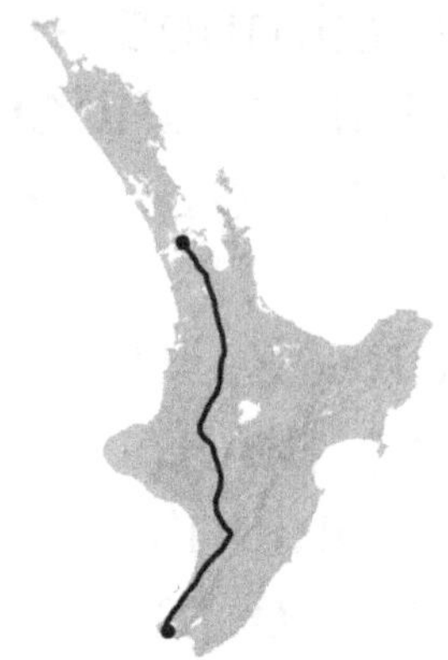

If the night trains sheltered this internal life, to the outside observer they looked like moving streets on wheels, at times lit up like cruise liners on New Year's Eve; at others, blacked out apart from muted vestibule lights, red tail lamps and the yawing sweep of the locomotive's headlight. In the days of steam, the glow and flare of the engine's firebox pinpointed the location of night trains in the lonely, shadowy landscape.

In the early days the North Island main trunk express and limiteds between Auckland and Wellington came to epitomise the classic New Zealand night train, but such beasts appeared elsewhere. One of the most ghostly night services ran in the pitch-black backblocks between Taumarunui and Stratford, and then on to New Plymouth. In the deep south, night trains travelling between Christchurch and Invercargill provided enough time and distance for the trains to take on a life of their own.

Troop trains, sporting specials, mixed goods and the occasional mysterious 'phantom trains' also plied the main lines of the North and South Islands. But night trains also ran on subsidiary lines, where they produced their own stories.

A passenger was harassed by beggars on the 'Cabbage Train', an overnight service taking its name from the fresh produce it carried north from Christchurch to Picton and the inter-island ferry. At a time when New Zealand wasn't supposed to have homeless people and beggars, night trains often enabled such opportunists to operate under the cover of darkness.

Image 2

Graham Hutchins at around age 10, soon to undertake a lone journey on the Wellington–Auckland express – and begin a love affair with trains.

Then there were the adventures associated with the 'Paper Train' – actually a railcar, which travelled on the midland line between Christchurch and Greymouth in the middle of the night.

For as long as night trains were running, the local railway station became a social mecca for many townsfolk, even if they weren't travelling. In the early days there was the Pied Piper effect of trains pulling into Te Kuiti at 2am, where the north and south night trains crossed. The town came alive at a most unlikely hour. Engines were watered, passengers refreshed and incoming land buyers stepped down at the beginning of their trek into the wilds of the King Country, where the frontier was being challenged. At the same time, disgruntled former farmers took their places on the train, only too pleased to turn their back on a lifestyle which had proved overly onerous. Drunken tipplers roused and joined the jovial crowds assembled for ten minutes on the Te Kuiti platform. Sometimes they were never seen again.

The night trains provided shelter and movement for a wide-ranging segment of society: prison escapees on the run, con men, ladies of the night, teenagers running away from home, foreigners seeking displaced family, alcoholics on the wrong train, freeloaders, rugby teams, hooligans and teddy boys, poets, singers and compulsive talkers.

Image 3

Heading for the night, the northbound Wellington–Auckland Express crosses the Otaki River. Te Kuiti is hours away.

Night trains also provided an important service for people living near the tracks. They weren't just a nuisance, keeping folk awake. Dairy farmers in several parts of the country relied on the night train's whistle to wake them in time for early milking, although it has to be said that some milkings started late. And of course the legions of women and young ladies who staffed the many refreshment rooms up and down the country were roused by the same shrill whistles.

I first became directly acquainted with the night train phenomenon at a comparatively young age. When I was ten I was put on the 3am Wellington to Auckland Express. Why it had to be that early I don't know. And this was an era when a 10 year old wasn't encouraged to ask. Some years later I heard that the 5am

Limited didn't always stop at Te Kuiti, which would be a pretty good reason.

Dad dropped me off at Te Kuiti Station on a foggy winter morning. I was half an hour early and still half asleep. The express was half an hour late, yet very much awake. You could hear it whistling down the valley. The fog had settled around the dim station lights, and you couldn't see along the platform – certainly not into the yard, where you imagined wagons waited to be pushed around as the next goods train north was assembled. That job could wait until the morning.

If you had fog, there'd be no wind. We had fog alright – and that meant silence as well, because without wind, there'd be no noise. No flapping of tarpaulins or rustling of leaves or pie wrappings. The silence was total, although you could just pick up a vague hammering somewhere off to the north. Could that be a drunk husband trying to get in the door after oversampling sly-grog? Something else we never asked about – and something we'd never be told even if we did.

Image 4

The typical NZR refreshment rooms, this one at Christchurch Station. Though much maligned, they often provided warmth and sanctuary. I had a soft spot for their rock cakes.

Suddenly footsteps sounded on the platform. They seemed to be coming from the south – and getting louder. Next minute a railway porter's legs could be seen as he emerged from the fog – to the north. Sound distorts in the fog, someone said. I was pleased it was the porter. Rather him than a nasty drunk on the prowl. Mind you, the porter was none too steady on his feet.

'What are you doing here, kid?' he slurred at me out of the fog.

'Waiting for the express.'

'On your own? In the middle of the night?'

'My father dropped me off. Anyway, it's morning.'

'Smart kid,' the porter leered and slurred. His breath smelt of sly-grog. Not so sly either. He had a flask of whiskey sticking out of his pocket.

Out of the fog a headlight shone. The express had made up time. A K engine was at the head, forcing its way through the swirl. It approached the station at pace. I figured it must be a long express if the engine was still motoring as it clanked past the platform. Behind the engine was a long rake of sheep wagons. It was just a goods train, scheduled before the express. The porter sensed my disappointment.

'You should've jumped on with the sheep, carrot top,' he leered.

I slunk embarrassed back into the shadows as the goods train gathered pace and cleared the yard. The smell of animal by-products from the sheep wagons remained, trapped in foggy pockets. Silence descended again but I became aware of the smell of sheep residue gradually being replaced by the agreeable odour of hot pies as they were made ready for the express and its hungry passengers. I wandered past the refreshment room door.

'Would you like a pie, young man?' one of the refreshment room ladies asked. I didn't reply 'rather', but then I didn't really reply.

'A bit shy, are we?' she replied. I nodded. She was the most attractive refreshment rooms lady I had ever seen. In fact I'd never seen her around town before. I thought I knew most townfolk, even if not by name. The refreshment ladies – all of them – could have been from a different planet. They were obviously someone's daughter or mother but I'd never noted them in the main street, or at church or the pictures, or the rugby – places where most townfolk went. Then I remembered my mother talking about the refreshment ladies and how hard life must be for them. Not only did they work at night, they worked broken shifts dictated by when the passenger trains and railcars came in. They slept when they could, during the day and night.

Lucy, my refreshment lady, gave me a free mince pie and a wink. She looked a bit like Kim Novak, or Grace Kelly from a certain angle. She sent me on my way with a tangy pie that threw off about as much steam as the AB shunter being fired up outside the engine shed. Under the hanging light Lucy's powdered make-up couldn't hide the bags under her eyes. Her heavily daubed red lipstick highlighted terse lips, and her smile took on an exhausted aspect.

Then it was time for the train to pull in and Lucy and her friends went into battle. A phalanx of strangers swelled the town's population by 400 for as long as it took the passengers to be refreshed and the engine to have its tanks topped up. I found my carriage – B non-smoking – and made my way to my reserved seat. Thankfully there was no freeloader occupying it, although the leather seemed warm. Perhaps a freeloader had been in residence and had simply ducked away for a pie. Would there be a situation to confront when he – it couldn't be a she – returned from the refreshment rooms? I was reminded of the macabre case where a boarding passenger found a usurper in his seat. He was sound asleep and no amount of jostling could rouse him. Eventually the guard became involved, whereupon he declared the man to be as dead as a doornail.

Night trains could be spooky alright. The people on the night trains were like blank canvases when they weren't asleep. At level crossings you'd see them staring out into the darkness, silhouetted by a carriage light left on by some selfish passenger reading a book, while the rest of the passengers sought sleep.

They were the passing-through night-train people, transitory strangers who looked down from the carriage windows at us small-town ants, scuttling in the shadows. We could have been inmates of some banished gulag. The sort of people Remuera aunts warned their nieces about – those living in the backblocks and small towns where ruffians held sway. In the land where Maori walked the streets and Europeans drank too much. And women didn't know a fascinator from a fascination; a gin and tonic from a gin.

Before we'd travelled on a night train, the passing-through passengers could have been from Mars. The night trains certainly had an aura about them. And it wasn't just the halo of steam leaking up from the heating systems and, if the atmospherics were in a certain aspect, enshrouding the carriage like a giant spider web. My sister imagined, as a young kid, that a giant spider was poised to swoop down and devour the carriage and its human cargo.

There was a certain mythology about the night trains. Some didn't stop. Some weren't allocated numbers. You'd hear about people who went missing in the depths of night out on the wind-swept plateau. There was a man who alighted to relieve himself after sampling too much sly-grog, choosing to do so while the train had temporarily halted near the old Mangaweka Viaduct. Someone heard a scream and two years later a skeleton was found in dense scrub beneath the bridge, beside a whiskey bottle.

The night trains had their hazards, even for young kids who weren't naughty whiskey drinkers. Under cover of darkness on the Wellington to Auckland Express, John went walkabout. He'd been sound asleep with his normally watchful parents when he sleepwalked down the aisle of the swaying carriage, entered the vestibule and rather than turning left to enter the toilets, he turned right and was able to open the external door – to blackness and certain death. The only witnesses would have been the smudge of midges around the vestibule lights. John was still asleep as he stepped into space. A mystery man, emerging from the toilet reached out a long arm and managed to hook a finger into John's nana-knitted jersey. Otherwise it was goodnight nurse. Not even hello doctor. The train was making up time through tiger country north of Taihape and at that speed you wouldn't need a doctor. Just an undertaker.

John's parents eventually rushed to the scene. The mystery man was nowhere to be seen, not that you could see anything. It wasn't the first recollection of some sort of male angel patrolling the night trains and keeping a watching brief.

Paul was supposed to get off the Limited at Feilding but at four in the morning and 10 years of age, it was quite understandable for him to be in a deep sleep as the train accelerated away from Feilding station. Paul woke with a start, disorientated and panic-stricken. He saw the 'Feilding' sign on the platform flash past. The train was already picking up speed. After a mad dash, Paul found himself contemplating the notion of defying the momentum of the train and leaping off. Before he could make up his mind he felt someone's firm hand on his shoulder.

Image 5

Feilding Station by day, with the Blue Streak railcar awaiting departure. At four in the morning it could be an even more shadowy place.

'Don't try it, son,' a voice rumbled. The man with a hand on his shoulder had a face like a relief map of the Rangitikei. Scars radiated out to every corner. Perhaps he'd tried it, Paul thought. So Paul returned to his seat and hoped his cousin would realise what had happened and drive the few kilometres south to Palmerston North to pick up young Paul. Sure enough at Palmerston, Paul's cousin – looking a bit bog-eyed – was waiting on the platform and Paul, wide awake by now, stepped unapologetically down from the Limited. He realised he could have been dead at the age of ten, at 4.27am, and several hundred metres above sea level.

As his cousin, ruddy-faced even in the chill of early morning, ushered him away, Paul glanced back at the train hoping to see some evidence of a firm-handed, scar-faced man. But the infernal external steam obliterated everyone, except a rotund man balancing three pies on a cup of tea. Then again, Paul didn't really expect to see his saviour. He still believed some things and some people happen along for a reason.

If night trains presented hair-raising moments from within, it was nothing compared with the chaos perpetrated on the outside. It was Christmas Eve in a small town where everyone knew everyone else. There were no mystery saviours. More's the pity. In the days before level crossing barrier arms came down, a young man behind the wheel of a Morris Oxford was hit by the Limited and killed.

'These things happen at Christmas,' mothers assured their children, as fathers clustered at the bloody scene and tried to do what they could, but were shunted back by the authorities.

It was Christmas Eve and Colin Harrison had been drinking. But the Limited took no prisoners. The news reverberated around the valley like the whoop of a JA whistle as it descended the southern bank into town. Christmas 1955 was as much about the Limited slicing open a Morris Oxford like a tin opener as rejoicing in the presence of a Hornby electric train set under the Christmas tree.

A few years passed. Night trains weren't just about guardian angels who sometimes got off before your stop, reneging on their duties. Night trains could carry you into territory you'd be hard-pressed to find back down the line at your whistle stop where nothing happened, and if it did you were too embarrassed to make a move.

Strange stirrings were carried on board in bodies that could betray as well as excite. For young men puberty protruded, with proximity in crowded carriages inflaming the situation. Perfect women strangers were seen to be just that – perfect.

Jerry spoke of a night-train encounter that was as much about embarrassment as excitement. At the age of 12 he caught the evening railcar from Dunedin to Alexandra in midwinter. It had been dark for hours as he sought a seat on the crowded Vulcan. While waiting at Dunedin Station he had been beguiled by a stately young woman who could have been Rita Hayworth, for all he knew. Why would such an attractive woman be travelling into the wilds of Central Otago, where people were usually ordinary to look at if not downright plain? Perhaps it was something in the soil, something in the schist, that leaked into the lives and profiles of no-nonsense ho-hum citizens.

There was one seat remaining as Jerry hustled on board after finding himself at the back of the queue. His blood pumped when he realised it was beside the extremely attractive young woman. At the age of 12 proximity can be a stimulating factor. The woman wasn't distant and unattainable – well, she was the latter for a callow, hormonally-awakening youth. Pre-pubescent or just about there, with pimples popping on his forehead and downy stuff protruding like Central Otago tussock on a weak chin. She engaged Jerry in friendly conversation. Up close she was even more attractive than Rita Hayworth. Up close – now that was the thing. Jerry tried to concentrate on monosyllabic responses, but he was distracted as a wave of horror swept over him. Her very proximity was leading to the last thing a 12-year-old boy would want to deal with in a brightly lit, crowded railcar.

As his body betrayed him, Jerry was able to align his school bag in such a way that the protrusion was largely concealed. As the woman continued becoming more and more attractive, Jerry's school bag began rising. Jerry and his mates had recently been sniggering about the couple who became ensnarled in one another during a display of passion and had to be rushed to hospital where a parting of the ways was facilitated.

Jerry wasn't sniggering now as he realised his stop was only ten minutes further on and he would fall under the harsh glare of passengers with nothing better to do than stare at what preceded him.

He closed his eyes and pretended to be asleep. At least that way there'd be no visual stimulation, although the gentle wafts of sweet perfume and dulcet tones of her trilling voice continued to assail him. He remembered a schoolmaster saying that, at times like these, the least stimulating mental exercise should be applied. Jerry loathed maths, and especially hated the rote dirge associated with reciting the times tables. Two threes are six etc. So between Wingatui and Hendon Jerry droned his way through the times table, his eyes squeezed shut as Rita Hayworth became concerned for the young man with numbers burbling out of his mouth.

Jerry alighted at Hindon, smooth from the waist down. He had escaped a fate worse than death and was pleasantly surprised to learn he knew seven eights were 56, when he used to think 64 was the answer.

Nothing anywhere near as exciting happened to me as I sat in the dark of carriage B non-smoking and contemplated my circumstances. No one smoked, no one spoke. A rotund man across the aisle snored like a chainsaw, but only when the train passed lit-up areas, such as level crossings and stations. The steam heating from the engine was so efficient the young man sitting in the aisle seat next to me peeled off his jersey at Otorohanga. He later loosened a few buttons on his shirt beyond Te Awamutu. The heat was still an issue, but that didn't stop him lapsing into heavy breathing – a poor man's snore – until we pulled into Frankton Junction.

Carriage lights went on as further refreshments were sought, and the young man beside me reached up to retrieve his bag from the baggage rack. At which point I couldn't help but notice the young man was a young woman. I didn't feel confused, betrayed or excited – just hungry. I needed a pie and perhaps a rock cake. Yes, a rock cake might do it – quell any welling arousal, as the young lady minced off into the fog. Thank God for the diversion of refreshments.

North of Ngaruawahia the train roared across the Waikato River. You sensed the wide, meandering flow of New Zealand's longest body of water. We used to rejoice as kids when the Wellington-bound express first encountered the Waikato River at Mercer. If the Picton–Christchurch line was famous for its maritime aspect, there was no train journey which formed the same affinity with a major river as those expresses, limiteds, railcars and mixed goods that shared the Waikato River bank with the main road to Auckland.

We always figured the railway held pride of place. As motor cars bounced around, the train, from a greater height, seemed to glide along the main trunk, leaving all the Morris Oxfords and Austin Cambridges in its wake. At that stage it seemed impossible the motor car would ever outwit the train.

Somewhere near Huntly the moon snuck through the clouds and the light reflected off the lazy Waikato. It was lake-like as it welled and glided northwards. Meanwhile the rabble who had climbed aboard at Huntly had the devil's own job trying to find their reserved seats. When they did, they found a family of four sprawled and sleeping in the enclosure. The mother expressed disgust when her shoulder was shaken. It had taken her since Te Kuiti to get to sleep and now she was expected to vacate the seat she had faithfully booked back in Taihape. The Huntly rabble, full of pre-dawn cheer, rechecked their tickets and found they were in the wrong carriage. They were in B but needed to be in D.

Apologies counted for little in the pre-dawn murk. The mother, a slip of a woman pushed at one of the Huntly rabble who, since the push coincided with a sharp lurch of the train as it crossed the loop points at Ohinewai, collapsed backwards in the gloom. The guard went down too and someone reckoned that was fair justice, seeing as how he had been slow off the mark to sort out the misunderstanding.

The Huntly rabble were coal miners from Rotowaro, heading for the big smoke to watch an important rugby match. They had caught a branch-line train from Glen Afton to meet up with the Limited on the main trunk. In those days it was possible to travel down the tendrils of rail that made up branch lines. The Glen Afton Branch was opened in 1924, and a massive bridge was built over the Waikato at Huntly to carry the line the final few hundred metres – or the first, if you were heading out.

It had never occurred to me that there was a railway line crossing the mighty Waikato at Huntly, to serve the Huntly West coal mines and related communities. As far as we were concerned, it was all about the main trunk and travelling to Auckland or Wellington. The notion of branch lines was completely foreign.

Perhaps, with the moon on the rise, I may have seen the train from Glen Afton ghosting over the Waikato River Bridge as the Limited slowed for Huntly Station. Images or imaginings of images may have appeared. If they had, what a sight it would have been. In hindsight I cursed our tunnel vision, as it related to the North Island main trunk. All up and down the main artery, there were branches and nodes bringing passengers to intermediate points to catch the major trains. Of course such expansive knowledge of the network didn't strike us then as being significant. Yet at a time when I recall everyone trumpeting road-based clichés such as *Are we there yet?* and *I wonder where that road goes?* no one seemed too concerned about branch lines.

Perhaps there was enough happening on the main trunk to take your mind off any shorter lines and the way in which they served the path of the big trains.

Beyond Mercer the Waikato River disappeared. So did the moonlight. Was that some sort of association between the moon and water bodies, to wit the mighty Waikato? A heavy cloud cover had descended, so heavy in fact that soon a decent rainstorm was pelting down. Blackness prevailed and I drifted off to sleep. I was roused by a squeaky-voiced woman across the aisle, who started up just as the rain stopped.

'We're coming into Buckland,' the old woman screeched. That gave me a fright. I thought she'd said *Auckland.* I went scrabbling for my bag. Then I thought things through. If we were coming into Auckland, that was where the train terminated. I'd have as much time as I liked to prepare myself for disembarkation. Then again, if the train was coming into Auckland and showing no signs of slowing down, which it wasn't, then perhaps the authorities had extended the train's range. Perhaps it now went out towards Newmarket as well. If so I did need to make haste to get off. We were still hiking along at a good clip – perhaps the train didn't even stop at Auckland anymore? It's funny what wild imaginings can emerge at five in the morning, after just two hours' sleep.

No one else seemed unduly perturbed in the half-light of dawn. Certainly not the old lady.

'I've got a brother who used to farm at Buckland,' she said.

Buckland! Not Auckland. I was greatly relieved. Apparently Buckland was a hamlet just south of Pukekohe, near Paerata, where a branch line arced away towards the west.

'That's the line to Wai-ook,' she reckoned. Apparently there used to be a passenger service, a virtual suburban train which turned off here and travelled for about 24 kilometres through the rolling country beyond Patumahoe before terminating on the southern reaches of the Manukau Harbour at Waiuku. If she was right, that was yet another branch line I knew nothing about.

As the sun rose over Penrose – where else with a name like that – the shafts of wan light cast shadows in the gullies and highlighted the upland reaches. Even at the age of ten I was aware of the peaks and troughs of young ladies who were no longer just angular girls – token boys really – in the days when PC was the kindly town cop who threatened to kick you in the arse if you were found loitering after dark. Young ladies of a certain type now favoured hip-hugging denim jeans and the one curled up like a cat, across the aisle, allowed the dawn light to dance all over her ample charms.

Just past Otahuhu as the train lurched over points and the train slewed, she stirred, arched her back and sighed. I wasn't allowed to see 'And God Created Women', starring Brigitte

Bardot, but that was one of the great things about being cast into the wide world on your own. No one could stop you looking at a young lady in tight denim jeans. As it was, I pretended to be asleep and only cast my evil squint in her direction when I was sure the square-jawed matron sitting next to me was diverted.

I thought of Bob Thwaite's wife. She used to parade in Te Kuiti's first bikini on a Sunday morning while washing the family Studebaker. How she washed that car. It was beautiful. We used to ride past on our bikes on the way to do a spot of what would now be termed trainspotting. While we didn't exactly *have* to ride down the street where Thwaite's wife lathered up a storm, the extra detour certainly had its own charms. This view was shared by several other cyclists – older boys usually – and at one stage there was a procession of male cyclists gawping and riding slowly past the cleanest Studebaker in Te Kuiti. In fact the only one. Mrs Thwaite was in no hurry to get the job done – she was still lathering and hosing away as we cycled back after watching the railcar pass through. Such small-town daydreaming passed the time as the express edged closer to Auckland.

A night train's arrival at the end of its journey can be a muted affair, particularly if the train arrives in darkness or semi-gloom and many of the passengers are still slumbering.

After all, there's no compulsion to be all alert and bright-eyed so that you don't miss your stop. If you're going all the way, it's just a matter of sleeping on until the train pulls into the terminus at the end of the line.

Image 6

The Auckland railyards on a busy day in later years, before Britomart. An exciting setting with its myriad platforms, perfect strangers and sundry suburban trains.

Auckland hovers and the lights are going on in suburban houses as the express attempts to make up time. A bit late for that, although the carriages are lurching and tugging, making egress to the toilets difficult. Kids are grumpy and fidgety. Hunger pangs gnaw and there are no more refreshment stops between here and Auckland station. Not that everyone is peckish. 'One more pie and I might have been done for,' I hear the rotund man across the aisle boom out to his wife.

With an almighty yaw the train suddenly heads to the east. Beer bottles are sent clunking across the aisle. A woman who has spent a good 15 minutes in the ladies and has somehow transformed herself into a Vivien Leigh look-alike takes a tumble off her high heels and ends up in the lap of the rotund man. Nothing is said but everyone goes a funny colour. Not unlike the hues of the shepherd's warning sunrise we are now heading towards.

The lurch to the right was of course the Express diverting to the waterfront approach to Auckland Station, through the newish suburb of Glen Innes, across the causeway at Judges Bay with early morning shadows dancing on the high tide; then on past the Parnell Baths.

Image 7

The Auckland–Wellington Express in later diesel-drawn days near Wellington. The end of the line is nigh in more ways than one.

There's a lot of action in the Auckland yards as the express is given right of way. Suburban trains hauled by squat WAB tank engines bring workers into the Beach Road platforms. The Rotorua Express, due to head out, makes preparations to depart. Another suburban train heading north angles away from the station, across the Parnell Bridge on its way to Newmarket.

It had been the first long train journey I could recall with clarity. Probably as much because I'd been primed for the whole journey by the knowledge that one false step, one moment's inattention and I could, confirming my mother's warning, come adrift and be taken by mischief, as the sheer excitement and sense of adventure got the better of me.

As the train drifted down the platform, hundreds of people waited for loved ones, friends, family, perhaps even perfect strangers. There was no sign of Aunty Peg, with whom I was scheduled to stay. A sense of panic set in when I realised I didn't really remember what she looked like. Then a few references returned.

'She's got a pimple on her cheek and a dimple on her chin,' my grandmother had said. 'You can't miss her. She's rather tall. Portly perhaps. Yes, tall and portly. She favours floral hats – ones with fruit on them.' So I kept my eyes peeled for a woman the size of an All Black with bananas draped over her head.

KA 945 at the head of the train is simmering as I walk past. The smell of hot metal is unmistakable. Still no sign of Aunty Peg. I wait to watch the disconnection of the engine as the claw-shaped, horizontal connectors are eased apart and steam hoses are left dangling. That was a pretty sure sign of an important train – claw-shaped connectors. Not like the vertical jobs you'd see on goods trains and the humble mixed.

KA 945 clanks off in a loose-limbed, relaxed fashion. Aunty Peg taps me on the shoulder. Even at 8am she's wearing an orchard on her head, but it's good to see her.

At one stage it became evident the 626 express running between Wellington and Auckland and the 227 express between Auckland and Wellington were about to be withdrawn. No express – it was a bit like Colin Meads being dropped from the All Blacks – and it happened twice. But while Meads fought back to remain a fixture in the All Blacks until 1971, the night express didn't make it.

Instead a new, refurbished train called the Northerner took its place, running the same route and mirroring a similar timetable. New Zealand now had the Southerner running from Christchurch to Invercargill and the Northerner covering the old night ramblings of the iconic Kiwi express. From 3 November 1975, when the Northener was unleashed, you could go south on the Northerner and north on the Southerner. Or south on the Southerner and north on the Northerner.

It featured refurbished steel-panelled first-class cars with each of two sets of carriages including a 48-seat buffet car. Dinner was served after leaving Wellington and Auckland, with light suppers available later in the journey. Continental breakfasts served in the buffet car were available before the train arrived at its destination in the morning.

Passengers were watched over by a head steward, four stewards and a cook. The emergence of the Northerner spelt the demise of the North Island main trunk refreshment rooms. The sacred stampedes disappeared into the night. Mind you, it took some of us a while to adapt to the new on-board feeding arrangements and passengers with a long memory still found it useful to run down the carriage aisles on their way to the buffet car.

The Northerner consisted of sleeper and seating cars, while its main trunk companion, the Silver Star, was sleeper only. In June 1979 the Northerner became the only overnight train when the Silver Star was withdrawn so some of its carriages could be converted into seating cars. When asbestos was found during the revamp, it became a paralysing union and health and safety issue, and the Silver Star remained off the tracks until it was sold to an overseas buyer.

Meanwhile, in a strange twist, the Northerner became an all-seater service. Someone suggested the sleeping compartments had become dens of iniquity, someone else reckoned it was simply a matter of economics. Few were prepared to pay for the luxury.

The Northerner was the last New Zealand night train. It last ran on the evening of 12 November 2004 between Auckland and Wellington – and Wellington and Auckland. Someone turned the lights out and an evocative aspect of travel life in New Zealand faded away down the tracks.

But when Aunty Peg met me in Auckland, no one considered for a moment that one day the night train would run no more. Yet nearly 50 years later, I was contemplating engine driver Dave Simpson's account of the final Northerner service, already the country's sole surviving night train, pulling out of Britomart Station on its last run to Wellington. Hammering the final nail into the coffin. Dave added an anecdote or two and also revealed the way deeply significant historical events can come to notice in a casual, everyday manner.

On Friday the twelfth of November 2004 we drifted to a stop short of the stopblock with train 200, the Overlander at Britomart Station. We were on time. It was only while checking the paperwork, I noted that the train manager had written on the bottom of the train list, 'Final run of the Northerner from Auckland'. Eventually we all realised we were taking part in railway history. This was the end of night trains on the Main Trunk. We had all heard the rumour that the night train was to be withdrawn. This was verified to the public in a media release on 29 October 2004. After the Overlander, train 200, we were scheduled to run the Northerner back down the main trunk.

We still had work to do. Reverse the train out of Britomart, down towards the Parnell Baths. Run up past the old Strand platforms, then reverse back down to Platform 3 in Britomart Station. We were now set, with service 203, the Northerner to depart at 2030.

Image 8

First day of the Northerner service at Hamilton: a new (or refurbished) night train with distinctive mustard-yellow carriages. An equally colourful DX engine provides the thrust.

Sitting back in the seat of DC 4790, with a cup of coffee in hand, one had time to reflect on the night service that would end with our departure tonight. These night trains had been running for 96 years. I had been fortunate to be associated with them for 41 years. My thoughts drifted back over my time in association with the night trains. There were good times, and those you would like to forget, thoughts of the characters you have worked with, and of the interesting people who have on invitation shared the cab with you.

How could one ever forget running out of fuel on train 202, the Wellington to Auckland Northerner, on a very cold and foggy morning, between Ongarue and Waimiha? Leaving my mate in charge of a rapidly cooling DX class locomotive, and to secure handbrakes on the passenger cars, I headed up the track to place the necessary detonator protection on the line to warn the driver of the relief locomotive to stop, and I would then guide them to our disabled train. That hour in the cold, standing beside the track was one of the longest I could remember, and there was a sense of relief on hearing the relief engine in the distance, and seeing the headlight coming out of the fog.

A couple of days after this incident a local newspaper printed a cartoon of a person carrying a couple of four gallon cans of diesel along a dark road with a dipstick under his arm. My wife's boss sent her home with a gift for me: a metre long wooden ruler inscribed at one end 'full', the other end 'empty' and in the centre of the ruler, 'Dave's Dipstick'. A few of the servicing people in Wellington were given a slap on the hand for not checking that the locomotive had sufficient fuel.

A couple of days later, while I was heading into Auckland from Westfield in a taxi, to pick up a locomotive from Auckland

Station, the taxi driver proceeded to give me his version of the fuel incident and then gave me his remedies for all the railways' problems and a general rundown of the pedigree of the crew on that day, asking me if I knew the driver. To which I answered, 'I was the driver.' The taxi driver seemed to slide down the seat somewhat, and the only sound I heard for the next 15 minutes until we reached our destination was road noise.

We are brought back to reality, with a bang on the side of the cab of DC 4790. It's the train manager with the paperwork for tonight's run. We have 38 passengers on departure, and 16 more to pick up at the four stops before Hamilton. A number of well-wishers have gathered around the cab. Some who are travelling on the train were unaware this was its final run, others were travelling because they knew it was the final run of the Northerner.

All too soon departure time of 2030 has arrived, and Graham, our train manager, gives 'right of way' over the radio, and we slip out of Britomart Station. The signalman in Britomart signal box calls us on the radio, wishing us a safe journey. As we pass under the walk bridge by the Parnell Baths we note a group on the bridge frantically waving. We give them a pop on the whistle in recognition. We hang on the whistle passing Westfield depot for there is quite a crowd of rail employees up on the bridge, waving torches in acknowledgement of our passing. The signalman in the Otahuhu signal box calls me up to say all is clear for our passage, and we give a pop on the whistle on passing the signal box.

Stopping at Papakura, we see that a number of well-wishers are on the platform to see the passing of the last Northerner. Looking back from the cab I watch staff from Papakura Station loading the luggage into the van, while the train manager sorts out the passengers boarding. All too soon I get 'right of way' over the radio from the train manager, and the Northerner departs Papakura for the last time.

We arrive in Hamilton on time. As I step off DC 4790 my relief driver Keith Jones is there to take over. I inform him all the paperwork is in order, and give him other relevant information as to the running of the train. We both stand in silence as we watch the activity on the platform. Keith climbs up into the cab of the locomotive, the radio crackles into life as he receives clearance from the train manager, and 203 slowly moves off for the last time.

As I watch the tail lights on the last car disappear into the distance, the night now belongs to the Northerner. I had run my last night train.

At the same time, something was dying in the soul of New Zealand rail transport.

2

Heading for the far east

The Gisborne Railcar

Image 9

The Gisborne railcar passing through Westshore. The best is yet to come: the railcar will straddle hill tops, thread valley floors and reveal sweeping ocean views.

Travelling to Gisborne by railcar in 1967 was like going to another country. It started out in confusion – Wellington to be precise. After a sleepless overnight jaunt down the main trunk on the faithful express, I joined my fellow zombies, who hadn't slept too well either, as we merged with men in grey flannel suits and women in largely sensible shoes – the incoming commuters – as we struggled for movement and oxygen in the echoing cathedral of Wellington Station.

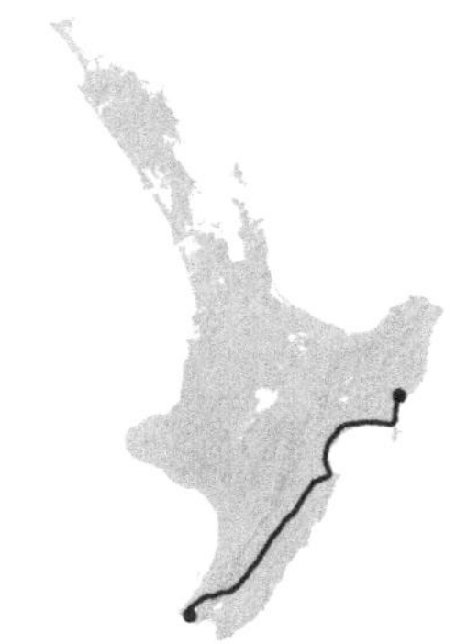

It was already like going to another country. I had communication difficulties with the ticket seller, not because he was speaking a different language or dialect, but because of the gales of sound generated by too many people talking at once in too small a space. It was hard to hear yourself think and that last pie at Palmerston North – or was it Paekakariki? – was repeating on me. My stomach was singing a song of its own, adding to the cacophony.

Another country too, when a tiny man wreathed in a blanket made eye contact with me.

'Got any money, sir?' he asked through, or around his remaining front tooth, in a distinguished British accent.

'Yes I have,' I replied foolishly, but innocently.

'My dear grandmother, at this very instant, has just passed away in Plimmerton. Can you lend me a guinea to travel to her funeral?'

'I'm running late, sir,' I said and hurried away. I was too.

'Anyone would think you had a confounded train to catch,' he yelled after me.

I did.

I still don't know what really happened in 1967, on that winter's morning. Through the dog-tiredness and diversions I had somehow managed to buy a ticket to Gisborne. Wellington to Gisborne. I went looking for my connection. The train I ended up on was a railcar travelling via the Wairarapa line, hopefully to Gisborne. *See Wairarapa by train,* the poster on the station wall back home in Te Kuiti had implored. I thought I was killing two birds with one stone.

Apparently there was another railcar, at another platform, which was heading north another way – up the main trunk, then through the Manawatu Gorge to Napier and on to Gisborne. I think my ticket was made out for the latter service. The guard got a bit grumpy when he discovered I was technically on the wrong train, although the destination, Gisborne, was valid.

'You've got the right ticket, but the wrong railcar,' he grumped.

'Or wrong ticket, right railcar,' I replied helpfully.

Image 10

A 1960s railway guard – an occasionally grumpy custodian who often gave you the benefit of the doubt.

The guard made a comment I didn't understand, but the important thing was that I wasn't thrown off at some hell-forsaken Hutt Valley suburban station, as we headed for the Rimutakas and Wairarapa.

It was pre-dawn as the railcar disappeared into the Rimutaka Tunnel. The suburban lights suddenly disappeared as the total blackness of the tunnel drew your focus to fellow passengers, most of whom had that early-morning look in their eye.

The tunnel was opened in 1955. I remembered seeing black-and-white glossies in the *Weekly News,* depicting the opening ceremonies, in which an English electric diesel – a DG – pulled the official train from one side of the ranges to the other. Pictures of what had gone before – the days of the Rimutaka Incline – also graced the pages of the *Weekly News.* The deeper the railcar delved into the tunnel, the starker my memories of the old incline became. My grandmother's voice describing the journey came back to me in fragments. She used to travel on the incline when visiting a friend in Featherston.

As the railcar swished and swayed through the eight-kilometre-long tunnel, I swore I could hear the disjointed huffs and puffs of the old Fell engines as they worked manfully to haul the incline trains up the steep gradients. Mind you, being half asleep probably bolstered the sounds of the railcar, with some of the sound effects coming from my own dream-like state.

It was amazing to contemplate all that rail history unfolding in the hills now safely behind us. I'd had enough trouble contemplating the current phenomenon of the Rimutaka Tunnel, which had been opened in 1955, and by 1967 already had a history of its own. And here we were thinking that the two Tawa deviation tunnels on the main trunk were as long as tunnels got on the New Zealand system.

The hills behind us used to pulsate with the sound and fury of the Fell engines. The old man sitting next to me painted a picture of those halcyon days. I guess he'd detected my enthusiasm for the landscape once the railcar emerged from the long tunnel, from pre-dawn murk as we entered the eastern portal, to the shadows washed by the rising sun as it highlighted Lake Wairarapa.

The latter was a large lake, one I didn't know existed. It stirred a sense of discovery in me, to think such a substantial body of water nestled on the plains beyond the Rimutakas, and it had never occurred to me to go looking for it.

'It's been there a while,' the old man said as I registered my surprise. His comment exposed my lack of knowledge of our country – off the beaten track. As the sun rose, the wide Wairarapa Plains revealed themselves to the traveller.

The old villas we passed on our way through Featherston were distinctive. This was another New Zealand entirely. It had an established look about it, unlike our neck of the woods and many of the main trunk towns. Time seemed to have passed towns like Featherston by – after all, the railway opened on this side of the Rimutakas back in 1878, but in subsequent years the more direct route north out of Wellington had gained in prominence.

The first train over the Rimutaka Incline – a sort of pilot train – was made up of a brake van behind the Fell engines. Temporary seats had been set up in the van. Four days later the first general train arrived in Featherston, creating quite a furore. One hotel proprietor was seen pushing a keg of beer in a wheelbarrow towards the station, where many had gathered. Some individual citizens were hot on his tail, their pockets bulging with celebratory bottles. It was quite a day for Featherston as townsfolk, passengers, and even train staff marked the occasion with much ribaldry and mirth. By contrast, the official opening ceremony at the station a couple of months later was a complete fizzer. There was no train at all and heavy rain dampened spirits even further.

Image 11

The Rimutaka Incline. The Fell tank engine, the central adhesion rail and the wind breaks all made the line distinctive.

My grandmother spoke about the Rimutaka Incline in wondrous tones, but we were too young to take on board her accounts of passenger trains with five small engines placed at intervals between the carriages, trains with a third rail for adhesion, such was the steepness of the gradients.

We pricked up our ears the time she spoke of the day a ferocious gale blew a train off the tracks and into a gulley. Three young girls were killed at that spot, known as Siberia, and the rail authorities erected a large protective fence to prevent such an accident ever happening again.

She also told of the time an express train became stalled in a tunnel and the choking smoke became a nuisance for the passengers. Some panicked and climbed out of the carriages to escape the smoke. Unfortunately, the smoke in the tunnel was thicker than that in the carriages and the panic-stricken took little coaxing to get back on board. Eventually the stalling engines got a grip and most people emerged with a little smoke damage, although several had suffered scrapes when jumping into the tunnel wall.

Up in the Rimutakas, serving the incline, were railway stations which were uniquely remote. Summit Station, perched predictably on top of the ranges, could be a god-forsaken place. It was totally exposed to the roar of prevailing winds and had an annual rainfall of 266cm. There was little escape for railway staff. At no stage was there any road access to Summit.

Cross Creek was regarded as a 'salt-mine' railway settlement, where wrongdoers were sent to contemplate their wild ways. The weather always seemed to be unwelcoming – not at all like today, when the Gisborne-bound railcar reflected the sunshine all day long, which soon burnt off lazy pockets of fog and mist.

We saw Wairarapa by train. It was a great way to touch base with the fertile plains and snow-capped mountains to the east and west. Greytown and Carterton flitted past with the sun filling most corners of the Fiat railcar. At Masterton it was time for refreshments and, although the hot pie and cuppa were welcome, the highlight was standing in the bright sunshine and contemplating a place I'd never seen before – certainly not by rail.

The rest of the morning and early afternoon passed in a flash. Wairarapa gave way to Hawke's Bay, where Eketahuna, Pahiatua and Woodville led to Dannevirke, Waipukurau and Waipawa. Then Hastings and Napier were upon us.

Napier seemed like the end of the line. By now we had been travelling for several hours and it was mid-afternoon. So many passengers alighted here you had to check timetables and departure times to make sure the final link with Gisborne to the north had been factored in.

Before long the railcar was swaying north. The suburbs of Napier receded. Those who had remained on board, or had caught the service at Napier, soaked up the seascapes as the line rimmed the ocean through Westshore and Bay View. I remembered my geography and history. This was the region so badly affected by the 1931 earthquake.

The line headed directly inland on encountering the Esk River outflow and now we were tracing the course of the river as it flowed through the hamlet of Eskdale, with its fruit growing and farming downs. A couple of kilometres beyond Eskdale the line did what railway lines do so well – it headed into territory unaccompanied by any road. The Esk River was our only companion as we headed due north.

I could now confidently say I was traversing genuinely personal virgin territory. I had been vaguely aware of being in the back of our car as the highway accompanied the line down to Napier, one Christmas long ago. Now we were also climbing, as we rejoined the Gisborne highway at Tutira, near the northern limit of Lake Tutira, a bird sanctuary.

The hills were parched. We were climbing into an environment I hadn't encountered before. Where the hills weren't parched, they had great white erosion scars down their faces, evidence of heavy rain. Obviously this was a region of extremes.

At Napier Ray had joined me in the aisle seat. He was middle-aged and had the close-cropped, windburnt look of a farmer. He didn't say much, but what he did say was significant. There was very little small talk with Ray.

'Do you realise that in 1957 the biggest landslide in the history of New Zealand railways came down at Wakakopu Bluffs, just up the track?' That was the first thing Ray said to me, about half an hour after we'd headed out for Gisborne. He had a certain tone to his voice, which almost made me feel responsible for the landslide.

'No. I had no idea,' I replied.

'Over a million tonnes of clay and papa rock slid into the sea, making a brand new peninsula.'

'Wow. That's a lot of clay.'

'And papa rock.'

Ray was nothing if not pedantic, and here was I about to make a disrespectful comment about Papa Rock being an American disc jockey. I refrained.

Another twenty minutes passed. Ray remained upright in his seat. His head seemed to lack motility. It barely turned left or right.

'People don't realise the Gisborne to Wellington Express that was in existence before this railcar, was the longest provincial express in the country. Five hundred and twenty-five kilometres.'

'That's a long train,' I replied.

For the first time, Ray turned his head to the left and gave me a withering stare. 'It ran for five hundred and twenty-five kilometres. No train could possibly be five hundred and twenty-five kilometres in length.' Was Ray a schoolteacher – a close-cropped, windburnt one – and was I the naughty schoolboy in a weird out-of-school encounter?

Luckily Ray wasn't long for the railcar. He got off at some obscure siding, but not before he had handed down some further pronouncements.

'Do you realise Beach Loop is only accessible by train?' I didn't. Nor did I know that Beach Loop was way up the track. I thought it was some sort of local summertime variation on the hula hoop, but I kept that thought to myself.

'Not many people know this, but the land at Beach Loop is moving all the time.' That was Ray's parting shot as he gathered up his briefcase, straightened his tie, and headed for the vestibule. Or so I thought. 'Just remember,' Ray yelled down the aisle, 'we're lucky to be here, what with earthquakes, depressions, floods, storms, slips and mechanical problems. Enjoy your journey.'

'He's right, we are lucky to be here.' This statement came from an elderly woman who had climbed on board just as Ray got off. This was Pam and her cheery interpretation of the 'lucky to be here' cliché was a million miles – and certainly 525 kilometres – away from Ray's dire, close-cropped, windburnt prophecies.

Pam replaced Ray in the seat next to me. Which was good and bad. Good in the sense that she was pleasant and predictable, bad in the sense that there weren't enough pregnant pauses in her speech patterns to enable untrammelled concentration when the railcar was climbing through vertiginous back country fit to take your breath away, or skirting dazzling bays you'd never seen before. At a juncture when a first-time traveller was keen to take in the matchless scenery, the constant prattle of your travelling companion was as irritating as the staccato clacking of her knitting needles. Or the occasional vibration and rattle of the railcar.

'Oh that damn rattle,' Pam said. 'You know, sometimes it rattles so much they call it the Red Rattler.'

The railcar entered a tunnel and the notion of the red rattler played on my mind. There are red rattlers all over the railway world. There was a classic old intermediate suburban service that met the Sydney to Newcastle trains before travelling downhill from Fassifern to Toronto on Lake Macquarie in New South Wales. Many years later I supervised the travel of my young daughter and two nieces on that particular old red rattler and we had an uproarious time. The girls jumped from seat to seat and only settled on their preferred seating arrangements when the train pulled into Toronto Station. Then, after ice creams and a bit of window shopping, we made a mad dash back to the station where I saw the return train was waiting. It didn't occur to me that the train which had deposited us there was the same one scheduled to take us back. It hadn't moved since we got off.

That didn't stop me cracking the whip, particularly when I heard what could have been the departure bell. One of my nieces later told me it had been a local bird, whose cry sounds a bit like a bell. My daughter and both nieces took tumbles as we scrambled down the gravel road to the station. Knees were skinned, and tears welled as we sat in the carriage for another 20 minutes. Serious looking women climbed aboard, glancing suspiciously at the three young girls gingerly dabbing their grazes with handkerchiefs. As their obvious guardian, I received the most withering stares.

The Gisborne Railcar was edging past yawning views of the Pacific as I returned to 1967 – and Pam's prattling. We had never met before but that didn't stop her assuming I knew everyone living in the Raupunga and Kotemaori area. Mrs Braithwaite's cousin's sister's aunt had almost fallen down an offal hole, but worse was to come. Mrs Braithwaite's cousin herself almost fell down the same offal hole. Near Waihua, Pam suddenly stopped her knitting, leaned across my bows and waved vigorously at a carload of elderly folk keeping abreast of the railcar, near where the line and the highway cross the Waihua River, heading for the sea.

Pam apologised for reaching across and wouldn't hear of it when I suggested that perhaps she might like to take the window seat, if she had any more cars she had to wave out to between here and Gisborne. It was a magnanimous gesture on my part, and I was secretly praying she wouldn't avail herself of the offer. Scenically the Gisborne rail route was a glorious surprise. I was still in another country. No one had told me it was this good. No one had told me anything.

Luckily Pam declined. Initially I preferred to think she understood my infatuation with the physical grandeur, but eventually as her clacking needles returned to their staccato pitch, she revealed something of the insularity of Poverty Bay, or maybe it was just those travelling on the railcar.

'No. You stay there, young man. I've seen it all a hundred times before. Besides, I've got no head for heights.' She was obviously referring to the yawning cliffs along which the line sometimes ran. And certainly the viaducts. Mohaka, a few kilometres back, was a case in point.

The Mohaka Viaduct. One minute we were rattling along, Pam keeping time with her knitting needles, clacking in unison with the clickity-clack of the rail joins. The clacking and the clickity-clacking were enough to take your mind off the enormity of the scenery. Next minute there was an almighty roar.

We weren't up in the clouds but we may as well have been. Countless metres below flowed the Mohaka River. It was impossible for the slat fence to hide the vertiginous gap in the land. If this was just a minor branch line petering out somewhere to the north, how come such a magnificent coathanger had been built on it?

The Gisborne line was full of such surprises, and made you appreciate just how stupendous were the feats of engineers and navvies. Of course you had to question the need for slat fences along both sides of the viaduct – through similar terrain on the main trunk, no such add-ons were deemed necessary. And that made the sudden emergence onto the Makatote, Mangaweka or even Waitete Viaducts all the more head-spinning. They made the girls scream. I know my sisters nearly fainted, and my mother had 'no head for heights' either.

As the Gisborne railcar seemingly took to the skies, I became quite animated. Why hadn't someone at school mentioned this feat of man-made engineering over a freak of Mother Nature? It wasn't the main trunk. That's why.

'This here's the highest viaduct in the Southern Hemisphere, young man,' Pam announced, halfway across. The chasm was like a moon crater. In the following weeks I was to learn the Mohaka Viaduct was 95m high and contained close to 1815 tonnes of steel. It was indeed the highest viaduct in the Southern Hemisphere. And our funky, spluttering Fiat railcar, a humble rail carriage, had taken it all in its stride. Oh, and it contained 450,000 rivets – the Mohaka Viaduct, not the Fiat railcar.

At this stage, what with the hulking viaducts, land carved up by nature, and place names I'd never heard of, things were becoming a little too unfamiliar. We could have been in Nepal or some South American republic near the foothills of the Andes. When the guard mentioned we would be pulling into Wairoa soon, I was reassured. I'd heard of Wairoa. And I could celebrate our arrival with another pie.

There was considerable celebrating when the line from Napier to Wairoa was completed and officially opened. 'A day of rejoicing' the press of the day claimed. The coming of the railway meant so much to the people living in the hitherto isolated town and region that, as a consequence, the locals and invited guests celebrated long and hard. Even now I could sense the magnitude of the line, and appreciate how it would have been seen as a saviour. It would have meant reducing reliance on the saddle-track roads to both north and south, which were often impassable and flooded. And it would have been a way to outwit Mother Nature, who had dredged up a treacherous bar at the mouth of the Wairoa River, able to thwart the attempts of even the smallest coastal vessels to relieve Wairoa's profound isolation.

Image 12

The Mohaka Viaduct hosting a passenger train from a later era. A stupendous feat of engineering and a hell of a surprise, it is the tallest viaduct in the land.

It was said that such isolation was exacerbated by the resistance of local Maori to the invasion of Europeans. This impacted on procuring land suitable for the passage of a railway line. As a consequence, the east coast line was one of the last to be completed and the Napier–Wairoa segment had more setbacks than many other major transport construction projects.

In 1967 Wairoa Station was quietly going about its business when the Gisborne Railcar pulled in. Refreshments were available. Another pie for sure. Yet back in 1939, on the occasion of the opening of the line, hundreds of expectant locals thronged the beflagged station and platform, waiting for the first official train. In fact three trains arrived in a short space of time and 1500 visitors from Hastings, Napier and most points in between climbed down to join in with the locals on the occasion of the opening day.

It felt significant to be travelling by railcar in 1967, for it was another railcar – a Standard model driven by the Hon. D.G. Sullivan, Minister of Railways, which transported political heavyweights to that long-ago opening ceremony. After the official party had been escorted to the dais, the mayor said a few words. Then the Chairman of Wairoa County Council, followed by the member for Hawke's Bay and the equivalent for Gisborne did the same.

Railcars also provided the first regular passenger services along the new link and beyond. A twice-daily service in each direction, utilising the new Standard railcars, did away with the need to trek for nearly four hours on the rough hill-country roads. Two hours ten minutes was all it took to get to Napier, and you could travel in comfort on the smooth steel road. The first railcars even had names: Tainui and Takitimu, named after canoes of the great migration fleet.

The 1967 railcar didn't have a name. Over the intervening years, the passage of the Gisborne railcar had become as everyday as the turning of the tide. As a result, the Wairoa Station experience was less than memorable. I barked my shins on a low-slung baggage trolley and my pie was lukewarm. Mind you, it was my fourth for the day after Masterton, Woodville and Napier.

And then there was a difference of opinion as passengers climbed back on board.

Someone said the railways should be likened to education, health and other social services which were not expected to function as business enterprises. In 1967, the Rogernomics revolution was still twenty years in the future. In 1937, as dignitaries gathered for the opening of the Mohaka Viaduct, the Minister of Railways felt constrained to remind onlookers of the need to see railways as being vital for the development of the country and not to be viewed from a narrow accountancy perspective.

As we pulled out of Wairoa and headed eastward towards the sea, it seemed daft that railways could be viewed as strictly a business. More than most lines in isolated areas, the Gisborne link served less tangible social and logistical purposes. Gisborne and large tracts of Poverty Bay may never have progressed without the ambitious railway that soon, after all that inland climbing and curving, was about to show off its other side.

Just beyond Tuhara, Whakaki Lagoon appeared next to the tracks, and beyond that the wide expanse of Hawke Bay. Apart from a brief flirtation with the coastline just beyond Napier, the ocean had disappeared. Such was the awe-inspiring, almost overwhelming presence of the ridges and valleys between Eskdale and Wairoa, you had the feeling this section of the line was all about rural backblocks, massive viaducts and rugged, broken country far from the sea. Admittedly, there had been a glimpse of the Pacific back at Waihua but beyond Wairoa the line took on a different aspect.

Mahia Peninsula became more prominent. Being a complete novice I thought the line might travel down the peninsula. And then what? Come back again? Perhaps the line travelled across the peninsula. I asked the man who had been sitting behind me since Wairoa. He didn't know.

Beyond Nuhaka the line carried on due east. The main road, which had been a constant companion, left us to it and veered away to the north. Before you knew it, the line was snaking around the edges of popular beaches such as Waikokopu and Opoutama, to take a northeast course towards Gisborne.

What a buzz it must have been, camping with the family at a beach settlement like Opoutama in the 1950s, where the Gisborne line came edging around the corner between the rocks and cliffs. If you were lucky, the

Gisborne Express roared past on its way north to the easternmost reach of the New Zealand rail system.

I remember seeing a photo of the Gisborne Express – a KA-hauled summer version with six steel-panelled carriages and a guard's van easing past a bunch of kids swimming at a beach – it may have been Opoutama. With its KA hauling steel carriages, it could have been the overnight Limited on the main trunk, but here it was, virtually running along the beach. In the photo none of the kids are acknowledging the train, although a few parents sitting on beach towels are inclining their heads towards the mighty KA and the Gisborne Express, which seemed totally out of place in such a backwater.

You can imagine the passing train full of happy faces – the bucket and spade brigade – on its way to Gisborne, or Bartletts or Muriwai, beach settlements south of the city – or even to Opoutama itself. It would certainly be a unique experience. The Gisborne Express might have looked like the Overnight Limited but I know, from personal experience, that there were no bucket and spade brigades on that particular landlocked, moonlit vessel.

In 1955 the express stopped running, to be replaced by the Fiat railcars. The Gisborne Express covered the longest course of any New Zealand provincial express – 525 kilometres, as Ray had it back down the line near Napier. Of course the 1967 railcar had to cover the same or a similar distance, which could account for the fact we began losing the light of day some distance from Gisborne. A group of railway track maintenance men climbed on board at some unscheduled stop. The fact that they appeared unheralded out of the murk caused murmurings. Were they taking over the railcar? Before their boisterous intrusion I was sound asleep.

We seemed to be descending on the outskirts of Gisborne. It was now quite dark. The railcar lights were on. The railways maintenance workers were chattering away as the railcar swirled and swayed. Suburban lights burned through the early evening murk.

The maintenance men were friendly, although they were a bit miffed that the railcar, their transport back to the city, was running half an hour late. At this time of year half an hour made all the difference between getting home in light or dark.

Image 13

The sweeping seascapes available from the Gisborne line at Nuhaka are enjoyed by passengers on the Gisborne Express in 1986.

'You off to Gisborne then?' one of the workers asked halfheartedly. It was a rhetorical question. There were no more stops and the railcar didn't run beyond Gisborne.

'Yeah. Never been there before,' I replied.

'Why didn't you come by plane?'

'I wanted to see the land.'

'It's pretty much all the same, whether you see it from thousands of feet or close up. Flying's quicker.'

'I like trains.'

'Fair enough, eh. You just got to make sure you fellas don't bang into a plane when the railcar crosses the airport runway. We thought you fellas must have crashed into a Fokker Friendship. That's why you were late.'

My mystified look motivated the maintenance worker to fill me in on one of the great oddities of the Gisborne line. Apparently the railway runs across the Gisborne Airport runway, or the runway runs across the railway, depending on your point of view. The runway needed to be extended when the new Fokker Friendship aircraft was introduced. Suggestions the railway line should be moved closer to the sea, and out of harm's way, were countered by cost considerations and the increasing reality of relatively light traffic for both trains and planes. So a carefully monitored security system enabled the railway to remain where it was and the runway to extend over the top.

I was fairly sure we hadn't crashed into any aircraft – in fact I didn't even see the airport. Perhaps I was looking out the wrong window. Perhaps I had nodded off.

A girl with a transistor radio had gone to sleep. 'Glad all over' blared out between the swishes and frequent honks on the railcar horn. Level crossings increased, with their jangling bells and flashing lights. The inner city was upon us. One or two passengers reached for travel bags from the skinny overhead baggage rack.

'Glad all over' was followed by a song that was immediately recognisable, yet strangely unfamiliar. A couple of months earlier the Beatles had sung 'All you need is love', on a worldwide satellite TV link-up. Then the song had retreated into the cosmos, as it was fine-tuned and later released as their new single.

Coming into Gisborne, at the end of a pivotal day in my rail odyssey, I was feeling exhausted and exhilarated at the same time. I had achieved something I didn't know was possible and found it to be mind-expanding in a railway sense – and I was hearing snatches of a song which would become the anthem of the era. 'Love, love, love' the Beatles harmonised. 'It's easy', John Lennon preached in the lead vocal spotlight. The immediate recognition of a half-remembered song, crackling out of a young woman's transistor, as the railcar eased off and pulled into Gisborne Station, cemented the memory. As the passengers stirred and shambled towards the exits, the young woman roused and turned her radio off. But I had heard enough. 'All you need is love.' Whenever I hear the song it always reminds me of coming into Gisborne as darkness set in, in a railcar that no longer runs, on a day I hoped would never end. I felt as if I'd climbed Everest. 'There's nothing you can do, that can't be done', John Lennon sang. Maybe. But I wondered how many of my mates would have discovered this way of getting to Gisborne. And how many would have heard 'All you need is love' in such a unique, unforgettable setting?

I found a nearby bed and breakfast, intending to catch a bus in the morning. It turned out to be more bed than breakfast. The spread in the morning consisted of burnt toast, cold coffee and some sort of mushed fruit. But the bed had been comfortable although I remained sleepless for a while, as the events of the day rewound in my mind.

You could tell the line to Gisborne had been a tough nut to crack. It wasn't just the lie of the land, which was often rugged and unstable, but the weather patterns as well. Tropical cyclones were prone to dump their rain load over the Poverty Bay region, and in later years Cyclone Bola wreaked havoc. Miraculously no lives were lost. This wasn't the case in 1938, when three or four days of torrential rain led to serious flooding. On the night of 19 February, a flash flood inundated a railway workmen's camp at Kopuawhara. Most of the temporary accommodation was swept away and 22 lives were lost.

The railcar had crossed the Kopuawhara Viaduct just north of Opoutama, or just before the line went walkabout and, unaccompanied by any road, found its way to Beach Loop before linking up with Bartletts and Muriwai. Just another unique feature of the Gisborne line – it had a mind of its own.

The novelty of seeing Wairarapa and Hawke's Bay for the first time by rail had been a delightful entrée, but the long haul from

Napier to Gisborne was a serious, memorable journey. The gaping valleys and massive viaducts, the towering ramparts and sheer cliffs, even the pronounced erosion at certain junctures, made the line unique. Then there were the ocean aspects with the railcar either providing spectacular elevated views, or virtually running along the beach at places like Opoutama. The land might be moving in some places but while it was still there it made for a wondrous rail setting.

Image 14

The view across to Young Nick's Head from the beach at Gisborne.

'Don't take this train for granted,' was the title of an obscure New Zealand train song. It could have been written specifically about the Gisborne railcar, one of New Zealand's most underrated rail journeys.

'Are you going all the way to Gisborne?' Pam had asked me as the railcar came out above the ocean at Beach Loop. The breadth of the Pacific and the depths of its blues took your breath away. So much so that I forgot to reply.

'Oh, it's just the sea, for goodness sake,' Pam snapped. 'You get sick of it after a while...'

Gisborne might have been the end of the line in 1967, but for many years there was an expectation that this was just part of the continuum. The line was to have carried on – and on – until it linked up with the Bay of Plenty line. Bearing in mind the latter got as far as Taneatua, that became the beacon destination, although alternate routes had been proposed, or even promised by local government and politicians of every colour.

Politicians. As delays, depressions and wars interceded, politicians continued to woo the people of Poverty Bay with assurances of a connecting line which would one day make it possible to travel by rail from Wellington to Auckland via a continuous east coast trunk line.

Despite the rugged landscape confronting engineers and line builders, hopes remained high. You could say the refinement of motor transport displayed bad timing. Politicians started duck shuffling when they began to sense an out – they could always point to the growing sophistication and clamour for buses, trucks and cars, as a worthy reason for procrastinating about an expensive railway line.

It was even suggested the railways shot themselves in the foot. In constructing rough roads to access rail construction sites they laid down much of the groundwork for roadworkers to follow in their wake, causing politicians to ponder less and less about the need to budget for rail expansion through the God-awful hills on the way to the Bay of Plenty.

That may have been an ironical touch but the biggest irony lay stretched out as far as the eye could see, northwest of Gisborne. Since 1917 the Moutohora Line had been in operation as a functional branch. The irony of the iron, the champions of expansion sighed, as the idea of extension beyond Moutohora slipped off the drawing board.

It's a funny feeling thinking you've made a remarkable discovery in a rail sense, only to realise the back story of Moutohora diminished your own sense of relishment. There may have been a rail buff on an earlier odyssey, who arrived in Gisborne on 14 March 1959, with intentions of travelling further north, only to find the Moutohora branch closed that very day.

3

Sea lions on the line

The Picton–Christchurch Railcar

Image 15

The Vulcan railcar at Kaikoura. It was our first encounter with the Vulcan. Kaikoura meant an opportunity for refreshments.

'If you think about something else,' Lance reckoned, 'it won't seem so bad.' The sea, bile green, crashed against the windows. Horizons swooped. Fellow passengers either screamed or went a funny colour. Some went deathly quiet. Some did both ... or all three.

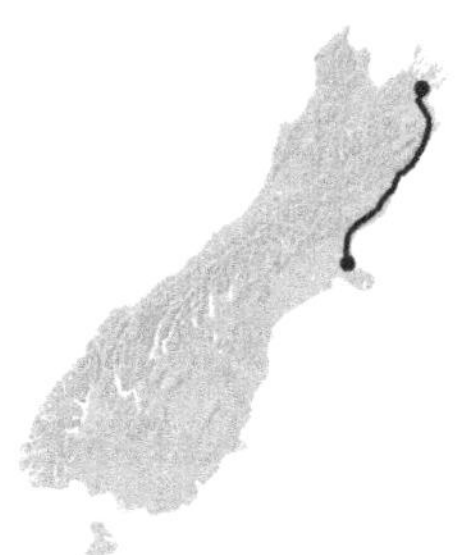

Passengers began heading for the toilets. Several children had already vomited. 'This is nothing,' Lance reckoned. We'd run into Lance on the overnight express and found him to be a garrulous and kindly travelling companion. He was heading south looking for work. Russ and I were heading south for our first real look at the South Island, on our initial rail odyssey.

After a day and night in Wellington we hoped to catch the inter-island ferry and the Picton to Christchurch railcar. Lance had it in mind to do the same thing. He'd travelled on the railcar before.

'It's a mighty trip,' he reckoned. 'But those railcars can throw you around a bit along the coast. Not at all like the engine-hauled carriage trains.'

Once Lance reckoned he lost a pie or two on the railcar, such was the biliousness engendered by the old Vulcan railcar swaying on the bendy track. And the small business of polishing off a bottle of rum with a mate the night before. On that occasion he was heading for Dunedin to look for work. That was back in 1965, when his presence in Dunedin coincided with a test match between the All Blacks and South Africa. He was looking for work in Auckland the day the same two teams fought out the fourth test at Eden Park.

In 1967, the whiff of fear and vomit was doing its best to overwhelm us.

'It's mind over matter,' Lance reckoned, as the man sitting in front of us suddenly cast matter before clawing his way to the toilet, his face the colour and texture of cheesecloth.

We were holding up OK but we noticed Lance had gone very quiet. All the colour had drained from his face. Then all the life went from his legs as he dragged himself down the aisle to the toilet.

It was a rough introduction to the South Island, the crossing of Cook Strait. We certainly hoped the Picton to Christchurch railcar would offer a smoother journey. It had been a long time coming, and so had we.

When you consider the northeast coast of the South Island has been a natural route to traverse when getting from the southern North Island to the centre and south of the South

Island for hundreds of years, the tardiness in opening a trunk railway was surprising. Perhaps it was because Christchurch, the major South Island centre, was located a third of the way down the coast. And this at a time when coastal shipping was regarded as the logical way to get there from Wellington, the capital.

It was certainly ironic. While the motor car and bus led to the demise of rail in many areas in later years, early on the pre-eminence of coastal shipping thwarted rail's development to the northeast, between Picton and Christchurch. Shipping in the form of inter-island ferries between Wellington and Christchurch would later impede any urgency being attached to the rail link. That was simply the way most New Zealanders travelled to Christchurch. Nelson and Blenheim were almost backwater centres and Picton and Kaikoura were little more than hamlets.

Once, on a school rugby trip to Christchurch, we had taken the express to Wellington and the inter-island ferry to Christchurch. I remember seeing the lights of Kaikoura late at night, and wondering why we weren't travelling by rail down this stretch. It would take half the time and we wouldn't have to put up with the wretched rolling in high seas and inevitable seasickness.

There were trains operating down the length of the Picton to Christchurch line in 1964, but for some reason the Wellington to Christchurch ferry was de rigueur. Perhaps it was historical. In 1962 the first roll-on roll-off ferry, the GMV *Aramoana* replaced the *Tamahine,* plying the waters of Cook Strait between Wellington and Picton. The main north line became more significant as a freight carrier as a result and, if nothing else, drew attention to the benefits of the line in general. Ironically, goods trains between Picton and Christchurch were shed of their passenger carriages at this time although railcars were still running.

Passenger services on the main north line had already been hacked back in 1958, with the 'boat train' connection from Picton to Blenheim having been replaced by buses. The authorities seemed to have a blind spot when it came to the line and were loath to maximise its potential.

In 1976, after the railcars had worn out and their replacement carriage trains hauled by DJ diesels had been withdrawn, the express goods 'cabbage train' was the only remaining passenger service. Locals protested loudly. The 'cabbage train' was a goods train with a carriage or two tagged on the end, and ran through the hours of darkness. Despite its 'express goods' tag it took a while. It carried fresh produce up the north line, to be forwarded on to the Cook Strait ferry and the markets of Wellington. Its sister service returned the favour, running from the north to Christchurch.

It wasn't much to come and go on for rail passengers and only confirmed the low status of rail travel in this corner of New Zealand, virtually from the outset.

When the Picton to Christchurch line was first opened in 1945, it represented the longest railway construction operation in the history of rail in this country. Not in the sense that it covered the greatest expanse of track, but in terms of time.

Construction of the line began in the early 1870s – from both ends. By 1876 the line north from Christchurch had reached Amberley, over 50km from Christchurch. Heading south, construction in Marlborough had seen the line from Picton to Blenheim bedded down. Beyond Blenheim and Amberley prevarication and politics set in, and it's unsurprising to learn the resulting delays were inevitable and protracted.

But all of that was behind us now as we took our seats on the Picton to Christchurch railcar, a Vulcan which looked very much like the son of the larger Fiat railcars.

Image 16

Overlooking Picton, heading south. We had overlooked it for too long, having neglected its charms and those of other places not on the North Island main trunk.

Climbing to Elevation on the rim of Picton, the old Vulcan spluttered. As a bit of vibration accompanied the swaying, a combination of dust and engine smoke rose through the floorboards near the vestibule. Doom-sayers may have said that this was another example of the steady strangulation of New Zealand railways. And yet in later years the elegant Coastal Pacific and TranzCoastal passenger trains covered the same lines. OK, the Vulcan had been around the clock and the block a few times, but a bit of smoke and dust never hurt anyone. Besides, the railcar was full. This was all enchanted territory for us. We would have been happy with a jigger or two.

When the railcar travelled on a massive horseshoe bend near Blenheim the train ride became surreal. The hills were so imposing and the bend so pronounced we felt as if we were travelling on a toy train. The railcar wheels screamed. We seemed to be on a merry-go-round, negotiating a complete circle, or as near as you could get.

Back in 1967, with no wine to speak of, Blenheim was regarded as a large small town, an agricultural servicing centre. Sheep, cattle, a bit of dairying, lots of orchards and lucerne, garlic and cherries. It was very much a country town, its streets filled with prosperous farmers with angular swaggers and ruddy faces. Tractor salesmen were very tanned, thanks to high sunshine hours and a goodly supply of melatonin.

On the station folded-armed farmers bid farewell. Check shirts, freckled elbows, slightly superior looks for us pastyfaced northerners with the beginnings of longer hair. We were still a bit pimply thanks to the King Country and Waikato fog and lower sunshine hours.

Russell's brother lived in Blenheim. He was an airforce engineer at Woodbourne Airforce Base, a feature of Blenheim which was distinctive. More uniforms than angular swaggerers out towards Renwick. On the surface Blenheim looked a bit like a Waikato agricultural

78

servicing town with sunshine, only healthier. There was certainly nothing to suggest that in six years' time the local rugby team, the Red Devils, would swipe the Ranfurly Shield off Canterbury and defend it meaningfully for six hard-fought defences. Suddenly people took notice of Blenheim and Marlborough. Very soon locals began planting vines and the eventual result was Blenheim becoming New Zealand's sauvignon blanc capital. Before that most of the ruddy-faced, freckled-elbow brigade couldn't even pronounce sauvignon blanc. Several decades down the track they were growing and making it to world standards and New Zealanders developed a different perception of the area.

Image 17

The Coastal Pacific at Hapuku in 1988, when the Picton to Christchurch route was becoming more widely appreciated.

Perhaps that was why it had taken the railway so long to get through and to gain credibility. The region just didn't seem to be on the way to anywhere. It was tucked away at the top of the South Island, somewhere near Nelson. Most had heard of Nelson, which had jumped the gun to cityhood by building a big church and calling it a cathedral, but Marlborough and its clutch of farming towns was in a bit of a grey area.

As we travelled on after climbing through the Dashwood Pass, the line swept in a massive curve across a valley floor. The Marlborough hills mesmerised. This could have been cowboy country – it was the colour of Wyoming, or perhaps North Dakota. The mid-morning sun shafted shadows on the brown undulations. This was another land. An upraised desert. Like nothing we'd seen in the North Island.

Beyond the town of Seddon we passed through Blind River, scene of a nasty rail accident in 1948 when AB696 derailed, causing a pile-up of carriages, six fatalities and 40 injuries. A combination of faulty brakes on the engine tender and marginally too much speed were discovered to be the causes of the crash, putting Blind River on the map for all the wrong reasons.

Not far from Blind River a unique feature studs the line. The multi-coloured salt lakes and stark white salt piles at Lake Grassmere provide an unusual obstacle. The Vulcan's trail takes to a causeway through the middle of proceedings. It is New Zealand's closest analogy to the long causeway across the Great Salt Lake in Utah, USA. What with the distinctive colour of the Marlborough hills – in places they had gone beyond russet brown and had an almost pinkish hue – Lake Grassmere added to the sense of being in another country.

We pass through Ward – like Seddon, another town named after a prominent Prime Minister – before the line headed towards the coast. Some travellers say they can hear the sea the other side of Mirza, but we reckon it's just a mechanical roar accompanying a puff of black smoke from the engine, which creeps through cracks in the vestibule running boards. When the smoke clears the ocean appears. At Wharenui great sweeps of coastline come into view. The revived railcar finds a more friendly gear and sways south, almost along the beach in places. Here the Pacific is grey-green with brown flecks following torrential rain earlier in the week. The coastline and rails disappear into the distance. They reckon the old Taneatua Express hugged the coast of the Bay of Plenty for a goodly distance, but the Picton to Christchurch line puts it to shame.

Down the track a bit the ocean clears at Kekerengu. Kekerengu presents a landscape that could have been daubed by the hand of an artistic God. Wavering tussock fringes the line. The hazy blue skyline highlights snow-capped peaks. The parched greys and greens of hillside vegetation contrast with the perfect blue of a benign sea.

The brown hills of Marlborough, the colour of Weetbix, rolled back towards a different back of beyond and yet most of the passengers, mainly mainlanders, took it all in their stride. Russ had spoken about the Picton–Christchurch line; how it spent a good deal of its time hugging the bays and open stretches of the Pacific Ocean coast. At times it seemed to be edging along the very sands adjacent to the water, like a tidal railway whose path shifts with the moods of the moon. Reputedly, once a train had to stop because sea lions were sunbathing on the tracks. But then Russ had only travelled along the line at night, on the 'cabbage train', so he couldn't confirm any sightings.

Going to the beach by train had always been a fantasy for landlocked rail fans who had read about the ultimate summer rail adventure. It had never occurred to us you could actually get right down to the beach by train in New Zealand – with bucket and spade. The trains on the main trunk dropped you off a long way from the sands of Takapuna and Days Bay, where we often stayed.

Image 18

The vineyards in Marlborough are now a major attraction for visitors.

Tales emerged of a game of beach cricket being played near a place called Goose Bay. When the railcar broke down in a clatter of gears and dusty smoke, several passengers wandered down to the beach, given their leave by the guard who reckoned it would take an hour for the relieving bus to arrive. When it was discovered half the passengers were North Islanders and half Mainlanders, someone produced a tennis ball, someone else found a piece of cricket bat-shaped driftwood, and an impromptu game of beach cricket took place.

There's no need for beach cricket today as the Vulcan railcar throbs manfully down the coast, unencumbered by faulty gears, sea lions or migrating crayfish. We approach a settlement of some substance: Kaikoura. Time for refreshments and a breather. The refreshment rush from the railcar was less like the Bulls of Pamplona, more a steady stumble with just thirty-odd passengers heading out, compared with the stampedes generated by carriage trains. It was an absolute amble back to the railcar – quite the most orderly refreshment break we could recall. And you didn't have to guard your booty, as you did on the express, when the engine reconnected clumsily with its carriages, sending hot tea raining.

Everyone seemed to be smiling. Perhaps it was the freshening breeze off the sea. The pies were good. It was a fond memory to store away – the Kaikoura refreshment rooms were the last on the New Zealand network, closing down in 1988 when the Coastal Pacific passenger train began running, with its onboard buffet.

In 1967 Kaikoura was a remarkable little town, very quaint. After leaving the station the line travelled over a viaduct bisecting the centre of town. Locals waved from the street below. A couple looked like fishermen. That might account for the waders they were wearing. But it wouldn't account for the fact they were pumping petrol in a service station. Perhaps they were just expecting rain? It was pretty parched down this way. Kids were tucking into ice creams, although they should have been in school. A young lady in a miniskirt and blonde hair strutted past. We both waved. She didn't wave back. So not everyone's friendlier than in the North Island. Mind you, we forgot to wave at the two thick-set, balding middle-aged men in cardigans talking on the pavement. One of them pointed at the railcar. It was that time in the 1960s when the generations were beginning to get on one another's nerves. Russ reckoned he could see derision in their eyes, from way down there, particularly the pointing man.

He was probably pointing us out – a couple of dropouts with lengthening hair and a poor work ethic, skiving off, going on nice long train journeys while the rest of the world had to earn a crust. You could just about see the RSA badges glinting in the sun.

There was more spectacular maritime scenery to come south of Kaikoura, until finally the line angled inland towards Ferniehurst and Parnassus, on the Waiau River. The show, to a certain extent, was over. We passengers, most of whom were not endowed with engineering nous, probably wondered why the line couldn't continue down the entire coast, around the rim of Pegasus Bay where dolphins barrelled and waves from South America broke. But there it was. Beyond Claverley and on encountering the Conway River, the line headed due west, away from the ocean, through Hundalee, across the main road.

Politics probably played a part. Some wealthy inland landowner no doubt held out for the line to serve his parish and, now the seaward Kaikoura Range had petered out, it was possible to leave the narrow ledge of coastal land. A shame really. It would have been nice to continue the maritime ramble across the Conway River, the Waiau mouth, the Hurunui and take in Gore Bay, Cathedral Cliffs, Port Robinson. Then you looked at a relief map of the area and couldn't help but notice there were no roads to speak of between Conway Flat and Gore Bay, a good distance, and no settlements. Obviously the ledge of land between the ocean and the cliffs was so narrow both the rail and road were driven inland for ease and because of the expense of construction.

Further south, over the Hurunui River, it would have been majestic to sweep along the ocean rim into Pegasus Bay, past Motunau Beach, before linking up with Amberley Beach, a few kilometres down the road from where the actual line ran through Amberley. But with 'cliffs' written in red on the relief map, at a point 20km north of the Amberleys, you figured it would have been too big an engineering task. Besides, passengers would be oceaned-out by all the maritime splendour. Wasn't 100km between Wharenui and Claverley enough?

In the real world Parnassus is one of the first inland settlements encountered after leaving the sea at Claverley. There's nothing much at Parnassus these days but for years it was the railhead of the line connecting with Christchurch. Many workmen occupied the Public Works camp and worked in relative isolation to push the railway further north.

Parnassus has its memories. One of the most startling was the running of a monthly train to Christchurch to provide the workmen with a well-earned day out in the big smoke. The 'Bob Semple Special', named after the Minister of Public Works, could be found at Christchurch station at 11pm, waiting to carry the workers back to Parnassus. Some didn't make it – not even to the station. It was a big day out for most, long deprived of access to alcohol. Those who made the train created legends of legless bravado and tomfoolery.

Alcohol was prohibited on New Zealand trains back then but that didn't stop the Parnassus crowd. It was easy enough to smuggle bottles of whisky on board. It was pointless trying to conceal a beer keg on your person, so no one tried. They just manhandled the heavy receptacles onto the train and rolled them down the aisle. The guard was invariably too preoccupied with passenger manifests and punching tickets to notice.

Levels of drunkenness were legendary. Thankfully for the guard and his young assistant many of the passengers, the day catching up with them, went straight to sleep as the 'Special' found the junction points for the north line and headed up country. It was just a matter of punching the tickets of those who were still conscious. No point troubling the snorers.

The guard carried on manfully, accounting for tickets, but he was worried about his younger, more gullible assistant. Chaotic scenes of lurching bodies and the din of caterwauling loudmouths blocked the aisles and communication channels. Some of the Parnassus people were well-known roughnecks and the guard figured his assistant may have come unstuck and could be, at that very moment, locked in a toilet or stumbling through the fields of North Canterbury with skinned knees and no direction home.

In the second carriage from the engine the guard found troubling evidence. A young woman was wearing the assistant's cap and had commandeered his ticket punch. She looked like the kind who would use her womanly wiles to get what she wanted – in this case the cap and ticket punch. To the encouraging guffaws of the passengers who were now playing games with pies, saveloys and fish and chips, she was punching up a storm. Most tickets were reduced to confetti. What had the assistant been reduced to?

Image 19

The Coastal Pacific of a different incarnation, near Parnassus. The town used to be the railhead of the old line from Christchurch. It was little more than a whistlestop in 1967.

At last, with some relief, the guard found his assistant in the car closest to the engine. For some reason this is the car that, over the years, has produced the most willing and extreme reprobates. Even on the express and limiteds this generalisation could be applied. Older folks tended to book seats in carriages further from the noisy, sooty, smelly engine, which left the first carriage to often younger passengers who found the noise, soot and smell less troublesome – and often agreeable.

Thus it was that the hatless assistant was found sitting around the keg of beer, caterwauling to match the engine whistle as it said hello to Nonoti at four in the morning.

Resistance had been fruitless for the young man, particularly as most of his drinking companions were also young people. Peer pressure on the Parnassus Special. The guard could have potted his assistant for defection, but remembering he was young once, he realised his assistant could be forgiven. After all, the latter had been battling great odds. A train full of wild, drunken, hard-nosed construction workers, and a few sporty young ladies to spice things up, amounted to an unforgiving clientele – a fatal mix.

In days when New Zealand Rail was almost the equivalent of the military, with its hierarchies, rigid rules and conservatism, the assistant could have been taken to task. Instead he was simply taken to Christchurch on an empty train, after being found asleep in the guard's van by the guard, who soon joined him. After all, the guard himself had reneged and after pocketing his ticket punch (a bit like putting your six-shooter back in its holster), he sat down near the keg and shared the spoils.

Our recollection of that story passed the time and mile-posts as the North Canterbury landscape became ordinary. After the glory of the ocean-girt stretch, there was always going to be a come-down. Wharenui to Claverley was a hard act to follow. The sun was also retreating. It had been a long, stimulating day. Beyond Cheviot and Greta Valley we stopped at a place called Waipara, just another whistle stop. Two attractive women struggled with the list of the railcar and a low platform to find balance on terra firma.

'Sensible shoes,' Russ grunted.

'What?' I replied. I was half asleep.

'Sensible shoes. If they wore sensible shoes they'd be able to touch down more easily.'

He had a point. The ladies finally made it, though it was hard to tell if they were getting on or off the railcar.

'Tight dresses.' Russ wasn't finished.

'What?' I replied. I was now half awake.

'They restrict your movements when you need to get off a train. Or on it.'

The two women's dresses were so tight their knees never parted company. The guard and several male station staff had to rush to the scene to support the women in their attempts to land on the platform – or in the vestibule.

'It must get lonely out here at Waipara,' someone said.

Mind you, Waipara was a junction station. The Waiau branch climbed away to the northwest. It was still operating as a freight line in 1967, but way back in 1939 passenger services had been curtailed. But it wasn't nowhere. Christchurch was nearby.

Like a lot of journeys in the South Island, the Picton to Christchurch run was a lengthy one. Nearly 354 kilometes in total. We were still over 64 kilometres north of Christchurch at a time when you thought it reasonable to expect the city to be just around the next corner. The sun had sunk behind the inland foothills. Amberley, Kaiapoi and Rangiora were negotiated and eventually the lights of suburban Christchurch were upon us. They went on for some time. It wasn't like coming into Hamilton. After all, Christchurch was the capital of another country – the South Island.

Lance, our seasick acquaintance off the ferry, wandered past. He gave us a wan smile and half a wave. He'd been keeping a low and ashen profile at the rear of the railcar.

Finally the railcar pulled into Christchurch Station. We knew we had been lucky to catch the service as it wasn't long for this line. It seemed to be a common trait afflicting the main north line between Picton and Christchurch. The Picton Express preceded the railcar – the shortest-lived provincial express in New Zealand. That didn't mean it only travelled a short distance, but that it lasted a little more than ten years. God knows how long the Cabbage train ran. Until the cabbages went off, someone suggested.

'Of cabbages and crayfish,' Russ mumbled as we walked along the Moorhouse Avenue Station platform. It had been a long day but his misquoted reference to crayfish was apt. At various positions of advantage along the Kaikoura coast, makeshift stalls and caravans sold the gnarled delicacy to motorists and, unofficially, train and railcar drivers knew when and where to stop.

We found cheap digs near the station, where we were able to kick back and ponder a truly remarkable train ride. We had considered the stretch of North Island main trunk which edged down the Kapiti Coast near Wellington to be hard to match, in terms of maritime and ocean scenery. But we'd just been on a train ride that put the Kapiti Coast in the dark.

It was enough to convince us to take a rest day in Christchurch, so we could digest the scenic grandeur and the uniqueness of the train ride. We wanted it to sink in.

Two days later we returned to Moorhouse Avenue Station with images of the Kaikoura Coast taken in and safely digested. We wished we could say the same about the hotel breakfast which we had bolted down. On the platform we were surprised to see the two women in tight dresses and non-sensible shoes. Obviously they had got on the railcar at

Waipara – not off. Or perhaps they had got off and, finding Waipara underwhelming, had got back on.

And yes, there was Lance, less ashen, heading out for God knows where, still looking for work, or wherever the All Blacks were playing next. Preferably both.

4

Seeking Mecca and finding the Rewanui Incline

Greymouth to Rewanui and back

Image 20

A miners' train at Dunollie near the base of the Rewanui Incline. To the workers, engine WE 375 was almost one of the family.

This sort of thing usually happens to other people. At Springfield we were told in a perfunctory tone by the guard that we would be vacating our nice, shiny Fiat railcar to the West Coast and transferring to a dusty, utilitarian Road Services bus. In this manner we would be linking with Greymouth after heading further north and negotiating the Lewis Pass road.

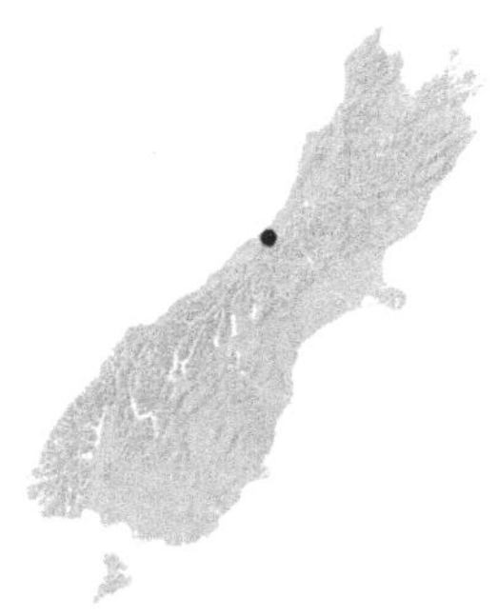

Ever since leaving Christchurch and curving through the western suburbs the expectation had grown. 'If you don't see another country in the world, make sure you see the West Coast by rail.' The pronouncement from an RSA digger at the local club, who had seen a fair bit of the world chasing Rommel and Mussolini, kept repeating. The Midland line cut away from the main line like a punctured umbilicus and our Fiat railcar dutifully followed. Across the western plains the mountains beckoned, until we were in the shadow of the Torlesse Range. Our Mecca, the railway to the West Coast, was luring us on.

Then we received the bad news at Springfield and transferred to the Road Services bus. A fellow passenger, an elderly woman, was philosophical about the change, caused by a slip on the West Coast side of the main divide. 'I've always wanted to see the Lewis Pass. Lovely scenery I'm told.'

We clumped disconsolately from railcar to bus. All this way to break our duck on a rail route which had developed mystical proportions. And now this. It was bad enough that we'd missed out on the steam-hauled expresses of the golden age with all that steam and smoke billowing in the freezing mountain air. And the novelty of electric haulage through the mighty Otira Tunnel, with another steam engine waiting on the West Coast side, amidst all those watercourses and vegetation.

The West Coast side. The West Coast had become a Mecca for more than just rail-related reasons. Years earlier a glossy photo section in a weekly magazine had highlighted trains on the Midland line of the South Island. Expresses, goods trains, coal trains, KB engines. I'd never seen KBs before, and I had little inkling as to where the Midland line was. As much as the trains fascinated, the physical settings of towering snowcapped mountains, deep gorges and wide, braided rivers were also captivating.

It looked like another land – certainly another island. Flashbacks of those glossy *Weekly News* photos returned as we lurched over the Lewis Pass and descended into West Coast rain. That magical Midland wonderland with the line going from east to west and coast to coast across the South Island, through several distinct vegetation types and varying microclimates had been denied us. Simply because the product of one of those microclimates – West Coast rain – had been falling for ten days. Something had to give and a massive amount of soil, rock and West Coast vegetation slid off the side of a hill and covered the tracks.

So here we were, feeling devastated as we squeezed into an uncomfortable bus, going over the Lewis Pass rather than under the Southern Alps in a railcar – or any sort of train.

The old dear sitting near us continued chortling about the opportunity to see the Lewis Pass for the first time. 'Besides, Mavis Moxham has family in Reefton,' she mentioned in passing. The bus itself passed through Reefton in a blur of driving rain and steamed up windows. No chance for a quick cup of tea with Mavis Moxham's family. No chance either to investigate the outside chance of getting some West Coast rail action by linking up with the Greymouth–Westport railcar at Reefton.

The bus driver was perfunctory. 'The Greymouth to Westport railcar stopped running on 11 September 1967,' he barked while grappling with his windscreen wipers. Exactly a month ago. We had missed the railcar on the

Buller line by a lousy month. Did they know we were coming? Paranoia descended. Certainly disappointment.

'Mavis Moxham has people in Ikamatua too, you know.'

Great.

We were now travelling down the highway next to the Grey River, approaching Greymouth from the northeast. Across the river from Ngahere the old Blackball line used to incline up into the hills. Nothing much to see today, as the rain splattered and misty clouds wreathed the hills. Passenger services on the branch had ceased on 3 November 1940 – so there was no point feeling paranoid about that. Just a chance to contemplate better days ahead – in a year or two when we vowed we'd return to do what we'd been denied this time.

There was nothing left of the rail bridge over the Grey at Ngahere. A year earlier a serious flood had swept it away and the announcement was made that it would not be replaced, thereby signalling the demise of another West Coast branch line. You had to be quick on the West Coast. If floods and slips didn't thwart you, declining patronage would.

Through the haze we saw an S-shaped rail bridge off to the right as we finally came into Greymouth. The bus pulled into the railway station. The elderly lady wished us well. She had people at Greymouth. She was hustled into a waiting car, which was quickly gobbled up by the rain vapour, and whisked away to a place called Blaketown.

We made our move just as another deluge descended and presented as drowned rats at the reception desk of the nearest hotel.

'Wet, boys,' a friendly proprietor proffered. Our documentation smudged as we signed in. The ink ran. Above us condensate oozed down the floral wallpaper. The rain thundered on the corrugated iron roof and you had to yell to make yourself heard.

'What brings you boys to the Coast?' the prop bellowed.

'A bus,' Russ yelled, with a certain savagery.

'Shame about the railcar. Still you would have seen some terrific scenery up through the Lewis Pass.'

'We couldn't see out the bus window.' Russ's disappointment was even more profound now that we had made it to the coast.

'The Rewanui Incline train's still running,' the prop mentioned as he left. 'Takes more than ten day of rain to stop that one.'

After squeezing rainwater out of our socks we sought out West Coast company in the hotel's public bar. Miners off the last Rewanui train shuffled into position. The barman, a taciturn type, nodded as he topped up glasses. Then he nodded at us. We nodded back. Then he nodded at us again. This, like the rain, could go on all day – or night.

'Two jugs of Westbrew, please.' Russ finally broke the cycle.

'Jugs?'

'Yes, please. Two.'

'Jugs?'

Russ nodded. A quick perusal of the bar revealed a surfeit of beer jugs. There were seven ounce glasses as far as the eye could see, a few handles, but no jugs. The barman disappeared into a back room, cussing and sloshing in that section of the pub where surface water had snuck in.

'Very few jugs down this way,' one of the miners said after draining his seven ounce with one glug. He'd been one of the miners who arrived in town on the Rewanui train. We asked him about the miners' train, expressing a desire to take a ride.

'It's a free world but it's not all plain sailing on the incline train, is it Monty?'

Monty the barman, having returned, nodded. He then topped up and presented us with two misshapen glass containers with no handles.

Image 21

A legendary KB engine hauls a special passenger train through Annat, near Springfield.

'Jugs,' he said. It was the only word we'd managed to get out of him so far.

'Jugs, be buggered,' Russ whispered. 'My beer's got petals floating on the surface.'

I nodded. Mine had sprigs of something. They were heavy duty, roughly-hewn glass vases.

We stuck to seven-ouncers once the 'jugs' were drained and looked forward to tomorrow's train ride on what would be our only 1967 West Coast rail experience.

The rain didn't stop and we wondered if the Rewanui Incline would slip into the valley, and a white-coated New Zealand Railways man with a wet clipboard would close down the 13.07km branch.

Engine whistles were sounding through the rain in the morning. We saw the early miners' train pull out from the station located on the Greymouth wharf. The early afternoon train called the 'wet-timer' appealed to us more. It ran specifically for those miners who worked in wetter corners of the mine and were blessed with shorter shifts. Initially we thought it got its nickname from the fact that over here it seemed to be wet all the time.

WW 679 was the motive force and soon it was coaxing its train out onto the S-shaped truss bridge over the Grey we'd noted on the bus the evening before. Images of Tangiwai surfaced as the swollen, brew-hued river buffeted. Besides, hadn't the Blackball line bridge been taken in 1966 by the flood-swollen Grey River? The fact that the S-shaped bridge was the only structure of its type in New Zealand somehow seemed to make it feel more sturdy. Certainly the miners took it in their stride.

At Runanga, the first stop, more miners clambered on board. Eight kilometres out from Greymouth we pulled into Dunollie, located on the slopes of the Paparoa Range, under Mount Davey.

Everything had a look of permanence. The Rewanui line had been around a while. Initially a private company seeking the lucrative coal had set out to build a railway to access the black gold. Because of delays, the government took over the coal lease in 1901 and began work on the line. By the end of 1904 the rail link was up and running as far as the state mine at Dunollie. Construction had been uncomplicated, despite the need for a bridge across the Grey River.

Things became more challenging when it was discovered there was more good coal higher up in the Paparoa Range. As a result, the Rewanui Incline, with a maximum grade of 1 in 26 was built up the steep valley walls of Seven Mile Creek. It was a considerable undertaking and such was the steepness, a centre rail was initially fitted to enable extra braking for descending traffic, and a Fell brake van attached. It was regarded as a mini Rimutaka Incline.

We were able to dine out on having travelled the Rewanui Incline. For a start, many folk weren't aware there was ever another incline in New Zealand, other than the Rimutaka, which had closed in 1955. Mind you, the distinctive centre rail which helped define the incline had been removed in 1966, a year before we arrived. When I first heard that piece of information I cursed our continuing rotten luck. Missing out again on a West Coast train journey by a smidgeon. It took me a while to come to the realisation that it was just the centre rail that had been uplifted. Not the entire track. The train was still running, but now only locomotives with two Westinghouse brake pumps for greater adhesion were permitted to operate the incline. A couple of years after our visit, DJ diesels and DSC shunters replaced steam engines, and they were required to have strong brakes fitted to handle the incline.

Luckily we weren't out-and-out steam buffs and fortunately we had been bitten by the rail bug before the mass closures of the 1970s. We could imagine the horror confronted by tardy steam fans post-1975, who found the Rewanui Incline in a state of dieselisation.

Such musings were obliterated in 1967, as the sound of the steam engine hammering echoed around the valley. Occasionally the wheels skidded on the greasy track, but there was no denying the fighting spirit of the WW engine. It may have had less pulling power than the heavier WE class, but it buffeted its way past private coal bins and through tunnels with a certain singlemindedness. It was a hectic climb up the incline but eventually the train levelled off on the plateau at Rewanui. We felt pretty chuffed with ourselves – although technically it was the faithful old WW engine doing all the chuffing.

The miners ambled off to commence their shifts at the Liverpool State Mine. Between Dunollie near the base of the incline and the summit was only 6.5 kilometres, yet Rewanui is over 190 metres above Dunollie. It was a serious climb.

Mist and rain shrouded everything. Workmen and miners moved in and out of a blurred landscape. Some headed for the bath house after emerging from the mines, their eyes peering out from coal-dusted faces. Others headed for the bridge fording Seven Mile Creek, normally a trickle but today carrying bucketfuls of run-off from higher ground.

We didn't have long to wait until the return service pulled out. On the way back the rain continued to fall. The train was forced to stop while a burst culvert was repaired. At Runanga, back on the flat, we noticed a short spur line heading west to Rapahoe. Two pennies dropped. Rapahoe was the site of the Strongman State Mine, the setting of a serious mine explosion which had killed 19 miners earlier that year. The miners, our fellow travellers on the Rewanui train, lived with danger every day. No wonder you'd be blasé about bridges being washed away. At least you had a chance of swimming for it. The area had a well-deserved tradition of true grit.

Image 22

A DJ diesel hauls a miners' train in 1984. Steam haulage has gone but some things never change: rain puddles remind you this is the West Coast.

The Rewanui area was not just on New Zealand's West Coast. It was part of our wild west. In earlier years gunfights were common. Once State Mine pay clerks were held up at gunpoint halfway between Greymouth and Runanga by a well-known robber named Eggers. Despite resistance, two clerks were shot and killed and Eggers was later hanged at Lyttelton Prison. Instead of sweeping the sad affray under the mat, a memorial was erected near the railway line. And lessons learned. Even in the 1930s when the pay clerk ascended the incline in the Fell brake van he had a revolver-wielding minder.

We felt a bit like usurpers. Freeloaders on a service carrying men to a dangerous place of work, although we'd paid our fare. We felt privileged to be there and wasted no time in claiming to be pioneers on a 'hidden gem' of a train. Of course many other travellers had already uncovered the service but it was interesting to learn the line became a genuine tourist attraction towards the end of its life.

Image 23

As two steam engines rest, miners amble to their dirty, dangerous place of work. We could have been in Wales or West Virginia.

As often happens, the coal ran out and impending closure lead to a running down of maintenance. Soon the Rewanui Incline was declared to be unsafe for passenger services and in 1985 the line was closed.

To think we might have overlooked the Rewanui train. After the disappointment of missing out on the Christchurch–Greymouth railcar, it was largely Russ's idea to try the incline train as compensation. To me it was just a workers' train going a short distance. Nothing significant. I didn't let on that the S-shaped bridge creaking against the flood in the Grey struck me as being a disincentive. You miss out on the railcar and get drowned into the bargain. The complete tourist package. Adrenaline junkies before our time.

The out and back journey on the Rewanui train was unique. The passengers were real characters. This was no light-hearted excursion junket for well-to-do city slickers off to see the pretty West Coast bush and gurgling streams. This was all about a trainload of miners with haunted eyes and hard dangerous labour to contemplate, treacherous rivers and driving rain for days on end. It was like no other train journey we had encountered.

There was time, too, on the way back, to contemplate miners' trains in general. In other corners of the country the miners' train was a common specialised passenger service. As our Rewanui Incline train came to a lengthy halt near the washed-out culvert above Dunollie, we talked about plans to travel on the coal-miners' train running from Huntly across the Waikato River to Rotowaro and the Glen Afton mine. Inevitably we were about a year too late again, when we finally got around to it. Passenger services finished in 1972, and once again, buses had taken over.

But now the steam engine waited and blustered, as something was done about the culvert. The rain, if anything, increased in intensity until sheets of it cascaded down the bush-covered cuttings and created temporary waterfalls off the ballast.

'We had a sort of miners' train back in Te Kuiti,' Russ reckoned. 'Well, more a miners' kids' train.' He was referring to the New Plymouth to Auckland railcar, which was utilised as a school bus for kids living in the coal-mining community of Benneydale. Te Kuiti High School was their destination but the railcar, after setting out at an ungodly hour from New Plymouth and having negotiated the meandering Stratford to Okahukura line in the bowels of the night, was often late. So were the miners' kids. If the railcar was very late they wagged school.

The Rewanui Incline train was due to be quite late because of the troublesome culvert. Several miners, despite the rain, abandoned the train and walked off the mountain. Finally the WW engine chuffed into life and we made good time through Dunollie and Runanga, discarding miners as we went. We were convinced the Rewanui train was about to plunge into the surging brown Grey River. The waters were now lapping the bridge rails and the engine driver wasn't hesitant about making up time. We pulled in 20 minutes late, the rain stopped, and a motley bunch of men headed for the bars in town. We did the same.

Image 24

At Rewanui, in 1951, a long train waits to take miners down the incline and home. And we thought that 1967 was a long time ago.

Our first trip to the West Coast may have been preceded by disappointment, but spending some time in Greymouth made up for it. The phrase 'see your own country first' seemed meaningless in a situation where we were indeed seeing our own country first, but from the perspective of seeing it the way it used to be.

Greymouth looked like New Plymouth in the 1950s, and bungalows abounded, with miners' cottages, their red roofs often rusting. Steam engines wafted that distinctive coal-smoke smell over everything. It looked well-established, yet some would say it was getting on in years. As were the people. We didn't see a lot of children, but then you'd be hard pressed to find knots of kids in public bars or on miners' trains heading for dangerous work environments or in dank hotel rooms waiting for the rain to ease.

We may have missed out on the ultimate prize – the journey by railcar from the east to west coasts, but we were able to appreciate other unexpected rail bonuses. It wasn't just the Rewanui Incline and other mining trains. The fact that Greymouth had a second separate station based near the wharves, but still within a stone's throw of the main station, struck us as being unique. As did the huge roundhouse shed to accommodate the many engines based in the town.

Image 25

Rewanui's existence relied on the incline railway. It wasn't just a conduit for miners – coal, goods and work trains operated too.

'That roundhouse for the engines is something else,' Russ exclaimed to a local at the bar.

'Yeah,' the local replied, while looking over his shoulder.

'Steam's still king on the West Coast, eh?' I added.

'Wouldn't know,' the local replied, looking us in the eye. One of his was bloodshot, the other ringed with coal-dust. An awkward silence was relieved by my coughing fit. I could feel a cold coming on. The damp was rising.

'You boys tourists then?' the local asked. I think he felt a bit sorry for us. Our obvious awkwardness. My indifferent health.

'Yep. We're North Islanders.'

'By the sound of that bloody accent you're from Auckland, right?'

'We're from a bit further south. King Country actually. Colin Meads country.'

'Who?'

An ugly silence descended on the bar. No one went for their six-shooters, but they wouldn't have been out of place. They went for their seven-ouncers instead.

'King Country, eh. Just south of Auckland. You heard of a player called King?'

'There was a Ron King from the West Coast who played for the All Blacks.' My interjection was meant to keep a lid on things. Some hope.

'Never heard of him,' the increasingly unpleasant miner replied. The floor was now his. 'Saw you on the wet-timer today. Bloody Aucklanders. You all swallow your Rs. You should have been on the Fanny train.'

'What're you trying to say?' Russ's question was wiped out like the Grey in full flood wiping out the Blackball Bridge.

'Yeah. The Fanny train would have suited you long-haired Auckland bastards. That's the train for the ladies. You would've fitted right in. Could have worn ribbons. You come down here, rolling your vowels, skiting about Auckland and the main trunk, and you have the temerity to travel on the same train as blokes who take their lives into their hands every time they go down the shaft.'

We were grateful for the West Coast rain. Its hammering on the pub's roof made the following silence less pronounced.

'Don't worry about Rod. He's been here since opening time. It's the beer talking.' The nodding publican proved he hadn't lost the power of speech. It calmed us down a bit at a time when Russ was about to take to the Greymouth streets, looking for a barber.

The barman wasn't hopeful. 'The only barber you'll find at this time of night is that wind whistling down the valley. We call it the barber. It'll cut you to the quick. Like the local barber.'

I was mystified by the chain of events, particularly as our hair wasn't even long in the accepted sense. You could still see our ears. But we were outsiders, non-miners and perhaps we did swallow our Rs and roll our vowels. And despite the miner's drunken blathering, we felt we had a right to travel on his train. He would be most welcome to travel on ours. But in all likelihood his type would have had us pigeon-holed and sipping tea at Mavis Moxham's people's place in Blaketown.

It was the only really sour note during our various odysseys. And as it turned out, he wasn't even a miner. He was a coal merchant. He delivered the stuff.

Late in the piece – we still didn't know if 10 o'clock closing had kicked in, not that the West Coasters gave a toss – we continued to sip seven-ouncers. Drinking toasts to a remarkable railway that couldn't be more important.

5

Change here for heaven

Christchurch to the West Coast on the Midland Line

Image 26

The West Coast railcar in its element. A thick blanket of snow covers the surrounds of Arthur's Pass Station, the Midland Line's highest.

Springfield on the western edge of the Canterbury Plains was our Waterloo. Back in 1967 we had been thwarted at Springfield this side of the Torlesse Range. It was here that we had had to leave the rail and take to the road because of a slip on the line.

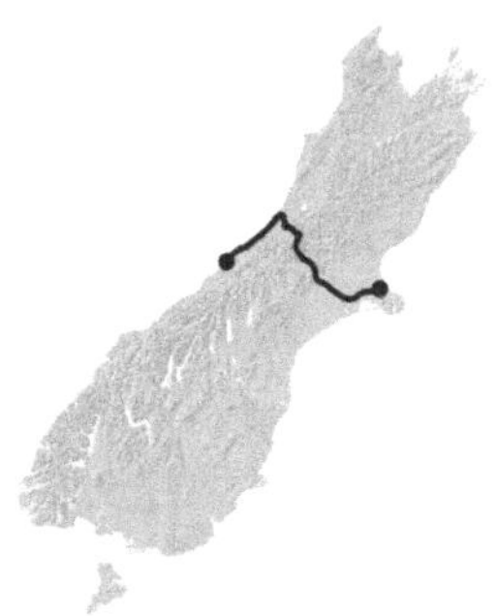

As the railcar pulled into Springfield in 1971 we half expected the laconic-voiced guard to come wandering through to tell us we could go no further by rail. In a moment of horror we realised it was the same angular guard with his distinctive limp. Would it be 'same guard, same announcement' – surely not!

There was no announcement. Nothing. Not even the usual advice about refreshments at Springfield – which there were, not that we were hungry. Our early 'big British breakfast' back at the Clarendon would keep us going till late afternoon. Sausages, bacon, black pudding, eggs, fried bread, tomatoes, toast...

Russell sensibly asked the guard about the lie of the land, the state of the track.

'Clear run to the Coast, Sir. Why? You expecting trouble?'

He wasn't. We weren't. This was it. We were finally off to travel the route that held more appeal for us than any other. We could only imagine what lay ahead. Russ had read several books on the Midland Line and I'd actually dreamed about it. And yet our breakfast companions at the Clarendon had been contradictory.

'One of the country's unsung treasures,' announced one man who'd ordered a double helping of black pudding. He breathed fumes and was probably still drunk from the night before. Did that make him a reliable witness?

'Totally overrated, I've done the trip hundreds of times,' reckoned another. Hopefully that was a case of familiarity breeding contempt.

As the railcar pulled away from Springfield, mountain-bound, Russ pointed out a feature of our rail travels I hadn't considered. In the space of five years we had now travelled the Christchurch to Springfield stretch twice. Nothing to dine out on really. Not even a double helping of black pudding, but I entered the fact in my diary nonetheless.

It was winter in 1971 when we assembled at Moorhouse Avenue Station, Christchurch, to catch the West Coast railcar for the second time. Same routine, same pack drill. It may have even been the same railcar. It was a Tuesday in July. School was in, winter was in full swing, and unlike us, few were on holiday.

The railcar was full though, and we were pleased we'd made bookings.

Squalls lashed the windows as we pulled out and headed west. Slightly northwest Russ reckoned, as the Fiat picked up speed through the suburbs and we watched citizens of Christchurch heading for work in the inner city. We've always felt a rare sense of privilege, being able to cock a snook at the worker bees, having to go to work in the wind and rain. We've always gone a bit against the grain in that sense, preferring to take our rail holidays at unlikely times. I think it made up for all the times we'd watched the 'passing-through people' on the expresses and limiteds, off on jolly adventures as we remained stranded in Te Kuiti, with our noses pressed up against the glass, as it were.

Addington, where the line north to Picton heads out, and industrial Hornby both flash past as we gather speed and continue westward. Southwestward now, if anything, Russ reckons. He always was a bit pedantic about these things. Beyond Rolleston the railcar takes the Midland Line. The West Coast line. Greymouth or bust, although it's really Ross or bust, as the railcar travels beyond Greymouth down the West Coast as far as Ross, 24 kilometres south of Hokitika.

The journey due west from Rolleston is flat, the line unusually straight, but you can already see we're heading directly for the mountains.

It's a time of reflection and some anxiety. There's been rain on the West Coast and we hope it's not sufficient to close the line again. We pull into Springfield with fingers crossed.

We probably didn't notice the KB engines at Springfield back in 1967, when our West Coast odyssey was cut short. Misty-eyed disappointment would have closed in as we contemplated and eventually climbed aboard the bus heading over the Lewis Pass to the coast. Had we been firing on all cylinders we would surely have seen and marvelled at the magnificent beasts that were the KBs. Coal-burning, unlike the oil-burning converted KAs of the North Island, the huge KBs were a class associated with a particular stretch on the New Zealand system. Springfield to Arthur's Pass. They were the behemoths who took over at Springfield to haul trains up into the Southern Alp foothills. More than that, they developed legendary status.

There was nothing more stirring to a rail-lover's soul than a KB hauling a train up through the grades, with its white exhaust clouds climbing into a clear blue winter sky; the white clouds losing themselves against the backdrop of freshly fallen snow on one or more of the many peaks that either prefaced the Southern Alps, or formed a link in the mountain chain itself. As long as steam was around, the scene would remain a favourite memory, easily on a par with the maritime vistas available on the Picton to Christchurch line.

Then steam was gone. The last KB ran on 22 June 1969 – two years before we were able to enter its orbit and relatively truncated 68km field of influence. The KB was the engine which featured prominently in the *Weekly News* pullout, in relation to the Midland Line. Everyone reckoned it was exactly the same as the KA, only it chomped coal and didn't guzzle oil. But somehow, to me, it looked more imposing. Its magnificence matched that of the mountains. The North Island KA was usually set against an easy rolling green plain, or at best the equally green Raurimu Spiral, and seemed less magnificent than a KB climbing through a mountain range. Perhaps it was illusory.

Image 27

A steam-hauled excursion train in a distinctive hinterland. This could be Switzerland – it certainly wasn't the Waikato.

Then Russ mentioned the KB had an auxiliary steam engine called a booster, which concentrated its power on the rear wheels of the bogie under the engine cab. This helped the engine climb the tough grades of the Midland Line. Russ had found this fact in one of the books he'd been reading. There was technical evidence the KB was more grunty – and had to be.

I guess size isn't everything. But if you're interested in songs about railway engines, the American 'Big Boy' and the New Zealand KB – monsters both – have each had songs written about them.

As we headed towards viaduct country, across the Kowhai River, we contemplated the extra thrill it would have been to be in a train drawn by the big, bucking, coal-chomping KB. We cursed our deal with time. Had we been born ten years earlier the KB would have been hauling the West Coast Express and we would have been on it. But we had little control over our passage into the world. 'We didn't ask to be born' (in the late 1940s) – to parrot the checkmating curse of all teenagers.

So we just swayed and rattled along in 1971, in a Fiat railcar with its own charms. It was like an intimate bus ride with people you knew, who seemed less dour than the heavy-set carriage-dwellers of the old expresses. The fixtures were more immediate. The speed was sprightly. The actual driver was just through the door where the seats ran out. There was no connection between the engine crew of the old KB and the passengers in the carriages, who must have seemed like abstract artefacts, perfect and complete strangers who could have been All Blacks, royalty, your mother – for all the driver and firemen knew. It wasn't a case of 'this is your captain speaking,' from the driver. And if the passengers only knew the working conditions of the crew in the cab of the KB they would be thankful for small irritations. A cinder in the eye. Smuts in the fruit hat. Smoke in the tunnels.

Up front it was dirty, dangerous, exposed, hard-edged and hot-surfaced. The only advantage was you could whip up a bacon and egg breakfast on a clean-enough shovel, prodded into the firebox, quicker than the passengers could run, stumble and grope at their pies, cuppas and rock cakes from the refreshment rooms.

It's a wonder more train songs from the steam era haven't been written. There was so much character in steam engines – and the men who worked them were often larger than life. Mind you, John Cooke wrote a paean to the KB, called 'The KB Cannonball', which was later performed by several Kiwi country and western singers.

It just so happened that by 1971 Russ and I had discovered songwriting. Russ was a promising poet. Good with words. A bit pointy-headed at times but able to touch base on most occasions. As the railcar weaved through viaduct country, high above the Waimakariri, across Pattersons Creek Viaduct, through 16 tunnels, over the awe-inspiring Staircase Viaduct, beyond which the line crossed an aerial, flat landscape, far above the river, seemingly wedged into the side of a mountain like a crampon, I scribbled our passage in blank verse. No time to rhyme anything up here. Broken River Viaduct, Slovens Creek Viaduct and then within minutes we were somehow at river level, with the wide, braided upper reaches of the Waimakariri stretching across to a cluster of chalets where we were told university students gathered to study the physical sciences – geology, etc.

Craigieburn, Cass and Cora Lynn – the three Cs – took us higher. All three localities ended up in songs, such was the lilting nature of the names. 'Craigieburn' became a border ballad about an old-time train guard called Craigie Burn, who not only threw freeloaders off the train, but managed to throw a few into the canyon. It was tongue-in-cheek, two-chorded and suitable for the repertoire of a tone-deaf sloth. 'Cass' had more chords. It was a lyrical interpretation of Rita Angus' painting of Cass Station, with a few references to the days of cattle-shooting from the mixed train, coming into Cass.

'Cora Lynn' was more substantial. By now the shadows on the greywacke mountains and the wavering tones of tussock, as we swayed down the Cass Bank, transported me into a dreamstate, not unlike the actual dream I'd had about another New Zealand, beyond the sea and plains, accessible only by train, available only to those who imagined paradise existed not far from their doorstep.

Russ was talking to some bloke in the seat behind us about accounting practices. Accountant to accountant. Balance sheets unbalanced. Here we were, going through heaven and all they could talk about was double entry and other daft stuff. We went past a small lake called Lake Sarah and I wondered if I'd ever seen a body of water so beautiful. The railcar blew its horn, disturbing my contemplation. The clouds flitted past the snow drifts on an unknown stand of mountains.

We were heading almost due west along the reaches of the Bealey River. Arthur's Pass wasn't too far away. I'd already personalised 'Cora Lynn' as a person – in song. I heard the tune in my head about the same time as the guard said there'd be time for refreshments at Arthur's Pass. 'Cora Lynn' was a landgirl, growing wild in the lonely ranges.' The song would be developed once we got back home.

Going from the edges of the Canterbury Plains, beyond Springfield, up into this absolute wonderland, made you wonder if going overseas was even necessary. 'See your own country first', sounded like a tired slogan – almost a boring obligation. What we'd already seen would take a lot of beating internationally. The slogan didn't seem so tired now.

Even Russ curtailed his chat with the Greymouth accountant. We just drank in the scenery. The shapes, the colours, the angles, the surprises. I wasn't too chuffed with physical scenery until I took the railcar from Christchurch to the West Coast. I was used to pretty grand stuff up north, but this was different. It was so overpowering you marvelled at the magic of rail engineers and construction crews who had the audacity to build the line in the first place.

I had been gazing down into the Waimakariri Gorge, astounded at the physical grandeur and feeling a strange pang of loneliness at the realisation there was absolutely no one out there – not even a dairy farmer, a deer stalker or an accountant. Certainly not a petrol station proprietor, given there was a railway, but no road. Perhaps there was an escaped prisoner on the run. Maybe the remnants of a lost tribe. When it became completely pristine, I grabbed my pen:

Last stop, Purgatory,

We should pull in at seven.
Time for a last try for glory,
Change here for heaven.

Arthur's Pass station saw the railcar cruise to a halt, 138 kilometres from Christchurch, and 737 metres above sea level. Eighty empty stomachs hit the platform. We were amongst them. In fact, we were so used to the stampede we were among the first. A cup of coffee, with that distinctive mustard taste, and an oozing mince pie later, saw us gazing up at the mountain walls.

'Who needs to go to Switzerland?' someone muttered, and we both agreed, never having been to Switzerland.

By the time we'd reached Arthur's Pass, it was obvious that everything they'd said about the Midland line was true – the positive stuff. We'd encountered some negative forecasts about how the line was overrated, yet at the halfway stage we had been rendered breathless, as much by the cold alpine draughts, as by the sheer majesty of the scenery.

It may have been because New Zealand railways were sometimes considered to be in decline in the 1960s, that people rather overlooked its surviving positive points.

Image 28

'Who needs to go to Switzerland?' The scenery at Arthur's Pass is stunning.

The burgeoning love of the motorcar, a fetish in many cases, clouded the issue. For some it was no longer the done thing to be seen travelling by train. You had to be out and about in the family Morris Oxford or Austin Cambridge, thoroughly British status symbols which meant you had made it onto the bandwagon, despite the fact the roads were little more than macadamised goat tracks.

In my many travels up and down the main trunk I used to puzzle over the pitiful state of our main highways. The aspect of opposing traffic with the new cars hurtling past one another with nothing more than a white line – and not even that at times – never failed to alarm me. Meanwhile the expresses, limiteds and railcars, safely confined to the steel lines, continued to outrun the Morris Minors and then later, in the 1960s, the Minis.

Road deaths began their upward spiral. Cars might be a status symbol but on those puny roads, head-on collisions were both inevitable and horrifying. I couldn't understand why New Zealanders were turning their backs on trains.

If Arthur's Pass and its environs seemed like a tiny European alpine state, the impression was enhanced when we saw the electric locomotives and the overhead wires which fed them. From the beginning it had been determined the steep gradient (1 in 33) of the long Otira Tunnel between Arthur's Pass and Otira, indeed between Canterbury and Westland, would be unsuitable for steam engines. So New Zealand's first electric trains were introduced, to take over from steam to haul trains through the Otira Tunnel.

We'd heard a fair bit about the Otira Tunnel. How, in its day, it was the longest in the southern hemisphere – at 8554 metres, it was over eight kilometres in length. Taking you through the great divide – the Southern Alps no less – it was as legendary a rail feature as the Mohaka Viaduct on the Gisborne line or the Raurimu Spiral on the main trunk.

I'd been through the Rimutaka Tunnel, on the way from Wellington to the Wairarapa, and it was marginally longer than the Otira. But the

Otira was different. From the Canterbury side it descended on a 1.33 gradient, which seemed to enhance the impression of speed. And it was well known that Fiat railcars really hooped along when they had a straight run. The Otira Tunnel was as straight as a die, slightly downhill, and the West Coast railcar was running fifteen minutes late. There was plenty of incentive to put the foot down.

The sound of the speeding railcar was shrill. The internal lights flickered like glow-worms disturbed by loud noises. Reflections of fellow passengers flickered too, like images of extras in an old silent movie. For the first time in my life during my train travels, I figured our numbers were up. The railcar seemed out of control. I looked to Russ for reassurance. He was sound asleep – or was he refusing to witness our inevitable demise? Then I heard him snore a couple of times above the screaming sound of steel on steel, and I began to relax.

Eight kilometres is a hell of a long way when you're in a huge hole, passing through the base of the spine of the South Island, and praying for daylight to return. My thoughts raced as the railcar seemed to speed up even more. This could be a time machine racing to meet our antecedents from previous archaeological eras a million years ago, when men walked on all fours through ancient cavern networks.

Some time later, just as you resigned yourself to a fate of travelling back in time in perpetual darkness, light appeared. Daylight. West Coast daylight. The railcar passed through Otira and into another land. Rain was falling. We gripped the armrests. Did this mean a slip on the line would consign us to another bus trip? I mean, it was heavy rain and rivulets ran down rock faces and water courses frothed. It hadn't been raining in Canterbury. That's why it looked like Canterbury. And now the West Coast rain gave rise to a different hinterland – damp, green and distinctively different.

Image 29

The great outdoors. The scenery ranged from spectacular to moody, serene to overpowering.

It was hard to believe we were still in New Zealand.

We followed the Otira River through Aickens, where it linked up with the Taramakau River. Beyond the settlement of Jacksons the line crossed the Taramakau. We would meet up with this river later in our travels. Aickens was named after an early settler in the district who subsequently married the daughter of Adam Jackson, after whom the settlement of Jacksons was named.

Behind us mist-covered mountains and foothills receded. The sky was full of flitting rain clouds, waiting to dump their load before heading for the alps. Westland is a smorgasbord of varying landscapes. Ancient forests hug the river banks or flank lakes of still, black water. In the clearings cattle graze on cleared, if soggy, land. Around the next curve gorse bushes and nikau palms replace the old forests. Native bush and ponga groves surround abandoned cottages and occupied villas standing alone in fern-lined paddocks.

Beyond Inchbonnie, surely one of the most lyrical place names on the rail network, the line passes Lake Poerua before heading through Rotomanu, Te Kinga and Ruru, to eventually arrive at Moana.

We stopped for quite a while at Moana Station on the shores of Lake Brunner. The setting was stunning. Beyond the waters of Westland's largest lake the distant ranges claimed the skyline. It was hard to imagine a more picturesque station setting in New Zealand, particularly as the rain had gone and blue sky dominated.

'It's usually raining,' the West Coaster from across the aisle reckoned.

'It was raining in 1967,' I replied. 'We couldn't get through on the railcar because ten days' rain caused a slip near Otira.'

'However, you can get days like this,' the West Coaster suddenly seemed defensive, taking up the cudgels of his home territory. 'Outsiders make too much of the West Coast rain,' he concluded.

We didn't bother mentioning he'd started the conversation.

Rain or no rain, I continued to feel miffed about the lack of promotion, interest and certainly status associated with train travel. Here at Moana we were grateful for the delay. The early afternoon usually sees me nodding off in such situations, but not with the blue, languid waters of Lake Brunner drawing you in. It isn't a massive expanse – about 41 square kilometres – but even when we first saw it in 1971 it was hard to understand why more people hadn't built houses and cribs on the idyllic site, or at least travelled by train to see it.

The River Arnold flows out of Lake Brunner and soon we were following its course. Thick native rainforests almost strangled the river in places, such was their prolific growth. Pukekos stalked through the occasional swamp. The localities of Kotuku, Kaimata and Kokiri were passed before the Arnold River met up with the Grey at Stillwater.

The line headed west beyond Stillwater, following the course of the mighty Grey River, which predictably was in flood.

'Minor flood,' the West Coaster interjected when we mentioned the river seemed to be uncommonly engorged with water – again.

I preferred it that way. It added an edge to proceedings, as did the increasing evidence of man's encroachment. After the picturesque passage from Otira to Stillwater, a stretch that seemed to feature more pukeko than people, the Grey's hinterland was more about the hand of humans. Larger settlements occupied the river banks on both sides. Brunner, Dobson and loose amalgams of old bungalows, villas and miners' cottages marked an increase of habitation as we approached Greymouth. The railcar was sounding its horn regularly now, as the level crossings increased. We recognised the S-shaped rail bridge across the Grey which had carried us on the Rewanui Incline train five years earlier. Then, as the rain stopped, we pulled into Greymouth.

The railcar in 1971 connected Christchurch with Ross, a small town 64 kilometres down the coast from Greymouth. We knew nothing about Ross and figured it was an odd name for a town – after all, it was a fairly common boy's name. We later discovered the town was named after a gold prospector, but we were never really sure whether Ross was his Christian name or surname.

Image 30

In later years the Midland Line was no longer taken for granted. The TranzAlpine train became a world beater. Here the sort of scenery we tended to overlook is reflected in a TranzAlpine carriage window.

Our tickets ran out at Greymouth, but such was the spirit of adventure we'd generated on our most excellent journey, we defiantly stayed on the railcar as it pulled out of Greymouth, heading south into another rainstorm. We figured we'd pay for additional tickets if required. After all, the guard seemed reasonably disposed.

Most guards of our experience were uniformly tall, rigid of uniform, narrow of eye, stubbled of chin. Often solicitous of young mothers with babies and children, they could be quite dismissive of most other passengers.

Then, on the Greymouth–Ross section, we came across a shorter, squatter, bow-legged, clean-shaven man who was quite garrulous. And he couldn't stand children. We first encountered him when he entered our carriage at a point when the railcar was bucking and swaying while making up time. His bow legs anchored him to the aisle, as he utilised his unusually long arms to position his hands to clip tickets. As he advanced down the aisle, speaking to all and sundry about the fate of mankind, the state of the nation, the rate of his train's acceleration, we swore he kept his balance by dragging his knuckles along the aisle floor.

'All tickets please, ladies, gentlemen and others.'

We cowered a bit as he approached but he gave us a wave as he bow-legged his way past us. It was a fair hike down to Hokitika with the line following the coast beside the highway. The rainstorm hit at Paroa, a virtual suburb of Greymouth. Heavy rain, then hail, clattered against the windows. Lightning lit up the darkening horizon. Whitecaps were barely visible in the gloom. If we thought we were getting a bonus in terms of unpaid scenic wonders, we were temporarily mistaken. Gladstone and Camerons were station names which barely cut through the gloom, but suddenly at Kumara Junction the skies cleared, revealing the remnants of a classic West Coast sunset. The sun had gone but the brocade of colour that exploded above the horizon – the melting pinks and purples, the drifting yellows, like egg yolks smudging the whites of remaining rain clouds – were spectacular.

We had crossed the Taramakau River a few minutes before on one of the last remaining road-rail bridges on the network. A line of cars and trucks with their headlights cutting through the sheets of rain, waited for their turn on the bridge. The river was running high, just as the Grey was doing back up the Coast. After our experience with West Coast rain in 1967, we began thinking about floods, slips and line closures.

Image 31

Was the delay at Moana station a planned move, the better to appreciate the view across Lake Brunner and beyond?

At Kumara Junction a fierce wind blew the storm northwards, just in time for us to appreciate the remarkable sunset. Mind you, darkness fell quickly as we pulled out of Kumara Junction, leaving us to contemplate the notion of ending our journey at Hokitika, rather than travel further south to Ross where, in the darkness, we might be hard pressed to find a bed for the night. Did they have beds in Ross? Our West Coast geography was undeveloped.

As the railcar bucked along the track adjacent to the coastline, through the whistlestop of Arahura, we had time to contemplate the unusual circumstances of

Kumara Junction. Further inland lay the township of Kumara and during the years the line was constructed, the mayor of Kumara was Richard 'King Dick' Seddon. Seddon held out for the line to pass through his town but the powers that be favoured the coastal route. When 'King Dick' became MP for Kumara he was able to bring even more weight to bear on the decision.

Hard times delayed construction and in 1880 the route of the line was put in the 'too hard' basket until later in the decade. Then a third attempt to have the line pass through Kumara township was mounted, but finally the coastal route to Hokitika was chosen and in 1893, it finally reached its destination.

So much rail history. Back up north the main trunk that served Te Kuiti wasn't completed until 1908. We mentioned this to the friendly, bow-legged guard as he returned to the rear of the railcar. In the process he caught my eye and regarding this as a signal for conversation, filled us in on the Kumara situation. He had a lot to say, but we were only able to decipher half of his spiel, because of the sound of the wheels squealing on bends.

'This started out as a timber line, you know.' We heard that bit and nodded knowingly.

'Headed south as a horse tramway running on wooden rails.' We thought he meant the original line carted wood out of the bush on steel rails but chose not to reveal our ignorance. Besides, we were expecting him to ask for our tickets at any moment, which would reveal our illegal-traveller status on his train. We didn't encourage him but he kept on, describing how the Taramakau River had to be crossed by passengers in a cage dangling from a flimsy wire. We felt tempted to mention he would have been in his element, with his long arms, in an environment where dangling cages and swinging from tree to tree was de rigueur.

The guard (we called him 'King Dick', because he mentioned Richard Seddon's name a lot, and claimed to be 'half-related' to the great man), kept talking about timber. Timber was the principal transportable commodity in the area. There were many mills and several had their own bush trams. So timber was being carted along lines made of timber. Were the steam engines made of timber too? The guard laughed, an unusual response for a member of a usually taciturn profession.

'Not to my knowledge, sir. But I'll tell you this. You'll be lucky to find a stone building in this neck of the woods.'

'You'd expect a lot of timber in a neck of the woods,' Russ replied. The guard laughed again, and we were beginning to feel more relaxed and less poised to strike in our defence of not having a ticket to cover the stretch from Greymouth to Ross.

The guard, well anchored, withstood the lurch as we crossed the Arahura River – on a bridge, not in a cage. The Tasman dumped its whitecaps on the black sand beaches to the west. Although night had all but fallen, the whitecaps were clearer than during the freakish storm that passed over like God wiping his nose.

'Bear in mind,' the guard continued, 'If you boys wanted to travel further south, beyond Ross, it might have been possible.'

I reached in my top pocket for a ten dollar note, expecting to be nailed and railroaded for the fare.

'Stuart and Chapman ran a timber tram from Ross all the way south to Lake Ianthe. It only closed in the 1950s and there were plans to continue this line along those timber tram formations almost all the way to Harihari. That would have been some journey, don't you think? I mean it would have been really something to take the railway closer to Fiordland. Could have gone through Okarito, Te Taho, Mount Hercules...'

'What happened?' Russ asked. 'Did King Dick put in a protest?'

'I know what you're saying,' the guard replied as off to the left Seaview Mental Hospital hove into view. 'It's all about timber, but it's not.' That's not what we were saying at all but we weren't given a chance to expand. 'Whitebait are big down this stretch too, the little buggers. It's not just timber. It wasn't too many years ago a box car full of whitebait was attached on a daily basis to a late train out of Ross, and soon lovers of the marine morsels in Greymouth and Christchurch were frittering them for their dinner.'

We still hadn't made a choice, in the dark, about Hokitika or Ross as our disembarkation point. We were getting hungry and the mere talk of whitebait was enough to start us thinking with our stomachs.

'Is there anything at Ross,' I asked. 'Motels, hotels, accommodation?'

The guard became strangely elusive. 'Let's just say that in the good old days when the West Coast Express was running, through coaches from Greymouth brought passengers on the mixed trains, all the way to Ross. There was a locomotive shed there too.'

Did the through passengers stay in the loco shed? Was that what the guard was suggesting?

'Have you boys booked accommodation in Ross?'

'No. But then we haven't booked in Hokitika either.'

'Seems you haven't booked anything really, if you know what I mean.'

This time Russ reached for a ten dollar note.

The station lights cut through the swirling mist as the railcar finally pulled into Hokitika. The thought of whitebait fritters and empty stomachs had finally tipped the scales in its favour. It looked like a largish town, one in which a bed for the night wouldn't be too hard to find.

Hokitika it was, and as we shuffled down the railcar aisle behind King Dick the Second, a stray bolt of lightning almost hit some sort of memorial and lit up the main street, complete with weather-boarded hotels and shops. Not a stone establishment as far as the eye could see.

As most passengers formed a queue at the railcar door, and King Dick counted heads and clipped the odd ticket, we both reached for our spare ten dollar notes. Only a handful of passengers were travelling on to Ross. As we passed King Dick at the railcar door he asked us for our tickets. We handed them over: Christchurch to Greymouth. One way...

Image 32

Beyond the great divide, the railcar – here in twinset formation – operates on the West Coast. Darkness was falling – and rain – when we first travelled this stretch.

He either didn't read the details, or chose not to. He simply clipped our tickets, giving them holes they already had, and handed them back to us. 'Enjoy the whitebait, boys,' he said. We grinned and said nothing.

Nothing was also the response of the hotel proprietor in Hokitika. No whitebait. They weren't running that week. So we stuck to fish and chips. They were very good. The fish was turbot, a flounder-like flat fish which made a pleasant change from the hunks of shark you usually got up north. The meal, in the hotel restaurant, was on the house. It was an old establishment and had seen better days. Our room was bleak and battered, and there was only one towel. West Coast condensate oozed down the scrim wall, in time-honoured fashion. We figured the free meal was justified. Boxes of books and rusting kitchen utensils waited in the corner for removal. Or just waited ... One of the boxes contained old cricket books by mainly English writers – John Arlott, Neville Cardus. I figured that was a bonus and retired on one of the twangy wire-wove beds that made a sound like the beginnings of the guitar riff from Duane Eddy's 'Rebel Rouser' while

reading about the ashes cricket series of 1954/1955 between Australia and England.
Image 33

Hokitika Station, where we finally decided to end our journey. A steam-hauled passenger service and a hovering Vulcan railcar can be seen.

The rain really hosed down overnight and we figured there would have to be a slip somewhere, endangering railway lines and causing cancellations. We felt relieved we'd booked flights out the next morning. No more traumatising, soul-destroying, sudden trips on bland buses for us. A Fokker Friendship would do the job, just so long as the airport wasn't underwater.

The rain became heavier at 2am. I know. I was still awake reading a fascinating account of the career of English cricketer, Trevor Bailey. The latter was famous for 'stone-walling', slow scoring and 'holding up an end'. It should have made for boring reading but it didn't. As our cricket coach once said: 'It's harder not to score in cricket than it is to make runs.' Maybe.

Russ, in the other bed next to the wall where condensate gathered, snored through it all: the storm that pelted the tin roof like buckshot, and the sound of an out-of-tune honky-tonk piano coming from the lounge next door. No doubt he was dreaming of a classic railcar journey four years in the making and 260 kilometres in the taking – Christchurch to Hokitika, no less. It could have been even further: Christchurch to Ross. But we figured we would probably return in a year or two and carry on to Ross to see what all the fuss was about. Right?

Wrong. A year later the railcar from Christchurch stopped running south of Greymouth. Ross, from a rail perspective, would always be a mystery.

6

The world's southernmost rail journey

The Southerner between Christchurch and Invercargill

Image 34

The Southerner at Gore. A new train on the block – a vital cog in the 'renaissance of New

Zealand rail' in the 1970s. Its distinctive blue livery contrasts with a drab sky.

In our youthful haste to travel on as many passenger trains as possible, we overlooked certain factors that, had we been more calculated and traditional, would have enriched the experience.

When we were in the South Island on our first odyssey, steam-drawn expresses and limiteds were still operating. The end of steam was nigh, so nigh in fact that when we were in the middle of our second South Island odyssey in 1971, they only had a few months to run. The final steam-drawn expresses between Christchurch and Invercargill pulled into their stations in October of that very same year. Not long before, we had been ambling happily around mainly on railcars. What a missed opportunity!

There was a hectic, desperate aspect to our rail odysseys. For a start we felt remiss, almost guilty. We had drifted away from the railways, and shifted allegiance to the car and bus, at a time when the railways needed all the friends they could find. That got us going. We had to make up time – and make up for our transgressions. It was as if we'd let the side down.

Then there was the awareness that there wasn't a moment to lose. Progress favoured the car and services were becoming truncated or simply cancelled, before you had any sort of chance. We snuck in with some services but missed by a nose with others.

Of course the sheer excitement and 'romance' of rail travel also prompted us. There was nothing terribly romantic about spluttering up the southern motorway in an ailing Triumph Herald with fumes drifting up through the floorboards making your eyes water. That's no way to see New Zealand – with fume-impaired vision! Nor was running out of petrol in an ancient Citroen near Te Popo, inland Taranaki, with owls hooting and only the stars to guide you.

Far better, now that you'd shifted allegiance, to be tucked up in a warm railcar, sharing scenic experiences with interesting strangers, going down valleys neglected by roads.

I guess we didn't have time to be staunch steam fans as well, tracing the demise of the volcanoes on wheels, like older rail buffs. The encroachment of railcars and diesels had been so much a part of our young lives living on the North Island Main Trunk that we regarded the casting out of steam as a done deal. Just like the inevitability of motor cars and buses. The smoke signals had dispersed. The cries for help fell on deaf ears.

In retrospect, in 1971, we should have factored in a journey on a steam-hauled express between Christchurch and Invercargill. My favourite steam engine – the JA – pulled the last of the trains and it seemed totally disloyal to pass up the opportunity to enjoy, for one last time, a steam-hauled train and summon the nostalgia that first attracted me to the railways.

Instead we caught The Southerner.

The Southerner was another shock to the system. When it was introduced at the end of 1970, it represented a wholehearted attempt to increase patronage on the route of the old Christchurch–Dunedin–Invercargill Express. This renaissance of rail passenger travel would come to encompass the Northerner, the Silver Star, the Silver Fern, the Blue Streak and the Endeavour, as well as the Southerner.

Increased speed of passage and operation was a primary focus and fewer stops were made. The trains were tarted up in more ways than one. New carriage liveries, design and amenities, a hostess service, buffet and/or dining cars and alcohol freely available. Not that kind of free – the other one. You had to pay for it.

We first encountered the Southerner in 1971, about a year after it had been plying the 'Great Southern Route'. We would travel on it several times in the next few years but nothing can match the thrill of taking your place on a new train travelling over tracks you'd never encountered before.

Image 35

A steam-hauled South Island Express. The end of steam was nigh, yet we were blithely oblivious or didn't care.

It suited us to catch the Southerner at Dunedin and travel south to Invercargill. A few days later, on my own, I caught it again heading north to Christchurch from Dunedin.

Before our first trip on the Southerner, we bunked down with friends who used to live near our home at Hamilton. Joe played the guitar and starred at student parties. He and I exchanged a few song ideas. Now Joe and his partner had transferred to Dunedin to further their studies at Otago University and they lived in a delightful, if slightly dilapidated, old colonial cottage with its roof sloping steadily from the front porch to the kitchen at the back. It paid to be shorter than 1.72m if you wanted to walk comfortably around the rear kitchen with its coal range and homely warmth.

'That's why in days gone by women did the cooking,' Joe reckoned. It was nothing to do with men being male chauvinist pigs, and refusing to do it. They just couldn't fit in the kitchen, being invariably over 1.72m tall. His partner Jill rolled her eyes. Women's rights were in the wind and staying in the students' 'ghetto' (Joe's word) ensured a climate of change would be the prevailing forecast.

We were allocated the side bedroom. Russ, at 1.75m, banged his head a few times. I, at 1.67m, emerged unscathed. Beyond the placards and banners proclaiming *Stop the Tour, Ban the Bomb, Kick a Cop* or *Punch a Pom,* canvas haversacks and smelly oilskins, we found two tiny beds – one with a half-folded tent as a blanket. It was cold at night.

'The boys are off on a rail odyssey,' Joe mentioned to Jill. 'The round trip in fact. Dunedin to Invercargill by Southerner, by bus up to Alexandra, then down the central line back to Dunedin on the old railcar.'

It was the old railcar trip which attracted most attention.

'We'd come to see you off at the station but we're going on a protest rally,' Joe said.

'What's the cause?'

'Stop the Tour I think.'

'What tour?'

'The Springbok tour of New Zealand.'

That wasn't scheduled until 1973. I knew my dates on this one. A week before we arrived in Dunedin in 1971 the All Blacks lost to the British Lions 13-3 at Athletic Park. Barry John scored a try.

'We're starting our protest early,' Joe replied shrewdly.

Jill corrected him. 'No, it's Ban the Bomb.'

Several other students dropped by. They were fascinated by these two North Islanders wanting to travel on the old railcar through Central Otago.

'That's cool man,' announced one duffel-coated oaf. 'Not many North Islanders would even know it was there. They might have heard of the Southerner though.'

We warbled the night away as Joe chose appropriate train songs like 'Last Train to San Fernando', 'Freight Train' and 'It takes a lot to laugh, it takes a train to cry'. As we caterwauled into the freezing night, a new song emerged. 'Train of thought' was a typical restless travelling paean to drop-out times. As promised to Joe I later wrote another one, inspired by the Alexandra railcar route – 'Goodbye Ida Valley'. I can still remember the words and hum the tune, neither of which made it a great song. But it made some sense committing memories and impressions to words and tunes, while travelling through matchless, hitherto unseen landscapes. And interesting places with interesting names. 'Goodbye Te Kuiti' would never cut it as a song, though. The mere thought of it set off a cultural cringe enough to permanently wrinkle a face.

After fighting for sleep in the tiny side bedroom, trying to quell the cold with oilskins, haversacks and placards, we were grateful for the chance to sleep in the following morning. The Southerner, after setting out from Christchurch, arrived in Dunedin in the early afternoon.

Just waiting for the Southerner was a wondrous experience. We'd never seen Dunedin railway station before. It is the most distinctive station on the system. Indeed, it's now regarded as one of the finest Edwardian structures in New Zealand. Its main body is built of stone from Hyde in Central Otago, while the ornamental work is Oamaru limestone. It has mosaic floors, a 37-metre-high clock tower and the longest station platform in the country – 500 metres.

As we pulled away from designer George Troup's impressive station, heading into the unknown, it seemed a little disorientating to be starting another rail adventure in the early afternoon. Clean beginnings in pristine morning light struck us as being the ideal time to commence a rail trek along virgin tracks, before industrial haze and horizon-shimmering heat have a chance to set in. When the mind is sharp and primed with a breakfast coffee or two.

Nonetheless, it doesn't take too much prodding to appreciate the southern Dunedin villas and buildings from the Victorian era, Carisbrook rugby grounds and the Mosgiel woollen mills, before the Southerner thunders across the Taieri Plains, past the still waters of Lake Waihola. We cross the mighty Clutha River at Balclutha and head across country to Clinton, before setting out for Gore and the deep south.

Back when it was introduced, on 1 December 1970, what appealed to travellers on the new Southerner as much as anything, was the on-board nosh. For the first time since 1917 meals were available on board. Buffet cars with long counters and a kitchen at one end were a feature. Old jokes about 'time for refreshments' died. This was an altogether different approach.

Old habits die hard though. When the Southerner stopped at Gore station, one puffing man was seen running down the platform, heading for a pie and a cuppa at the refreshment rooms. He hadn't travelled on a train for years.

Others weren't drawn into this trap but they nonetheless expected pre-packaged, re-heated airline-type food. A plethora of pies perhaps? Certainly the battered teapots had gone – but three-course meals, cooked as required, offered a genuine touch of sophistication. It felt like being in an American diner, which are often carriage-shaped, with long counters and individual stools.

Rail food for passengers travelling on trains plying the South Island Main Trunk line had come full circle – twice. In the very early days refreshments were provided at various stations. Then in 1899 dining cars were attached to express trains running between Christchurch and Dunedin, but in 1917, because of war-time austerities, the dining cars were converted into conventional carriages and station refreshment rooms returned as the accepted means of replenishment.

Image 36

A good place to start a journey: Dunedin railway station, the nation's finest. You could spend a week exploring it before actually catching a train.

Now, in 1971, as I tucked into a ham omelette on the Southerner, the thought arose that the railway refreshment rooms of myth would soon go the way of the long-drop toilet. We would be back in 1899, taking all our sustenance on board. The Southerner was a little ahead of itself though. Railcars and night expresses were still running along the South Island Main Trunk and refreshment rooms would continue to be required for their passengers. Indeed, the final refreshment stops on the line weren't made until September 1979, when the last conventional expresses called at Clinton Station in the deep south.

Initially we enjoyed the refreshment room stampedes. As young boys and later uncouth youths, such mad-headed scrambling and skidding was something you weren't allowed to do at home, but in the middle of the night, in the murk of station lights, who was going to haul you out by the ear and dress you down? Certainly not the guard who was more concerned with securing his own cuppa and rock cake.

As young men it was semi-tough and laudable to take on the tirades and physical jerks often required to place yourself and your order at the refreshment counter and somehow spirit the well-gotten gains back to the bowels of a darkened carriage, where you were pleased to take up the challenge of being able to juggle a cup of hot tea and a plate of food while easing yourself back into your seat. Particularly if that attractive young lady sitting opposite seemed to be taking an interest in your progress.

Image 37

The Southerner, part of the new fleet, reaches Clinton, where a more familiar but fading Fiat railcar waits at the platform.

As mature adults the stampedes and tirades lost their appeal. It suddenly seemed like a daft way to get yourself topped up. And you felt sorry for older folk, shaky of grip, who often lost control of their victuals in their haste to get back to the train in time – rather than being stranded in a place like Clinton.

It was harder to feel sorry for Noel Thomas, who would have been an adrenaline junky today, but back in the 1960s was a fully-fledged fool. It was Noel's habit to beat the stampede by jumping off the train while the carriage was still moving at a considerable clip, break into a sharp sprint as his winkle-pickers hit the asphalt, and be the first to return to the train with two steaming hot pies and a look of invincibility. One night he came a cropper. A porter had positioned a luggage wagon on the part of the Palmerston North platform Noel would normally have negotiated and when he saw his path blocked he swayed a bit to the right. Right into a concrete column holding up the roof. The column took all the pace off Noel and he went down for the count. He lost a couple of teeth and missed out on his two pies. Some kind travelling companion bought him a single pie while Noel limped back to the train, but he found it very hard to eat a hot pie with bleeding gums.

'Time for refreshments' was a bit like 'Time gentlemen, please'. Not everyone liked the six o'clock swill either but, like the refreshment stampedes, it was around for long enough to make you think it was immutable. A bit like the guard's van situation of the 1980s when guard's vans – and guards – suddenly disappeared off the end of trains. Some accountant reckoned they weren't necessary. They were just 'nice to have' add-ons – and cost a lot of money. So guard's vans went the way of the long-drop toilet. Trains didn't fall off the line as some traditionalists reckoned they would.

There was much speculation when refreshment rooms starting closing. Time for refreshments was up, in many places. Those who disliked the stampede figured some important person had finally listened to reason. Those for whom the institution held a certain fascination, were not saddened to learn many refreshment rooms would be retained, long beyond the introduction of more civilised eating arrangements associated with the Southerner.

'Beats me why they don't close them all down. Refreshment rooms are a shambles and a poor reflection on New Zealand railways and New Zealand in general.' The portly man dressed like a public servant sitting next to us had a point.

'As long as we've still got steam-hauled passenger trains in parts of the country, why close the refreshment rooms on those lines?' the young buffet attendant said. 'The engines have to stop regularly to take on water, so why not utilise that downtime topping up the passengers at refreshment rooms?' Until that moment I had never made the connection between the needs of steam engines and the survival of refreshment rooms on steam-hauled routes. Sometimes there's a reason that things don't happen.

By the late 1970s when Perry Rice, a fellow rail enthusiast, travelled on the Southerner, steam-hauled services had gone. As had refreshment rooms, at least on the Southerner's route. New Zealanders had become used to on-board food, and there were fewer incidents of rogue refreshment-rooms-bound runners, who still harkened to the time-worn summons that echoed the call, 'if you don't run you won't eat.'

They had become used to the ease of procuring alcoholic beverages on the Southerner too, with which to cement friendships – or mere acquaintances – with the increasingly exotic international travellers who now frequented the service.

Perry Rice recalled one such encounter:

It must have been at Oamaru that a typically brash Aussie boarded the Southerner. The sort who has a voice like a TV sports commentator – a high-pitched, rasping, guttural slur that only suburban Sydney can produce.

'Funny liddool treks yewr 'ave heer myte!'

'Really?' said I. 'Good for a laugh then ... sort of keeps you amused as you travel.'

'Trynes are liddool too!'

'Compact,' said I. 'Compact.'

This loquacious larrikin was rapidly becoming a pest of great persistence and no perception. After a bit, after he'd delivered a damning critique of NZR – 'Thur seeneries good but!' – he suggested we should have a beer. My mind started to race – here's my chance. A hot day, hot railway carriages and beer.

We proceeded to the bar. The train manager (no waiters or guards – managers), a red-haired southlander of moderate years, probably from Gore, asked what we would like. The 'orrible Aussie asked for a cold 4X – none on board. He then asked if there was a VB in the fridge.

This was my cue. 'VB mate? VB?' You're travelling mate! Travelling about; experiencing different cultures and customs mate. You don't want to spend all that money coming down south just to drink cold VB!'

'Oh yeah, whaddya got?'

'Ever tried Speights mate?'

'Na.'

I nodded to the pile of boxes on the floor behind the bar and said to the train manager, 'Two Speights thanks mate – my shout!'

'Good on ya mate,' said the Aussie.

The train manager reached to open the wee caravan fridge. 'No no!' said I, 'we'll do this in the Southern way,' again nodding to the boxes on the floor. The train manager raised an eyebrow quizzically, and I nodded again. He sighed a conspiratorial sigh and pulled two cans of Speights from the box. The Aussie observed the cans were not cold. I told him they were bang on.

'Here's to the ANZACs,' I said and quietly told him you have to guzzle it down. Like any good Aussie boozer the can was tipped up, jaws parted and Speights flowed. It took the train manager several minutes and half a roll of paper towels to clean the beer off the window after the Aussie involuntarily sprayed the unfamiliar, room temperature beer all over the place.

New Zealand 1, Australia nil.

Back in 1971 it had been a long day on the train but it could have been longer had we caught the Southerner in Christchurch. For all that, fatigue set in as the train turned left at Gore and headed virtually due south towards Mataura. Russell started rolling his Rs. A worrying symptom, I figured, of having been engulfed by local customs and perhaps a deep-south virus.

Perhaps we should have been contemplating a drop of the hard stuff. A dram of something to stiffen our sinews and thicken the blood against the looming cold of New Zealand's southernmost city. A fellow passenger was warning a young English tourist about the perishing perils of Invercargill. How it was the last city before Antarctica, which as the crow flew, wasn't that far south in the southern ocean. Why, the train could yet be derailed by an iceberg reckoned our fellow passenger, a ruddy-faced man from Makarewa who rolled his Rs, making his home town sound like an outpost in the Hebrides.

Image 38

The Southerner at Timaru. Tales of loquacious Aussies and room-temperature beer surfaced here some years later. Or was that at Oamaru?

As we passed through the suburbs of Invercargill, night had fallen. Deep southerners could be seen clustering around open fires, coal ranges and bar heaters as the night came down. There were many bungalows and many streets. Invercargill was surprisingly sprawling. It had been easy to forget it used to be regarded as a large New Zealand city. Its heyday in the 1950s was past but that didn't mean it had reduced in size. Just because population growth eases doesn't mean houses are torn down, suburbs bulldozed over, and wide streets narrowed.

In the warmth of the Southerner carriage the air temperature outside was a matter of pure speculation. In the bungalows beside the track, fireplaces roared, bar heaters really glowed. Prompted by the man from Makarewa, the young English tourist was invited to check suburban station fixtures for ice stalactites and the roadways for sheet ice and snow deposits. The man from Makarewa gave us a wink.

Invercargill Station at last – at 5.30 – was large enough, but compared with the caviar of Dunedin's grand edifice, it was like rolled oats – and cold at that. But nowhere near as cold as we had anticipated, and certainly not the icy hell alluded to by the man from Makarewa who was first off the train and soon gone. The platforms were long and windswept, yet if anything the wind was warming. Or perhaps it was the fact we'd rugged up with all available windbreakers, duffel coats, scarves and woollen hats.

The Antarctic seemed a long way away. Mind you, it was a wonder there wasn't a junction connection to the ice-shelf from Invercargill Station. There were connections to just about everywhere else.

The Seaward Bush line radiated out as far east as Tokanui on the edge of the Catlins. The Kingston line headed almost due north for kilometres before coming to rest at the southern edge of Lake Wakatipu. The Tuatapere branch headed east via Makarewa, off the Kingston line, and the Bluff line snaked for 24km south towards the icebergs. There were other branches as well, and on learning this mine of branch line information from the proprietor of our hotel, Russ was adamant we should dally a while in *Inver* (he was beginning to abbreviate his words, which was as obvious a warning sign as rolling your Rs) to partake of the branch line smorgasbord.

'It gets cold in them branch guard's vans,' the proprietor reckoned while holding up my cheque to the single swinging light bulb. It was his way of saying that conventional passenger services were no longer available on the branch trains. We cursed the march of progress as we were shown to our digs at the back of the hotel. The demise of the steel roads and the iron horse, eh? There was a sad irony, too, in the fact that not six months after passing through Southland, a brand new passenger service called the Kingston Flyer – steam-hauled and everything – started running from Lumsden to Kingston on the old Kingston branch. It first pulled out in its modern incarnation on 21/12/71. We had been too early. At other junctures and junctions we had been too late.

We didn't dally in Invercargill. Really cold draughts were now whistling in from the Antarctic. The weather change clicked over at about 2am, as we were dreaming about the journeys that lay ahead and thrashing a bit at the frustration engendered by our poor timing in regards to the rolling out of the Kingston Flyer. The wind change found out every crack around the window frames and under the basic brown door. Four blankets were now not enough and to the accompaniment of the mounting moan of the southern blast, Russ and I emptied our bags to create layers of socks, underpants, singlets, spare jerseys and shirts, shaving gear and other weight-bearing toiletries, every towel from the bathroom, the bath mat, even the carpet square from the middle of the room (which covered some ugly cigarette burns in the lino). Despite all this additional bedding it was still impossible to get warm. Russ threatened to rip the flapping wallpaper off the scrim walls and swaddle himself in that, but he seemed placated by several layers of the *Southland Daily Times* which, as luck would have it, featured thick 'properties for sale' and 'situations vacant' supplements. We curled up like homeless vagrants and waited for the dawn.

'A bit bracing today, boys,' the hotel proprietor reckoned, while doubling as our breakfast waiter in a dining room smelling of pork and disinfectant. The knives and forks were icy to the touch, but the tea was hot. The day was grey and turning. The scheduled storm was right on time – just like the Southerner – only going the other way.

Image 39

The 'Seasider', sole survivor on the famous southern route. In recent years it has been the only regularly scheduled service. At least the mutton pies in Palmerston enhanced our experience.

We contemplated catching the warm, friendly Southerner back to the north, but as this collective thought rose to the surface we realised that at 8.15am the Southerner would already be 15 minutes into its journey north.

So we stuck to the original plan, which was to catch a bus or two to get to Alexandra via Queenstown, and take the Central Otago railcar running from Alexandra all the way across country back to Dunedin.

I don't think it was my idea to travel on what I imagined would be another back-country, beaten up 'social' service. We'd been spoiled rotten on the Southerner, swayed by the newness and convenience of on-board food, and cans of beer on call. And heated carriages. Someone said the Central Otago railcar could be quite cold in winter, and anyway, wasn't going through the sparsely populated backblocks of Central a bit like travelling through the backblocks of any other New Zealand rural area? If nothing else, it would provide a stark contrast with the Southerner's passage.

When you consider the notion of the line between Christchurch and Invercargill, via Dunedin, you had to marvel at the sheer expanse of the connection – 601.4 kilometres. In 1879 it was New Zealand's first trunk line to be opened, and over the years expresses, limiteds, railcars and mixed goods trains were common people-carriers, as the major cities of the South Island grew.

It defies belief that in 2014, apart from the tourist operator Taieri Gorge Railway scheduling an out-and-back journey from Dunedin to Palmerston called the Seasider, this historic, pivotal stretch of track does not accommodate a passenger train.

Image 40

The railway line at sunset, near Dunsandel on the Canterbury Plains.

I caught the Southerner north to Christchurch from Dunedin in 1971 after we'd arrived back in 'student city' from Central Otago. The train, at the end of its scheduled journey, ran all the way through Christchurch to Lyttelton for the convenience of passengers catching the overnight ferry to Wellington. This extension continued until 1976 and I was later to curse myself for not staying with the Southerner until Lyttelton, thereby chalking up another stretch of track – albeit short – still covered by New Zealand passenger services. Then I recalled I *had* been on the Christchurch–Lyttelton line – at a time when such a feat lacked the significance I now placed on my rail odysseys. It was back in 1964 – the year of the Beatles and rugby. During the course of a first-fifteen junket to Canterbury, we had caught the boat train from Lyttelton after getting off the ferry, and travelled through the Lyttelton tunnel and pre-dawn darkness as the electric loco hauled the train through the southern suburbs of Christchurch and on to Moorhouse Avenue Station.

The Beatles, at the height of their fame, toured New Zealand in 1964 and our first fifteen prided itself on being pretty slick. There were other passions to absorb us back then. The boat train was just a means of getting from A to B. We were still buzzing after seeing the Beatles in concert at the Auckland Town Hall (we would see 'A Hard Day's Night', the Beatles first movie while in Christchurch) and plotting rugby manoeuvres for our games in the land of Lancaster Park. Mind you, the buzzing had subsided temporarily as we nodded off in the boat train. It hadn't been a great crossing on the ferry and we had an early start in order to catch the rail link with Christchurch.

Apart from our many trips up and down the North Island main trunk, the short haul along the Lyttelton line was the first time many of us had wandered from our main trunk stamping ground. It was only the second New Zealand railway line we'd travelled on. Except Russ of course, who'd been on the North Auckland and Bay of Plenty lines while on holiday. And Tim Scott, our halfback, who reckoned he'd travelled from Taumarunui to New Plymouth on another line, which seemed a bit far-fetched. We were more impressed by Tim's trick of wearing a fedora hat and being able to sneak into bottle stores on the rim of Cathedral Square – at age 17.

Vague memories of the boat train returned. The grimy electric engine which nonetheless pulled powerfully and quietly, the reflections of faces in the carriage windows as the train went through the mile and three-quarter tunnel, which was how we measured it then, how washed-out our coach looked in the half-light, commuters clustered at Opawa Station, Tim Scott with his fedora pulled over his eyes, the horrible rumbling of pre-breakfast stomachs, the lights of Christchurch going off as the winter sun peeped through the cloud banks.

Image 41

When you got sick of eating, drinking and sleeping you could always take in the Otago scenery as the Southerner headed north.

Considering the time of day and winter's haze, the boat train was surprisingly warm, the result of an AB locomotive having provided steam-heating while shunting the boat train around a tight corner and the wharf. We scoffed a bit at the sight of the old steam engine, unaware it was responsible for heating the carriage. Diesel was the new steam where we came from and we felt a bit smug about that – a feeling we would experience again the following day when we beat Riccarton High School.

History was happening all around us though, on the 1964 boat train. Earlier that year the Lyttelton road tunnel was opened, inevitably consigning the boat trains to the scrapheap. We should have shown more respect for a rail institution which had been serving New Zealanders since the early days. We were a bit more passive after travelling back on the evening boat train a few days later – after losing to Burnside High School and being ticked off by our coach for poor behaviour at the team hotel. Two boys filled a condom with so much tapwater the fire brigade was called out. Tim Scott was caught smuggling bottles of Canterbury Draught up a fire escape, but everyone got a bollocking over that because no one turned down the buckshee beer. The coach was further miffed when we had to hurry our dinner at the hotel in order to make the boat train in time, and things went from bad to worse. One of the waitresses serving our meals somehow managed to get a blob of mashed spuds stuck to the bottom of the plate of meat and three veg she was rushing to the table where the coach was sitting. She did a bit of a pirouette with the plate, hovering momentarily over the coach's bald head. At the crucial moment the mashed spuds came unstuck and slopped on the coach's head, whereupon 15 first fifteeners and all the reserves – and anyone else who was watching – roared with laughter.

Such potential for mayhem came to a halt in 1976, when the inter-island ferry from Lyttelton stopped running. Boat trains and the Southerner no longer needed to link up with the Wellington-bound steamer.

In 2014 the Southerner runs no more – in 2002 it made its last connection between Christchurch and Invercargill. *These things happen,* you might say. Established trains lose their lustre and new, upgraded services take over. But since the Southerner was cancelled there has been no regular, scheduled passenger service linking Christchurch with Invercargill.

Not long before the Southerner stopped running, a friend and I spoke about the possibility of undertaking an ambitious rail trek all the way from Invercargill – the southernmost railway station in the world – to Murmansk, in Russia – the northernmost. We would walk the walk and come back home and write an account of the round journey. It seemed like a good idea. One book publisher showed interest. Before we had a chance to develop the idea, the Southerner was gone. It had left the station for ever. We could have thumbed a ride on a goods train from Invercargill but bearing in mind the book's major focus would have been passenger interaction, much of the appeal died. And *From Christchurch to Murmansk* didn't have the same ring.

Image 42

Te Kuiti High School first fifteeners and a few Otorohanga College travellers assemble during their Christchurch rugby junket, 1964. The author is fourth from left in the middle row, with Russell Young third from left. We beat Riccarton High and forgot whom we lost to.

The demise of the Southerner affected many people in various ways. For many years it was considered New Zealand's friendliest train. It made the world's most southern rail journey. Deep down you hope somebody, august or otherwise, will bring about its reinstatement. It needn't be called the Southerner. The Southern Phoenix might fit the bill.

7

The railcar that could

From Alexandra to Dunedin on the Central Otago Line

Image 43

The Central Otago Vulcan railcar at rest in the Cromwell Gorge, as the crew undertake some essential maintenance to coax a few more kilometres out of the ageing craft.

I don't know how it came up in general conversation, but it did. A group of us were sitting around talking about tourist options ('things to do in the holidays') when a younger person offered up the Central Otago rail trail as something new and novel.

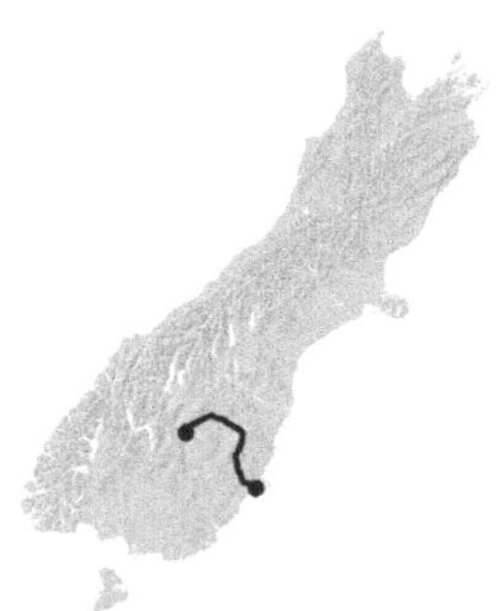

'Have you been on the Central Otago rail trail?' the young woman asked.

'Yes I have.'

'Did you walk or go by bike or horse?'

'I went by train.'

'Yeah right.' She didn't believe me. People had forgotten the trail traced the meanderings of the old Central Otago railway line and some of us were old enough to remember what it was like.

'A mate and I travelled on the Alexandra to Dunedin railcar in 1971, when the rail trail actually had rails. And trains.'

There was a discernible gasp. It was a bit like saying you'd been to the moon, or had attended a Beatles concert – or saw Colin Meads sent off against Scotland. But we travelled by Vulcan railcar along tracks long gone, and now occupied by new generations, who had claimed the embankments, cuttings and bridges of the old line as their own rail trail.

Back at the beginning, when the Central Otago line was still a dream, people wanted a railway to transport the fruits of Central Otago, considered the garden of Otago, to Dunedin and further afield. The old rutted roads were rough on the produce, not to mention the coach drivers. So they built a railway through some of the most desolate, yet scenic South Island corners, crags, gorges and plains.

The line was never profitable for most of its length, and when the line was closed, there was a certain irony in that its last job was transporting supplies to the Clyde Dam construction site – the same dam which created Lake Dunstan, which in turn compromised the line's path.

In 2013 all that remained of the line was the Taieri Gorge Railway from Middlemarch to Dunedin and, of course, the Central Otago rail trail. But back in 1971 the Central Otago line was a going concern, although it was New Zealand rail's best-kept secret.

The preliminaries to taking our journey on what we called the 'round trip' saw us catching Road Service buses which travelled along roads that included the one through Lumsden, the intended southern destination point of the new Kingston Flyer train. The round trip involved the Southerner from Dunedin to Invercargill and buses to Alexandra, the railhead for the Central Otago railway back to Dunedin, winding across country. The Central Otago railcar waited. The greatest show on wheels, some said.

If only a proposal in the 1880s, to construct a line from Kingston, around the shores of Lake Wakatipu to Queenstown and further on to Cromwell, had been persevered with, way back then. A complete rail round trip could have been undertaken – Dunedin to Dunedin, utilising the southern main trunk, the Invercargill to Kingston line, the proposed rail link between Kingston and Queenstown and on to Cromwell, and finally the Central Otago line back down to Dunedin. It would have been an exciting and head-spinning journey.

However, the spoilsports of the Royal Commission on Railways reckoned rail couldn't compete with the cheap water transport which had already established a reputation between Kingston and Queenstown, and the link in the 'round trip' chain was off the drawing board. Miraculously, in this conservative era, the idea of another line was entertained, heading west from Lake Wakatipu over difficult territory to a port planned for Lake McKerrow near Martin's Bay on the wild West Coast of the South Island. Now that *was* a romantic notion and quite cavalier, for its sole purpose would be to establish a line of communication to a port closer to Australia, the better to serve the Wakatipu goldfields. Predictably it disappeared off the drawing board. But what a train journey that could have been! New Zealand's remotest, the only one serving the South Westland and Fiordland Coast. Wishful thinking was very much a part of the Kiwi rail fan's emotional portfolio – and it wouldn't have helped in providing a spoke in the round trip. But still...

And so as the bus bore us away towards Cromwell, we could at least thumb through our yellowing timetable booklet uplifted from a secondhand store in Invercargill, and dream. Under 'Invercargill and Kingston Station' in 1879 a mixed train headed out for Kingston from Invercargill at 6.50am – a tad early perhaps, but dreamers can't be choosers. We would have gladly set the alarm to catch such a train. Makarewa Junction, where a branch line headed west to Riverton, was scheduled for a 7.22am arrival, then came Royal Bush, Wilson's Crossing, Forest Hill and Gap Road, place names redolent of a province still being broken in and establishing itself. Centre Bush at 8.43am, Caroline, the stop named after someone's girlfriend, at 9.46am, then the oddly-named Elbow (which would become Lumsden) at 10.16am. Finally the mixed train angled down towards Lake Wakatipu and pulled into Kingston at 12.30pm – 140 kilometres from Invercargill. If it had kept to our yellowing schedule.

Dreams dissolved. It would be a long, trainless day. We'd bus many kilometres from the South, via Queenstown, and finally sit in a pub and be happy enough to knock back a glass of Speights. The beer was cold, the day was cold, but the pub presented a warm, quiet ambience. Russ pumped a few coins into the jukebox, made his selection, returned to his seat, drew his drink to his lips and waited for the opening riff of 'Day Tripper' by the Beatles. As George Harrison ran through the first unaccompanied triplet, a terrific commotion obliterated all sound. It was as if a stock truck had left the road and was on its way through the pub wall. A cloud of dust cleared to reveal a workman of the pre-hardhat, pre-high-viz days presenting himself at the hole in the wall he had just created with his pneumatic drill.

Image 44

Until we encountered them at Picton and Alexandra, the Vulcans were new to us, yet they'd been around a while. This one, on Omoto Viaduct, was snapped in 1951.

The drill was stilled but the damage was more than peripheral. His lips moved but we couldn't hear. Plaster flakes floated on our Speights. He lay down his drill, stepped gingerly forward, by which time our hearing was returning.

'Sorry fellas,' he yelled at us.

'She was a day tripper,' the Beatles sang (the barman had turned the sound up).

'Turn the bastard down, Basil,' the drill guy yelled. 'We can't hear ourselves think. And bring these fellas a couple of fresh beers. The fallout's like Hiroshima over here.'

Jack the drill guy apologised again. A bit of demolition work had been necessary in the bar. Extensions and all that. Then Basil apologised too, for allowing us to use the bar while demolition was in progress, but then he thought Jack had finished for the day.

'Have now,' Jack reckoned as he joined us for a drink, shaking us vigorously by the hand thereby creating further dust clouds that made Russell's briar pipe flare.

'Just passing through then?' Jack enquired as he picked plaster flecks out of his beer.

'We're catching the railcar in the morning,' I replied.

'You're not rolling your Rs then?' Jack observed. 'Bet you're North Islanders with that accent.'

'Te Kuiti, in the King Country. Not far from Hamilton.'

'I know it well. Had a sister in Tokomaru Bay.'

It was all North Island to Jack, who went on to say the railcar to Dunedin on the Central Line could be a bit disappointing if travellers were expecting the Orient Express.

We weren't. In fact we didn't know what to expect.

Sometimes the Central Otago line was referred to as a long branch line, at other times, a short main. It had an identity crisis for a lot of travellers. When we first began exploring the wider New Zealand rail network in the mid-sixties, we figured the Central Otago line was no different from the short branches which left the southern main trunk and headed west, until they were halted by the imposing obstacle of the Southern Alps. A simplistic appraisal of course, but it was hard not to treat the line from Dunedin to Cromwell in the same way as the Timaru to Fairlie, Ashburton to Mt Somers, Studholme to Waimate, Palmerston to Dunback and several other deep south spurs. But then you remembered your geography and realised Cromwell was located about halfway across the widest stretch of the South Island. And on the rail map it had a distinctive and long-winded kink in its course that would make it much longer than most other South Island 'branches'.

In 1927 the Royal Train carrying the Duke of York around the Dominion travelled along the Central Otago line from Dunedin to Cromwell. While some observers were more transfixed by the fact that two beautifully prepared UB engines were allocated to the special, it was the fact the line was considered important enough for the Duke which impressed others. It was obviously a line of some distinction.

In 1958 the Central Otago railcar ceased operating from the railhead at Cromwell. Patronage was down and it made more economic sense to use Alexandra as the starting point. It didn't improve passenger comfort in winter though, for plans to build a railcar shed at Cromwell were scrapped with the establishment of the new departure and arrival point. Had the Cromwell railcar shed been built, the railcars would not have had to shelter under the veranda of the Alexandra goods shed. In severe frosts there was no nullifying the cold completely, although a power lead to the railcar's heaters from the goods shed prevented the water system freezing. And a battery charger in the shed helped make the Vulcan less reluctant to start on cold mornings.

Image 45

Central Otago landscape near Cromwell. The colours are a majot tourist attraction in autumn.

Despite the indications of a decline in patronage, a rather unexpected development occurred when a Sunday afternoon service was introduced in June 1971, close to the time we travelled on the regular service. The new schedule saw the railcar leave Dunedin at 12.40pm and Alexandra at 5.40pm. It became something of an institution for day trippers and such was its popularity that on occasions as many passengers were standing in the aisle as were seated. So it may not have been the Orient Express – but it wasn't train 542 either, the mixed service that tried really hard between Taumarunui and Stratford, a long way from Tokomaru Bay.

By the time we presented ourselves to catch the Central Otago railcar in 1971, Alexandra continued to be the terminus. Yet coming down the Cromwell Gorge by bus with the road, rail and river sharing the narrow cleft, you figured they could have scheduled the railcar to run the total length of the line, starting in Cromwell – if only for our benefit. It would have been a stunning way to view the mighty Clutha – from a railcar running on a ledge closer to the clear blue water than the potholed road.

After checking into a bed and breakfast establishment built out of great, grey stone squares, we half expected the pneumatic guy to be on the guest manifest. He said he was staying locally – on a temporary basis. We did share our digs with the railcar driver and guard, which lent a decidedly local slant to the whole operation. We even shared the cost of a taxi in the morning to get to the station.

Unlike Invercargill Station, where we expected to feel the cold and didn't, Alexandra Station was a modest wooden affair, where we expected to feel the cold and weren't disappointed. It was minus something and snowing or sleeting. The bed and breakfast had been so toasty, despite the great, grey stone squares, that it took a while for our extremities to register the cold. The woman who sold us our tickets was warm and cheery, although her cheeks were the colour of red apples.

'Off on the railcar then,' she said, while exhaling a huge cloud of condensate.

I attempted to say something like, 'Yes, two single tickets please,' but my lips appeared to be frozen shut and my tongue wouldn't move.

'You're not locals, are you?' she replied astutely.

I shook my head and a dusting of snow or sleet broke loose from my frozen rigid hair.

Meanwhile Russ was thumping his torso with his arms in an attempt to either restart his heart or force air into or out of his lungs. He resembled a rogue ape attempting to define his jungle territory. I had so much trouble picking up my change – either my fingers had frostbite or the coin was frozen to the ticket counter – that I just left it there.

The cold was so cutting our senses were on the blink. Literally. It hurt to blink. Moisture on our eyelashes had frozen into sharp little pins which seemed to graze the eyeballs every time we tried. So we tried not to. After securing our tickets our brains gradually began processing information relating to our immediate surrounds.

Alexandra Station was a remarkably nondescript, anaemic light-yellow wooden building, which had last been painted at some long-distant and earlier time. Station lights were burning brightly in the pre-dawn gloom, highlighting the snowdrifts on the slushy platform. It had obviously not been designed by George Troup. The originating station at Alex and the terminal at the end of the line were beyond chalk and cheese. Dunedin's grand edifice was eons and a million kilometres away from Alexandra's crib-like box. Our thawing brains processed that much. They also picked up a latent high regard for the railcar driver and train drivers in general, as portrayed by the ticket seller.

They were the brave men in hats and distinctive overcoats and ties who could get you out of Alex in winter. We had shared digs and a taxi with our driver, and he seemed a nice enough guy. The ticket lady was under no misapprehension. Bob (or Ted, or Tom) was the knight in trenchcoat armour, who would ride the Vulcan steed out of the dark and desolate cold of dawning, into the golden pastures of Central in daylight. Bob (or Ted, or Tom) deserved the highest praise.

Given the Vulcan's stuttering bronchiality, a lot of credit had to go to the driver for coaxing the kilometres out of a run-down, ageing railcar. Bob (or Ted, or Tom) was also noted to be tallish, rakish, with a straight-toothed smile, factors which increased a driver's popularity. It was a bit of the 'this is your captain speaking' syndrome associated with handsome airline captains, although there was no denying our driver had injected life into the Vulcan and was now shepherding it out and away from the Alexandra goods shed, where it had sought solace through the freezing night. Its headlight cut through the fog and smog, a proportion of which had been contributed by the smoke from the many frost pots burning close to fruit-tree groves to mollify frost damage.

It seemed appropriate that the range of mountains to the southwest of Alexandra was called the Old Man Range. Not that our driver was an old man, but you got the feeling he was no greenhorn either.

Respect for the Vulcan drivers carried on until Anzac Day 1976, when the driver of the last Central Otago service to Alexandra was presented with a flower and foliage arrangement and a bottle of wine by a group of women. There were no blokes from the Old Man Range with a firm handshake and a dozen DB. Not that anyone noticed. It wasn't the sort of thing men living in the lee of the Old Man Range would do.

From Alexandra we headed out into the Manuherikea Valley as the sun began to rise, peeking around edges of the Raggedy Range. At least we'd get a fine day out of the icy situation, although it was easy making such presumptions thousands of kilometres from home. We didn't contemplate too hard as the Vulcan swayed along beside the Manuherikea River, but should have consigned the 'icy dawning, fine morning' old wives' tale to the scrapheap.

Come to think of it I don't recall such a situation always applying to our North Island meteorological environment, although sometimes it turned out to be true. Most often an icy dawning led to a wretched morning.

The other passengers on the railcar were dotted around the carriage swathed in hats, large coats and scarves. They sat so still as the Vulcan coughed and spluttered in the cold they could have been piles of dirty washing, for all the animation they displayed. Russ and I were jumping around a bit, as much to keep our blood circulating as to take in the Central Otago scenery stretching away on both sides of the line, once the dark disappeared.

Scenery, no matter how eye-catching, increases in attraction and intensity for me if you watch it from a train window. The Central Otago railcar often went where the road didn't, which was a huge bonus. It almost took your mind off the cold.

Russ reckoned he had to jettison one of his gloves when it froze to the windowsill. That was earlier, before the heating made its presence felt in the railcar, but the spectre of cold weather took a while to pass. At Ophir, a couple of kilometres from Omakau, one of the lowest temperatures ever recorded in New Zealand – minus 21 degrees – was to put the hamlet on the map and things in perspective.

When we crossed the Poolburn Viaduct, a further feature of the line became evident: the use of stone and masonry, as well as steel, in the construction of bridges and viaducts. North Island viaducts were more often than not of steel, and steel alone.

If we felt we were in another country, and we did for much of the passage of the Central Otago railcar, we could be forgiven. Fellow travellers on the Southerner, Mainlanders mainly, said the line from Alexandra to Dunedin wasn't unlike the Denver and Rio Grande Railroad in the USA. We figured they might have been exaggerating a bit, but as we meandered in a great semicircle through river valleys with mountain ranges defining and confining our course, we realised Central was unlike any other part of New Zealand. Russ reckoned it was like Peru, not that he had been to South America. Neither of us had been to Denver or the Rio Grande, but we'd seen hundreds of western movies back at the State Cinema on double-feature Friday nights. Sometimes both features were westerns – back-to-back black and white cowboy flicks. Some of them were set in the Rio Grande hinterland (or perhaps it was just down the road from Hollywood). Whatever, the movies had provided the images which had you imagining, at various junctures along the Alex to Dunedin run, that you might spot Joel McCrea or John Wayne positioned behind rocks waiting to ambush some ne'er-do-wells on horseback. Shoot-outs from behind the schist columns in the Taieri Gorge wouldn't have raised an eyebrow. The Jesse James gang might storm the Vulcan after galloping across the Maniototo Plains. Chatto Creek, fifteen minutes down the line from Alexandra, sounded like a settlement out of Rio Grande country, a lawless place where Jack Palance would escape on horseback, Randolph Scott hot on his heels.

It took a while for the railcar's heaters to have an impact but by Ida Valley, with the snow beginning to thaw outside, we became aware we still had toes. It had been at Ida Valley, when it was the railhead of the line in 1902, that the issue of warm feet became pressing. Footwarmers, strange-looking oblong metal containers filled with sodium acetate solution, were the railway's answer to the biting cold before steam-heating from the engine was utilised. Yet it wasn't until late 1902 that a footwarmer heating tank was set up at Ida Valley. The footwarmers were immersed in the tank's boiling water and the sodium acetate enabled the clunky devices to retain heat for lengthy periods.

Footwarmers weren't the greatest thing since sliced bread and the sheer harshness of Central winters and loose-fitting carriage windows nullified their usefulness. It was one thing having warm feet – but when the rest of your body was being racked by zero and sometimes sub-zero temperatures, the need for more effective carriage heating became pressing. Besides, footwarmers often went the way of railway crockery – missing. One day archaeologists will find layers of sedimented earth, studded with NZR cups and saucers from an earlier age in which a mode of transport called trains ran on steel rails for varying distances, until they went the way of the dinosaurs. A few long-discarded footwarmers will share the rail stratum with broken crockery and portions of something they used to call guard's vans. Schoolkids who tended not to feel the cold as much as adults, sometimes cast the odd-shaped footwarmers into rivers and streams from carriage windows and platforms along the Otago Central line, thereby making their contribution to future archaeology.

Between Lauder and Oturehua the rail and state highway parted company. We entered remote, snow-speckled territory where the line stretched out in long straights towards the unknown. After crossing the Manuherikia and Poolburn Rivers we stopped at Auripo, a tiny station that must rank as one of the loneliest on the New Zealand system. Further along this remote shortcut the Ida Valley station was more substantial, but not as big as the first version, which in 1919 was consumed by fire. Snow covered the Hawkdun Range to the north, although it was impossible to get your bearings in such a wide-open wilderness, so north was only a guess.

Image 46

Footwarmer House was not a congenial Central Otago guest house, but an area set aside at Hillside Railway Workshops in Dunedin where the oblong footwarming metal containers were serviced.

The sky changed from pure, blinding white, to deep, distant blue as we travelled between the great ring of mountains – the Dunstans, the Hawkduns, Raggedy Range, Rough Ridge and Northern Rough Ridge. Passing through Oturehua it was hard to imagine a more stunning rail setting. We were in another land. And yet it was surprising to learn some of the locals cut up rough when the halt was given its first name, Rough Ridge. You'd think anyone blessed with the opportunity to live in such a paradise would be above such taciturnity. Yet within a month of the Rough Ridge Station opening someone defaced the name board with a tar brush. Even the final name, Oturehua, was only accepted grudgingly by some.

Our radar suggested we should be heading southeast towards the Taieri Gorge and Dunedin, but the line was already halfway through its sweeping semicircle that took us towards the northeast and would soon, after we joined up again with the state highway, take us southeast beyond Oturehua and frozen Idaburn Dam. Here iceskating and the game of curling took place at this time of year (though perhaps not at this time of day).

And then we pulled into Wedderburn, the highest station in Otago and Southland, as the husband sitting behind us did his best to explain to his wife that the curling which occurred on Idaburn Dam had nothing to do with women's hair, although it did involve brooms.

Wedderburn was a bit of a watershed. From here you sensed the railcar was now heading towards the south, which was where we had to go. Wedderburn was also a lonely place. Layers of downlands swept towards blue-brown horizons. The surrounding land was parched and bare, bereft of animals. There might have been a sheep wagon or two in the stockyard siding but there was no sign of life, no sheep.

We took a special interest in a place called Gimmerburn, home of an Otago All Black named Ian Smith. Smith had been a surprise selection in the 1963–1964 New Zealand team who toured Britain and France. They called him the Gimmerburn Ghost because he had fulfilled the Kiwi dream of anyone from anywhere being able to make the All Blacks. Yet Gimmerburn struck his team-mates as being beyond anywhere. It was hard to recall an All Black coming from such a remote locality. That, plus the fact he was a genuine shock selection, led to the 'ghost' tag. Soon they were calling him Spooky.

North Island rugby fans were fascinated by Smith's emergence. We were anyway, given that the Meads brothers from over the craggy hills to the west of Te Kuiti came from another decidedly remote location. I asked the guard if the line passed through Gimmerburn.

'It goes close but you'll have to get off at Ranfurly.'

I left it at that, not wishing to enter into a long-winded discussion about how I didn't want to get off at Ranfurly to facilitate my travelling to Gimmerburn. I only mentioned Gimmerburn as a matter of interest.

'That's where "Spooky" Smith comes from,' I told the guard.

'Who?'

'Ian Smith, the All Black.'

The guard clipped a ticket and moved down the aisle. Something else I was learning about New Zealand in a wider sense was that quite a few people either didn't follow rugby or simply didn't like it.

Ranfurly was the next stop after we'd dropped perceptibly along straights heading southeast. It has been said that travelling along straights gives you an appetite, and sure enough, as we pulled into Ranfurly, stomachs were gurgling. It was time for refreshments – lunch in fact. And yet Russ couldn't remember stopping for refreshments anywhere along the line. A later perusal of the timetable for the former Otago Central express indicated refreshment stops were made at Ranfurly and Hindon. Railcar passengers would surely have had the same privilege. Russ could be a bit perverse – particularly when hungry.

I ended up in the art deco Centennial Tea Rooms beyond the station, where a roaring trade was done in friendly, unhurried surroundings. I had a pie on a plate and shared a table with a besuited man on his way to a funeral in Dunedin. He had a pie too. Life goes on.

Russ nodded off after we left Ranfurly but I found myself wide awake as the railcar passed through Waipiata, where some passengers alighted to visit family at the nearby prison, and Kokonga. The husband sitting behind us kept us informed at this stage. He and his wife were due to leave the railcar at Hyde and had useful local knowledge of this stretch of track. The first passenger train to pull into Kokonga carried a cricket team who played a game against a Naseby eleven. The husband sounded like a sporting type. He'd earlier raised the issue of curling back at Idaburn. I asked him if he'd heard of 'Spooky' Smith and he had, although his wife hadn't.

The line had become the constant companion of the Taieri River by now as the husband and wife prepared to de-train. The railcar was belting along, making up time. The husband chose this moment to tell us about the rail crash in 1943, which accounted for 21 lives when the Otago Central passenger train derailed south of Hyde. The train driver had been speeding and was later convicted after being tried for manslaughter. Russ roused, wide-eyed, when he heard the account.

We pulled into Hyde almost on time. The husband and wife clambered down. The fact that the town was named after John Hyde Harris, a former mayor of Dunedin and superintendent of the Otago Provincial Council, was less momentous to us than the notion of a town being named after someone called Hyde. Two of our boyhood mates back home had the same surname and it seemed just as silly as naming a town Hutchins or Young. Hydetown or Hydeville might have made more sense.

Image 47

The railcar's predecessor, the Central Otago Express, takes on water at remote Kokonga. Was there a cricket team on board – or 'Spooky' Smith?

The railcar continued south at a useful clip and it was hard to get the thought of the 1943 derailment out of the mind. Beyond Rock and Pillar we had cleared the fateful stretch. The mind's a funny thing. Hearing about the derailment opened our senses to every lurch, sway, creak and rattle as the old Vulcan went on its merry way. Rock and Pillar was a strange name for a station. We figured Rock and Roll would have been more apt, now we'd become aware of the rollicking passage of the railcar.

Yet many considered the Vulcans to be very comfortable and steady on the tracks. They had a five-speed gearbox capable of providing a top-gear speed of 120kph. Once a Vulcan hit 125kph on the Midland line without too much trouble. We were going nowhere near that speed but still we felt every little lurch, untoward or otherwise. The mind's a very funny thing.

This negativity was relegated beyond Ngapuna, Middlemarch, Sutton and Pukerangi – we had entered a new wonderland – the Taieri Gorge.

At Waipiata the line had met up with the long Taieri River and further south the Taieri Gorge in all its broken splendour would provide an awe-inspiring finale. We thought we knew gorges. There was the Awakino Gorge providing a prelude to the open ocean of the northern Taranaki coast, which owed its appeal to the way it provided panoramic views of the ocean after a long, landlocked plunge – where the prospect of ever seeing the ocean seemed a pipe dream. The Karangahake Gorge in the Bay of Plenty had a certain appeal – it was a genuinely narrow cleft in the Coromandel Range, where road and rail squeezed through, but not without difficulty.

The Taieri Gorge was different. Littered with schist rocks – random sprinklings from the hand of God. Sky-scraping columns, often layered and uniform, but more often than not random as well. Tufts of yellow broom, and drifts of snow caught in the ever-present shadows, destined not to melt. Unlike other gorges, in the Taieri the railway sometimes edged along the narrow, natural right of way near the top of the cliffs, while at other times it descended closer to the river. Most other gorges we'd encountered saw the rail and road winding hand in hand next to the river, at the base.

Middlemarch was the last of the significant towns before Sutton, where the line veered southeast, leaving the main road behind. Beyond Pukerangi we were entering lunar territory – the true spectre of the lower Taieri Gorge. Pukerangi used to be called Barewood, in the days when the line surveyors found the locality bereft of firewood. It was impossible to take it all in at this stage with the late sun glaring and kids jumping around in the railcar.

A group of high school pupils climbed aboard near Big Mount Allan. Railcars often operated like school buses in various parts of the country, down rural branches and intermediate lines. As one example, the Gisborne railcar was said to have drawn kids up to their very front gate, just beyond the track.

Tony Thorpe reckoned railcars stopped at the drop of a hat. Or the flick of a thumb. Once he reckoned he nearly got the New Plymouth railcar to stop and pick him up when he missed his ride back from the rugby near Mangapehi in the King Country. He had given the hitchhikers' salute with his thumb while traipsing along the track and Tony reckoned the driver began slowing down, until he must have remembered the railcar was full to overflowing and running two hours late.

Then we remembered that if Tony was trying to get home to Te Kuiti after the rugby near Mangapehi, the New Plymouth railcar would be going the other way at that time of day – south towards New Plymouth. Then we also remembered it was the same Tony who reckoned the *Titanic* was actually called the Titanekai, after the male lead in the story Hinemoa and Tutanekai. He could be a bit fanciful at times.

The accounts of kids getting to and from school by jigger along the Central Otago line were more believable. Surfacemen became temporary school bus drivers as kids living in the rugged, largely road-less Poolburn Viaduct area enjoyed a novel way to get to school at

Ida Valley. In midwinter, they enjoyed it rather less.

We were afforded a staggering view of the gorge at Flat Stream and another at Deep Stream. The latter, none too original, was named by early wagoners who probably preferred Flat Stream to Deep Stream, in their attempts to get across the river to the antimony mines.

Hindon was locked in a bit of a clearing and was another refreshment stop, although Russ couldn't recall that one either. We were both nodding off at this stage, stupefied by the grandeur, but were brought around by the man sitting across the aisle who was telling his mate an old Hindon story.

Buggering Jack was an engine driver in the very early days of the line, who came to grief at Hindon. They called him Buggering Jack because he swore like a trooper and one day he cursed his way through a cup of tea at the Hindon refreshment rooms with the guard, before heading out on their train. One of the reasons for stopping at Hindon was to enable Jack's train to cross another going the other way. What with the swearing and sweet tea and exchange of witty repartee with the ladies working in the refreshment rooms, Jack and the guard, the latter a bit of a novice, completely forgot about the other train. A head-on collision resulted, Jack said more than 'bugger' and not long afterwards a safer electric train tablet working system was introduced on the route.

Image 48

Taieri Gorge Railway interior. A faithful reproduction of what a carriage looked like in Buggering Jack's day.

Image 49

The jaw-dropping cliffs of the Taieri Gorge from the train.

From Hindon time seemed to fly. Passengers began folding newspapers. After all that grandeur we felt a little cheated when the last stretch opened on to the Taieri Plains and comparatively ordinary-looking landscapes. We roared across the Wingatui Viaduct, the largest wrought-iron structure in New Zealand, before stopping at Wingatui Junction on the main south line. Night was falling.

Back in Dunedin after a typically brisk crash and clatter through the southern suburbs beyond Wingatui Junction, memories and images washed over us. The Central Otago railcar ride wasn't one of those journeys you could simply cross off your list. The physical landscape produced flashbacks as we wandered through Dunedin's Octagon and back to our digs in the north city. And no one had slipped anything into our last cup of coffee. But we couldn't help flashing back as we contemplated the Central Otago scenery revealed by the game little Vulcan. In contrast to what was whizzing past our windows now, back up on the plains there were ridges and hollows, variegated and vegetation free.

Image 50

AB694 pulls the old Central Otago Express through Hindon in 1950. Twenty years later it was the Vulcan railcar's turn.

Image 51

Russell Young standing next to a Taieri Gorge Railway service in 2007. 'Better to see all this with a friend': the mantra was just as appropriate then as it was back in 1971.

At other points, like the horseshoe bend on Tiger Hill, you could look back the way you'd come and see the broken landscape, upthrust into ribs of small hills, with the afternoon sun casting shadows when the clouds allowed. The optical illusion created the impression of folds of green and yellow land buckling and rolling, like ocean breakers heading for shore. And then the railcar swept on a wheel-screeching curve through the heart of the apparently moving land.

Better to see all this with a friend, I thought. At one stage, as endless horizons and windswept plains showed no sign of human habitation or animal life – not even a rabbit or two – an intense feeling of loneliness swept over me. It was melancholic in a way no other stretch of New Zealand had ever been. 'Savage beauty' didn't cut it. This was neither savage nor conventionally beautiful.

At another stage the railcar angled down into what looked like a large, fenceless paddock. The line curved around the perimeter like one of those small trains taking kids for rides at the A & P Show. Rocks were strewn about the flats, and a couple of babbling brooks emerged from what looked like large puddles or sheets of surface water. Rocky outcrops barred ease of passage to the north, so the line slalomed through close-cropped vegetation which looked like a well-manicured lawn. It was as if the line had taken a short cut through someone's private property. Perhaps I was hankering for signs of human habitation, even if it meant gate-crashing.

Yet the colours – the greens and greys and browns – were like no shade of vegetation I had seen before. It was as if we'd travelled to the Russian steppes or to one of those Columbian wetlands that looks like a regular farm in the dry season, yet spends most of the year underwater. This was the Central Otago I had figured was just another rural backblock, with the railcar running through it relegated in my mind to a screeching, rusty 'wobbler' connecting whistlestops, to uplift or set down yokels.

It was much more than that. Much, much more. And right then, under the moonlight, back up on the ranges and in the gorges, ghostly, unexpected shadows and images were probably emerging. It was almost worth taking the evening railcar along the Central Otago line to check out the moonlit plains where rabbits ran in response to the intrusion of a lonely little Vulcan railcar.

8

Train to Morpheus

From Auckland to Wellington on the Silver Star

Image 52

The pristine Silver Star express at Hamilton Station, about to enter service. DA 1463 has the solemn duty of providing the motive force for the signature train. Were we ready for this?

We'd heard a few things about the Silver Star. How the cost of the rolling stock was $3.5 million. How the stewards would polish your shoes if you left them outside your compartment door. The same stewards provided a drinks service to your personal cabin until 23:30 – mind you, we had to ask around what 23:30 was in laymen's terms. It sounded late.

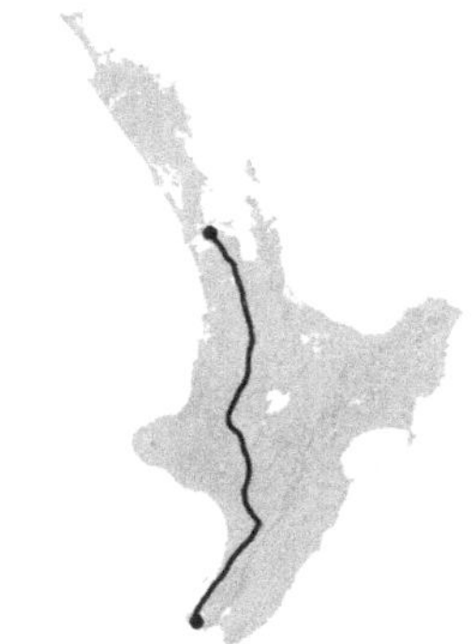

Some of the other numbers were equally as impressive. The Silver Star could house 42 passengers in its buffet cars. There were only six designated stops. Frankton, Te Kuiti, Taumarunui, Taihape, Marton and Palmerston North heading south. This was not a stopping service – and there was nothing local about the way it connected Auckland with Wellington.

The Silver Star was a stainless steel shock to the system. It replaced the old Auckland to Wellington Limited and made the former look like something out of an earlier, faded New Zealand. The Silver Star, more than any other of the new services introduced in the late 1960s to early 1970s, represented the renaissance of

New Zealand rail, a time when the powers-that-be made sincere efforts to keep up with the competition provided by air travel and the motor car.

The Silver Star came highly recommended. International travel writers judged it to be among the top six trains in the world. One went so far as to describe the train as the world's third best. We figured it was the best. Naturally.

Each carriage was fully air-conditioned. Sixteen passengers could be accommodated in a choice of double-berth twinette compartments or single-berth roomette cabins. Foldaway wash basins and toilets were a unique feature of each compartment although only the twinettes had their own showers. Was the lack of individual showers in the roomettes the thing that knocked the train down from second to third best in international eyes? The buffet car was, to all intents and purposes, a genuine restaurant car. Passengers sat at tables and were served by stewards. Meals were cooked on board. There was none of this trying to eat a scalding mince pie sideways in the pitch dark, while absorbing the jostles of fellow passengers in a crowded express or limited carriage.

More than anything though, the Silver Star was an all-sleeper service. Where would people sit? Did you have to spend the entire journey in bed? Or in the buffet? That aspect of the revolutionary new train wasn't well explained. The rail authorities were more inclined to bang on about their new baby being among the sleekest trains in the world – Japanese-built along the same lines as the highly successful Southern Aurora running between Sydney and Melbourne in Australia. Not surprisingly, the 'all-sleeper' aspect caught a few out, particularly those who'd spent half a lifetime sitting bolt upright in the old Auckland to Wellington Limited.

There was the tale of the farmer who climbed on board the Silver Star at Hamilton and went looking for a seat. He scoured the sleek new carriages and eventually confronted one of the bowtie-bedecked stewards.

'I can't find my seat, sport,' he trumpeted. 'In fact I can't find any bloody seats.'

'Precisely sir, this is an all-sleeper service.'

He was ushered to his compartment and folded away into the wall, so to speak. There was an altercation of sorts, but nothing too serious.

When I first travelled on the Silver Star it smacked of international sophistication. From my compartment, the lights of passing towns were disorientating. You could almost imagine Taihape was a village in Luxembourg, until the train pulled into the humble New Zealand station and local passengers prepared to climb aboard. The traveller might be smartly dressed, in keeping with the new train's image, but those wishing them bon voyage reminded you the train hadn't suddenly dematerialised somewhere south of Otahuhu and been reconstructed on foreign shores. The son who drove Mum to the station was wearing an All Blacks rugby jersey, faded jeans and jandals. Dad was all in brown, New Zealand's favourite colour in the 1970s – brown hair and beard, light-brown cardigan, faded wood-coloured corduroys and dark-brown slip-ons.

The comments were pure Kiwi.

'Make sure you lock your door, Mum. Those train guards look dodgy,' the son said.

'Their bowties are really cameras, dear,' Dad added.

'Go easy on the plonk, Mum,' both yelled.

'Don't forget to give Mavis the pavlova recipe when she calls around on Tuesday,' the woman beseeched from the carriage door, as the bowties did their best to hustle her along to the right compartment.

The arrival of the Silver Star and the other new services of the 1970s coincided with the second of our rail odysseys, yet it wasn't until 1972 that I first travelled on the Star from Auckland to Wellington, on my own. Russ and I had completed the part of our second odyssey which saw us travelling on the Southerner, the Central Otago railcar and the West Coast railcar in 1971, before he snuck back to work and I found myself between jobs. At this stage I classified myself as a student/writer. I was halfway through a BA degree, but I was an extramural student, which meant I didn't have to attend lectures. I had yet to crack the freelance market and most of my 'writing' was creative. Poems and song lyrics poured out of me. Most didn't amount to much. Some of the paeans were rail related. Many were elusive.

Life was a bit loose just then and appropriately I nearly missed the Silver Star as it waited patiently at the platform at Auckland Station. A fairly starched steward showed me to my compartment. He prattled on but I was too keen to settle in and absorb a unique rail experience to listen closely. The steward, without any prompting to my knowledge, brought a can of Steinlager to my cabin. I must have nodded at a critical stage. In fact the steward returned a few times with cans, so I must have nodded more than once.

Image 53

The Wellington to Auckland Silver Star heading north across the causeway towards Auckland Station. I was happy to be heading south, away from the city.

Soon we were drifting south, going past all those familiar landmarks I'd seen over the years, from older trains, peering hard through begrimed express windows to decipher passing features. Reclining in my Silver Star compartment seat, which I figured would eventually be transformed into some sort of sleeping arrangement, I drank in the lowering sun and manmade suburban lights of Auckland coming on, like a glowworm colony stirring. I also drank a quiet toast to the setting sun. Any excuse. The air conditioning was sucking the cool air of a summer night into the compartment, but air conditioning cannot slake the thirst of the inner man. Hence the soothing properties of Steinlager as I glanced back to the house lights clinging to the hills above Judges Bay, where my Aunty Peg and her humble, yet homely bungalow used to angle down a suburban street. She'd welcome me after I'd survived the travails of the early morning express or limited from Te Kuiti. She'd passed on several years earlier – a kind soul. I drank a toast to Aunty Peg.

I learnt very early that travelling on a modern night train where you've got your own thoughts to keep you warm, and not some sleeping sprawled stranger in a musty second-class carriage, had a unique appeal. Extroverts probably hate single compartments – where solitude and claustrophobia become issues for them. As the Silver Star eventually passed into the dark of the rural recesses south of Auckland, I came to treasure my privacy, just so long as I could think and dream, scribble and sip...

It's funny what you remember as a night train rumbles through your home town. It was dark in Te Kuiti as the Silver Star eased past railway town and confronted the level crossing. Lights laced the length of Ailsa Street where my folks still lived and where the bullying and bravado, good times and bad, played out to the soundtrack of Patti Page and all the other post-war favourites, Elvis and the rock anthems, the Beatles...

I was drawn to the villa in George Street with a single light glowing. That was where my passion for railways was further fuelled by being allowed to sleep over at my grandmother's place with carte blanche to stay up and monitor the ghostly path of the night trains, screeching to the heavens with their whistles, yet providing a compensating, smooth steel-on-steel roar which put you back to sleep.

How times had changed. Te Kuiti Station was largely deserted, compared with the days when the Limited arrived at 11pm. The latter service was now replaced by the Silver Star, with its bowtied attendants, instead of the Limited with its guard stalking his train like John Wayne heading for a shootout. The new train's quiet, enclosed detachment, as opposed to the wild but willing, and in some ways, endearing, stampede and stumble to the refreshment rooms, was marked.

I climbed down at Te Kuiti. It was a scheduled stop, although one of the attendants told me not to wander too far. The pie cart was still pulsing just beyond the platform. A couple of carloads of youths were revving impatiently, waiting for their burgers and chips. Once the handful of passengers had climbed on board, the platform was deserted, apart from a couple of attendants who jostled one another good-naturedly as pockets of fog swirled.

Back on board I drank a toast to my home town as the train pulled away from the station where I swore I could see the murky outline of the poster extolling the virtues of seeing Wairarapa by train. And the swirling images of my Friday-night mates, eating their fish and chips, Harry the grumpy porter and Melanie Hayward, who a year or two ago had died in a car crash.

Image 54

The last incarnation of the Te Kuiti piecart located next to the station. Appropriately it was a converted railway carriage – but it, too, has now gone.

Right at the end, where the trains inched past the rear of the piecart, I imagined I saw my father making a late run to jump on the carriage steps before the platform ran out, and made such a manoeuvre dangerous. He used to delight in keeping his adrenaline pumping as if he was hooked on the stuff and the war was still raging. Mum and us kids, already on the train, used to be really concerned that one day Dad would miss his jump and not be able to accompany us to Wellington for a long weekend. Still, we hadn't had to fight in a war like Dad.

Just south of Te Kuiti I ventured forth, in search of the buffet car. A large man had anchored himself in the vestibule near the door, accompanied by a large suitcase. He and his suitcase were blocking access to the buffet car.

'Excuse me please,' I yelled above the clatter of floor plates and other fixtures. The man did his best to oblige but in the end I had to clamber over his box-like suitcase. Better than climbing over him, which was emerging as a drastic option.

I couldn't work out why he was waiting in such an obstructive manner anyway. Taumarunui, the next stop, was over an hour away.

'I get off at Te Awamutu,' the man yelled. He sounded foreign.

'But this train doesn't stop at Te Awamutu,' I yelled back.

'I thought Te Kuiti was Te Awamutu, but the spelling was different. Yet the train – it stopped at Te Kuiti, but I didn't get off. Now you tell me the next stop is not Te Awamutu. Someone told me it was.'

The man was largely confused and becoming breathless. He must have been anchored in the vestibule for an hour or more. Luckily, an attendant was on the case.

'Sir. You were supposed to get off at Te Kuiti,' the attendant yelled.

'No, no. I get off at Te Awamutu, not Te Kuiti. I am sick of not getting off the train.'

The attendant looked flustered. *Still that's what they get paid for,* I thought to myself, and ducked into the buffet car.

The latter was about a quarter full. A couple of business men were in suit and socks. Apparently they had availed themselves of the quaintly American service of having their shoes shined. They'd placed them outside their cabins, before deciding they'd like a nightcap in the buffet. The overzealous attendants had whisked their shoes away for a damn good polishing in the split second it takes to change your mind. Either that or somebody had nicked them, I suggested, something which had happened to a friend of mine earlier in the year. He had felt a bit awkward putting his patent leathers outside the door. It smacked of servants and other anti-egalitarian forces, and it wasn't the done thing for a Kiwi to rely on strangers to maintain shoes and keep up somebody else's appearance.

Image 55

Scarred hills and gentle farmland, so typical of
the North Island countryside.

The thief must have thought all his
Christmases had come at once. Either that, or
the gullibility of people who don't secure their
property properly. The two businessmen downed
their whiskies and tiptoed sheepishly out of the
buffet, presumably to round up their shoes,
while hoping no snake-in-the-grass had beaten
the attendants to their shoes, which were nice
Italian jobs and worth a bob or two.

I was pleased I favoured suede slip-ons, or
lace-ups if the occasion demanded it, although
I noticed a pair or two of suede boots
assembled in the corridor. Which proved Kiwis
were often less sophisticated about such tourist
services, having grown up on expresses, limiteds

and railcars where if any footwear intervention occurred it would be the half-drunk business of someone tying your boot laces together.

There wasn't a lot happening out the buffet car window, but then the train slowed as it passed an unusual configuration of bright lights close to the tracks. Level-crossing lights were also flashing. You could just make out the silhouettes of workers in the fields and huge, slow moving harvesters. Something was being gathered.

'Could be a UFO landing,' someone suggested. Someone else laughed. Heading for Taumarunui and midnight I was now wide awake.

The Silver Star was an all-sleeper service, yet I couldn't sleep. Not really. If it happened it happened, but what was the point of sleep if your only reason for being on board was to experience the total excitement of travelling on New Zealand's first all-sleeper overnight train? Awake.

Coming into Taumarunui on the Silver Star was a new experience. Normally in the past the train, be it express or limited, would convulse as passengers stirred and then set out strenuously for the brightly lit refreshment rooms. The engine's whistle cut like an air-raid siren and people would evacuate the carriages as if bombs were about to obliterate the train. Now, with the arrival of the Silver Star, you'd be lucky to see ten people on the platform, and they certainly weren't scrambling. It was true that a couple of elderly gentlemen were fumbling on the ill-lit platform for the refreshment rooms, until they were told by one of the attendants that the Silver Star had its own buffet car – and on-board food.

Back in my cabin I still didn't sleep, or if I did I wasn't aware of the fact. Come to think of it, I couldn't account for the stretch between Mangapehi and Ongarue, so I might have nodded off. There weren't many lights in the bowels of the King Country. Even with the blinds open and a bit of a moon-glow, it still felt as though the train was edging across the surface of the moon, such was the remoteness of the hinterland.

I had stirred at a deserted station, where the name board said Okahukura. Taumarunui was a few kilometres south.

Insomnia City. Somewhere south of Oio. The moon was on the run or perhaps it had yet to burst completely through the thin clouds. Would it be a bad moon rising? I was now feeling dog tired. The excitement of travelling on New Zealand's first all-sleeper service can only sustain you for so long. The idea now was to get to sleep. That was the obvious destination. Morpheus Junction.

I'd been told that if you stayed up expecting some of the night-train action once associated with the express or limited, you could be disappointed. Most passengers were sequestered away in their compartments like battery hens. Some even sounded like battery hens. Was that the 'new snoring' vibrations believed to be set off by modern air conditioning and unnatural draughts? There was no chance of mingling, as we did in the old days of open carriages. I said goodnight to Manson's Siding and closed my eyes.

Some hope. Soon the train was snaking its way up the Raurimu Spiral. I opened the blinds again, defying sleep. Soon the train reached the level it was seeking. Moonlight now bathed the volcanic plateau with playful patterns, shadows leaping from rocky outcrop to clumps of trees, depending on the movement of the train. Tongariro National Park wasn't far away. A set of headlights glowed like possum's eyes on a nearby side road. Street lights of a small settlement blinked in the distance. I was too tired to think what the settlement might be. Perhaps it was Waiouru army base and its railway station, the latter the highest on the Silver Star's route? In fact the highest station in the North Island. This was nose-bleed territory according to John McPhee. Any higher, John reckoned, and NZR would have to provide oxygen for the passengers. 'Next stop Waiouru, time for oxygen.' Reliable main trunk reports suggested McPhee, a cantankerous bigmouth, fell foul of an alighting army cadet whose elbow connected with his nose as they jostled in the vestibule. The army cadet considered the long-haired McPhee a threat to national security during the 1964 chaos created by the Beatles tour.

I had either over-calculated the amount of time I'd been asleep, or simply didn't know my mid-North Island geography. It wasn't Waiouru but some other town kilometres to the north.

At some lost hour we passed through Ohakune, where rain was falling. Ohakune used to be a junction with a 13.7km spur heading west as far as Raetihi. There was talk of the line being extended all the way to Wanganui but it all came to nothing in 1968, when it was closed. Before that, in the mid-1960s, I had an encounter with the Ohakune to Raetihi line.

One year our high school first fifteen were billeted out to stay with local townsfolk and farmers. In this manner we could be based in the Ruapehu College hinterland, the better to play a game of rugby against Ruapehu College first fifteen. I was allocated to a farming family who were obliged to cross the railway lines to reach their farm house. When I declared I wasn't aware the main trunk went this far west, I was gently corrected.

'That's the branch line, son,' the farmer advised. 'It goes west until it reaches Raetihi. Not much traffic these days. Maybe a weekly shunt. But you've got to keep an ear out for it. A couple of cockies got a fright a year or two back when they were nearly hit by an unscheduled service.'

That night both teams and supporters gathered at the school hall to celebrate the day's events – which hadn't amounted to much. The big game was drawn – nil all – in the mud and slush. Stan Reid, our tight-head prop, was sent off and later at the dance he was dumped by his girlfriend Jess Cribb of the netball team – who didn't win either.

Stan hitched a ride to where he was staying, packed his gear and waited defiantly next to the railway tracks, where he intended catching the express north and getting the hell out of there. We came across him at 2am, dusted with snow, huddled over his suitcase next to the tracks running along the front of the farm next door to the one where I was staying.

'What's wrong Stan?' I yelled.

'Got sent off, played like a girl, then got dropped by Jess.'

'Can't win 'em all Stan,' I yelled back. 'Anyway that line only goes to Raetihi and then only once in a blue moon. The main trunk's twelve kilometres back that way.'

Ohakune was the setting many years ago of one of the most macabre accidents on the main trunk. It all related to the tablet exchanger. No, not the means for one of the engine crew of a passing train with a headache to upgrade from an aspro to something stronger. The 'tablet' in a rail sense was a small object train crews had to uplift if they were to use a particular stretch of line ahead. At the same time they had to hand over the tablet for the line they had just vacated. The tablets were exchanged using a sharp arrow-like object mounted on a pole at the edge of the station platform, with a corresponding exchanger attached to the side of the engine.

One of the Ohakune station staff was designated platform porter and acting shunter and when the Wellington to Auckland Limited approached, he had to get from the yard, back to the platform. He didn't realise the train was almost upon him as he scrambled from the line to the apparent safety of the platform. The sharp steel exchanger on the side of the engine impaled the poor man and he died some days later.

Ohakune wasn't all about lost love and horrible death. It was near Ohakune that an acquaintance told me he 'scored' on the Silver Star, and it was every bit as exciting as touching down under the posts at Eden Park. Or was it one of those towns starting with T? The acquaintance wasn't sure. It might have been near Taihape.

We'd heard about the Silver Star, how it was not unheard of for couples to retire to their compartments to check out more than the scenery – couples who had climbed aboard as separate individuals. In tune with the times that had a-changed, young folk could be expected to express their sexual emancipation anywhere the mood struck, or the vibe was cool or inhibition-kickers struck the right chord. At times it happened on solid ground, but it was not unknown to erupt on anything that moved. Such as an overnight train. Under cover of darkness. Behind locked doors. Matrons may have applauded the locked doors. Chaperones from an earlier, constricted era may have felt cheered by the demise of the rank actions of a minority who, under cover of darkness and blankets on the old trains did stuff they wouldn't have done at home.

But the minority was becoming a majority and the Silver Star developed a swinging reputation with some. Rod, a work colleague had heard of this reputation. He was also a rail buff so he needed little prodding to catch the train and check out the action. Rod was a striking looking man – tall and angular with flowing brown hair hiding unhunched shoulders. If he dipped out on this new swinging service what hope did the rest of us have?

He didn't ... or at least he said he didn't.

Not far from the actual Waiouru, the train lights dimmed momentarily. The moon went behind a cloud and a huge shadow swept across the central plateau. A shiver went up my spine, although the train's heating was toasty. The train slackened pace as we approached an insignificant bridge over a trickle of a stream – the Whangaehu River. Someone had been talking about Tangiwai earlier, in 1953 the scene of New Zealand's worst rail disaster, where 151 people died. People who knew about these things say the ghosts of Tangiwai still make their presence felt on passing trains.

Back in 1953 I had dreams of Tangiwai, how I was travelling on the train that fateful Christmas Eve. How someone dressed as Santa – it may well have been the real Santa – went floating past the carriage window with bubbles coming out of his mouth and passengers swam past in strict formation as if they were swimming in the 4x4 relay at the local Centennial baths. The sort of dream a six-year-old innocent would have.

Like a lot of kids back in the golden-weather days, dreams were sanitised and painful events kept from us. Fathers didn't speak about the war, things were hushed up. As we sat down to Christmas dinner the low drone of a male voice reading out the names of the victims of Tangiwai disturbed the festivities. My grandmother couldn't hide the tears as the low drone told her an old friend from Wellington was amongst the casualties. We weren't supposed to hear the low drone. Christmas was a time of good cheer and presents.

The Silver Star slowed down further as it crossed the Whangaehu River, the conduit for the freak lahar from the Ruapehu crater lake which had caused the disaster by wiping out the rail bridge. A couple of stewards could be heard conversing in the corridor as the train gathered pace. They sounded exactly like the radio's low drone we heard on Christmas morning, 1953 – the one we weren't supposed to hear – and in my half sleep the dream returned, only this time there were screams and dead bodies and kid's teddy bears floating face down.

I woke with a start, grateful the train was still securely on the tracks. The feeling of languid comfort I had succumbed to on the other side of somewhere, seemed a long way back up the tracks.

Image 56

Mt Ruapehu, snow-covered in winter, offers splendid views from the train. It had a dark side though: its lahar caused the Tangiwai disaster.

Tangiwai had been the great betrayal for Kiwis. The trains were our friends. Utterly reliable, even if a little late sometimes. They were very much in our lives, so much so that at Easter in 1939 eight expresses ran each way between Auckland and Wellington. That equated to thousands of travellers being hauled up and down the island by the friendly, chortling steam engines – big, bluff monsters who wouldn't hurt a fly. After Tangiwai, our trust was shattered.

Further up the line, and a few years earlier, the Auckland to Wellington express hit a washout, just out of Oio. This accident seemed to be representative of the era. No one died, only two needed medical treatment, yet carriages were thrown around like Hornby toys. No one spoke much about the accident, although it had occurred close to Taumarunui, which was close to Te Kuiti. Someone seemed to be watching over us in those years, when New Zealand developed a reputation for being just about the greatest country in the world. Godzone in fact. The best place to raise kids. Safe trains. Kind people. Mind you, it didn't go unnoticed that express carriages were strongly built. Perhaps bad things didn't happen in New Zealand then for a reason. Common sense and true compassion were as valued as equality, eating your greens and repaying a favour. And making sure people were safe.

Ominously, in an earlier era and again, not far from Taumarunui, the Auckland to Wellington express hit a landslide. On that occasion in 1923, 17 people were killed and 28 seriously injured. The accident placed the township of Ongarue on the map and made you wonder about how privileged and protected we seemed to be in the fifties, when 'she'll be right' first emerged as a catch phrase.

Now it was 1972, and Taihape in the early morning. This used to be a pick-up point for sly grog in the days when the territory we had come through was 'dry', completely bereft of booze. They even had a brewery here called the Cascade, which released its fine products into the cat-and-mouse shenanigans of slygroggers trying to outwit the forces of the law, and prohibition do-gooders. Somewhere in-between, ordinary blokes just wanted a beer.

A large man with a large suitcase got off the Silver Star at Taihape. Surely it wasn't the foreigner who originally wanted to get off at Te Awamutu? At that stage I figured I could have been hallucinating, what with travel weariness and a sleep state which fluctuated wildly between wide awake and virtual coma. Utiku, Mangaweka, the Rangitikei River were some of the main trunk places and features tumbling around in my mind.

I returned to the buffet car. Milly, who was off to Marton, Dan a young scrubcutter/poet with whom I had a few things in common, and Andy, a bearded Aucklander who was going all the way, were some of the buffet people. I needed to sleep but couldn't. Much. That accounted for the frequent transfers from the buffet car to my compartment and vice versa.

Marton Junction – Milly got off. Then Feilding and Palmerston North passed, or rather the Silver Star passed them. Someone thought Palmerston North was Wellington and tried to alight. One of the attendants stepped in and defused a developing situation. Perhaps he was wearing a fresh bow tie.

Somewhere near Paraparaumu my train to Morpheus came in. I fell into a deep sleep. Next minute, it seemed, I was being presented with a cup of tea and biscuits and a copy of the local newspaper as we came into Wellington.

The Silver Star travelled over familiar tracks, but by the time we reached the capital, I felt as if I'd been to another, murky world. The heartland of New Zealand by night. Earlier trips by night train were attended by the fight to get to sleep, or by actually sleeping. On the Silver Star I probably slept more than I realised, yet the intention had been to stay awake to experience the inner workings of the most sophisticated of New Zealand night trains. In a sense a night on the Silver Star was like travelling through a continuous tunnel all the way from Auckland to Wellington. The lights of towns and cities could have been glow-worm grottos on the tunnel walls. Talking with the 'night people' in the buffet eventually became tedious. At times you felt entombed in the long tunnel from which there was no escape.

Image 57

Towards the end of the line, the Silver Star generates pace as it approaches Wellington. Soon there will be harbour views and a good cup of tea.

If the Silver Star all-sleeper service was the future of New Zealand long-distance train travel, some Kiwis would take a bit of convincing. It just didn't seem like a Kiwi train without the seating accommodation option. Soon the trains were losing two million dollars each year and inevitably, in 1979, the carriages were withdrawn to be converted into a combination of sitting and sleeping arrangements.

The Silver Star became NZ Rail's *Titanic.* It didn't strike an iceberg, but it came up against several issues of the day: strident unionism and one of the first major health and safety scares in New Zealand, when it was found that the conversion to seating cars would involve exposure to dangerous blue asbestos. The alteration work was delayed until the asbestos issue was solved, and for seven years after the Silver Star was taken off the tracks, the trains sat rotting in rail yards in Auckland and Wellington. Finally they were sold to rail interests overseas, but not before a private tourism firm called Pacific Trailways had announced in 1987 its intentions to convert all 27 passenger cars into a luxury tourist train, which would carry those who had a thousand bucks around the major routes of both the North and South Islands of New Zealand. Instant odyssey. What a hoot that would have been, but the project never got off the ground.

In 1990 the British luxury travel company, Oriental Express Trains and Cruises, had the carriages regauged for the Thai and Malaysian rail networks. Most of the cars went to Singapore to be rebuilt and painted and became part of a regular five-star luxury cruise train between Singapore and Bangkok – the Eastern-Oriental Express.

It could be ventured that the ghost of New Zealand's old Silver Star still stalks the corridors of this new train. (The ghost would have lengthening hair, a scruffy beard and bow tie and would be half-cut and shoeless.) However, the Silver Star didn't run long enough to develop a life, or after-life, of its own.

It was fun while it lasted.

9

The Dreamlander

The Silver Fern Railcar on the Main Trunk Line

Image 58

Following lunch at Taihape, the Silver Fern prepares to depart. There had been no mad dash for refreshments as there would have been in the old days. It was almost an anticlimax.

Occasionally we'd see a daylight passenger train going through town – usually during the school holidays. Its configuration was similar to that of the night express and limited and at first we just thought one of those trains was running dreadfully late. There were a lot of kids with parents on board, a few nanas, but none of the sloe-eyed, sleep-deprived passengers you'd see on the express and limited if they were behind time.

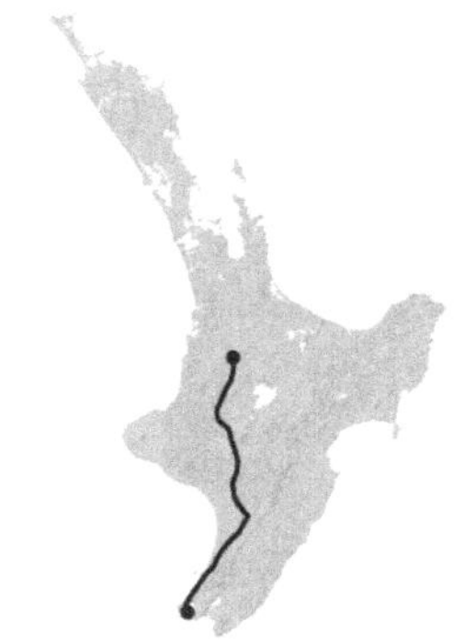

Eventually we learned the 'late' train was the Daylight Limited, running between Auckland and Wellington. Initially it was hard to grasp the significance. We'd been raised on the notion of trains disappearing south into the night, with everyone supposedly in dreamland. In fact, when I was really young, I thought southbound trains disappeared into a vortex – a black hole, or even one long tunnel and only emerged when the trains were coming into Wellington.

But that wasn't the case. In fact, the scenic wonders of the central North Island – the volcanic plateau, the mountains, viaducts and

Raurimu Spiral – had been lauded as long ago as 1925 when the first Daylight Limited plied the sacred course of the night trains. Yet in its first incarnation the Daylight Limited ran for less than a year.

It seemed the appeal (and convenience) of night travel had become ingrained in the psyches of New Zealanders. It was how we got from A to B, or precisely A to W, Auckland to Wellington and points in-between. Many passengers obviously considered it a waste of a day just sitting there watching the central North Island flit past.

So the Daylight ran only occasionally at Christmas and Easter until 1929, when the authorities had a change of heart and it became a regular service again. It now carried lounge cars, indicating Kiwis were slowly becoming aware of the matchless scenery and wide open spaces available to those who travelled south by day. Tourists too, who seemed to appreciate our wonderland more than we did.

But then the Great Depression came and the Daylight went, except for holiday trains. World War II knocked it on the head completely until 1949, when it reappeared, again as a holiday option. Eventually it emerged in 1963 as the Scenic Daylight, hauled by DA diesels, at a time when we tended to look north, rather than south, where the Daylight was in its element.

When we first began exploring the New Zealand rail system in the mid-'60s, it was still the night trains we favoured to get us to Wellington – and on to the South Island, or up to the east and west coast lines of the North Island. Even when the Blue Streak railcar, a daylight service, was introduced in 1968 it didn't occur to us for some time that we could be missing out on a unique rail experience – the Central North Island wonderland. When the Silver Fern railcar was introduced on the daylight run between Auckland and Wellington, we decided we needed to have a cut of that action, if only to marvel at its uniqueness.

The Silver Fern was certainly silver. It looked like no other railcar that had ever run on New Zealand lines. The notion of the old red rattler – or even a new red rattler – was turned on its head. In 1972 the Nissho-Iwai Company of Japan constructed three specially crafted railcars to run a daylight service on the North Island main trunk.

The future had come calling. When the distinctive Silver Fern railcars first appeared, they looked like commercial airliners without wings and made very little noise. Their engine compartments were insulated, concealing a 670 KW diesel engine, which drove a direct-coupled alternator. Direct-current power was converted from the alternator, to drive four 149 electric traction motors attached to the railcar's bogies.

Image 59

Precursor to the Silver Fern, the Blue Streak railcar at Puketutu, south of Te Kuiti. It seemed a bit ho-hum at the time – just a Fiat railcar with a fancy colour scheme.

The Silver Fern railcar caught the sun as it came down the straight into our station. I was travelling alone this time and watched several other locals chirping with excitement as they took their seats. For the uninitiated it could have been a UFO; however, I had boned up a bit on its external physical characteristics. The exterior was made of ribbed stainless steel sheathing over a carbon-steel frame. It looked futuristic and was light years beyond the old black steam engines – and even the grubby red DA diesels – that usually presaged train journeys to the south.

Wall-to-wall carpet greeted us, and our seats were covered with woollen fabric. It was quite an adjustment coming to the conclusion that, unlike earlier journeys to the south, we didn't have to eject sleepers from our reserved seats – and the sun was shining. There were adjustable footrests, refreshment trays which disappeared into the armrests, hostesses in miniskirts, and air conditioning. It was future shock.

Image 60

A new presence in the rail hinterland. The Silver Fern at Amokoura, looking a bit like an airliner without wings.

If I thought I'd gone to another country during my first odyssey travels on virgin track, the Silver Fern presented me with the conundrum that I may well have been catapulted forward in time. This was 1972, yet the last time I'd set off in the same direction a year or two before, the night express presented slashed seats and air conditioning of sorts, simply because my window was jammed open. If there was any wool to be sat on, it would have been the residue from clothing of the shearing gang who had thankfully vacated our seats while seeking out the company of the Maori guy playing 'Ten Guitars' in the gloom of the toilet lights.

Image 61

An eye-catching piece of product branding: the Silver Fern name-tag resplendent in red on black, and a little white, amidst all that silver.

The blinds on the old expresses had seen better days, and sometimes you figured there was little point trying to pull them down. I remember someone doing just that. The whole blind and fixtures came crashing down and bonked someone on the head. A bit of blood flowed. The guard was called and after establishing that no one was actually dying, he simply returned to the guard's van with the errant blind under his arm. On other occasions you might think you'd used the blind appropriately to keep harsh station lights from stirring your slumber, but later in the middle of nowhere in the pitch dark, the blind would suddenly spring up like a jack-in-the-box with a hell of a racket and most of the carriage would be awake.

The Silver Fern's windows were double-glazed, for noise control and insulation purposes. There was even a third pane, enclosing the venetian blinds, which could be opened and closed by rotating a cute little handle. Why you'd want to shut out the view was beyond us, although Brett, a friendly fellow traveller heading back from the toilet, reckoned the lowering sun further down country could be dazzling on a fine day.

Image 62

On the Silver Fern it was nothing like the surreptitious beers of old. It was all above board – and above the knee in the case of the hostesses.

If we felt uninformed about the features of the futuristic Silver Fern, Brett brought us up to speed. We were being propelled by a D398TA Caterpillar diesel engine, direct-coupled alternator and direct-current electric motors – horsepower available for traction was 970, while a small, auxiliary engine (Caterpillar D330T type, rated at 115 horsepower) was connected to an alternator with a 415 volt 3-phase output and available for lighting, heating and air conditioning.

We felt weighed down with technical information as we passed through Puketutu, Kopaki and Mangapehi, with the King Country becoming more stratified and rough. Pasture gave way to scrubby outcrops of rocks and forests. Puketutu, Kopaki and Mangapehi. They reckoned the people got rough too, the further you travelled south down the main trunk. Yet the kids who had been to school with us from this neck of the woods were nice enough. One or two of the Benneydale boys were inclined to late tackle on the rugby field but the fair-headed guy from Waimiha was OK.

The Poro-o-tarao Tunnel before Waimiha had always held a mystery or two. Childhood folklore developed around it. The land through which it was built was so wobbly that trains were crushed and trapped. It leaked like a sieve. There were monsters with eyes that glowed like steam train headlights, and fire-breathing dragons lurked beyond the portals, spitting fire and rolling it off their long sooty tongues. Nightmares in dreamland.

No trains were crushed, but it was often a tight fit. Gouged grooves where wagons had scraped along the tunnel wall attested to its instability. Goats and cattle used to shelter in the tunnel and one night when a railway serviceman entered the tunnel with his torch he was spooked by what looked like train lights bearing silently down on him. Even when it was explained as simply the reflection of his torch in the eyes of wandering cows, he was loath to enter the tunnel again.

The tunnel had its positive side. In some situations it was the quickest means for the local doctor to reach a patient, in a region where roads were few on the ground, although the doctor had to be wary of animals and trains.

At Waimiha I was fascinated by a ramshackle old hall with what looked like the word *Talkies* fading on its front wall. The Picture Palace. Waimiha's Picture Palace had been a focal point of the town, the movies a highlight of the week. Tarzan, cowboys and Indians, Yankee musicals – all were favourites, but for some the movies themselves were secondary as the serious business of establishing romantic entanglements, often as yielding as supplejack, was played out in the murky shadows towards the back. At some stage someone painted *Talkies* on the front and a rail excursion fan took a snap of the priceless old building before it was demolished.

Image 63

You can barely see the word 'Talkies' painted on the front of the old Waimiha 'Picture Palace'. History fades and passenger trains no longer stop at Waimiha.

The railway impacted on Waimiha in all sorts of ways. At the Picture Palace young boys rolled marbles roughly hewn out of rail-track ballast between the seat rows, disturbing the concentration of those older youths attempting to forge unions with members of the opposite sex. In the late 1950s when the hamlet's population was temporarily swelled by a camp of railway workers relaying the line, the Picture Palace threw open its doors twice a week to cope with demands.

Now there was the Silver Fern, no longer stopping, in all its gleaming arrogance. There were even plans to re-bore the tunnel, make it less of a tourniquet, enabling the new Silver

Fern to swish and sway away from making a commitment to a stretch of by-passed land. To cock a snook at a rusty, fading backwater which owed much of its existence to the railway and could now attribute its demise to the same sinuous divining rod – the main trunk.

Waimiha was one of those whistlestops encountered on the main trunk in the dead of night. In 1960, writer A.H. Reed, on his long trek from North Cape to the Bluff, had slept a night at Waimiha railway station. No sign of him now. No sign of the station either. And now the Silver Fern was the first railcar to bypass Waimiha. Locals were aghast, although the stocks of the town in general had taken a dive. It used to have a 30-metrelong platform. Expresses stopped there, and the sidings could house 45 wagons.

Some kids used to get to school at Mangapehi from Waimiha. Once they didn't go to school for a week. Instead they climbed on board the train, waved goodbye to their mothers, then shuffled off the train on the goods shed side, out of view of the authorities. They'd spend the day at the pa and down by the river.

Image 64

The Silver Fern near Poroo-Tarao tunnel passes a goods train. The railcar still threaded an old, unstable tunnel, which itself was soon to be upgraded.

The Silver Fern swung south towards Ongarue. Pureora Forest Park dominated the eastern horizon. They always reckoned this part of the King Country was scary and remote. The main roads avoided the stretch, and without the main trunk its loneliness would be doubly profound.

The very country on which the main trunk was built, from Mangapehi to Ongarue, was dodgy. The Poro-o-tarao Tunnel was never up to it. Mind you, locals reckoned it had a mind of its own and when it was announced the flash new Silver Fern wouldn't be stopping at Waimiha, the tunnel sought revenge. On one of its early trips the railcar was squeezed by the tunnel like a boa constrictor. It ended up limping into Waimiha, dented and grazed, its shining new silver sides blackened with old soot.

Image 65

In the heart of the King Country, the Silver Fern passes through remote Ongarue. The main trunk was critical to such backwaters.

The unstable land which made the tunnel such a liability was also responsible for several nasty accidents. Wash-outs and landslips after heavy rain made the line vulnerable. In the same year that saw the introduction of the Silver Fern, the Wellington to Auckland express ended up all askew in a wash-out caused by a cloudburst. The driver sensed danger and slowed down, so that by the time the line buckled beneath, only the engine and steam heating van were seriously disrupted. Things could have been a whole lot worse – just 800 metres further on another wash-out could have swallowed a good part of the train. The hard truth was that sections of the main trunk weren't ready for the new trains.

In the 1970s what with the all-sleeper Silver Star and now the Silver Fern daylight railcar, it was possible to believe New Zealand passenger services were keeping up with those in the rest of the world. Other worlds, perhaps, as UFO believers reported one of those strange intergalactic craft had landed – pretty close to the North Island main trunk. On sunny days in the heartland, the lowering sun's rays often glanced off the 'new age' railcar as it climbed the Raurimu Spiral or traversed the high plateau skirting the flanks of Mt Ruapehu. If you'd never seen the sun-kissed Silver Fern before and you were wary of a close encounter, the Silver Fern could resemble a grounded UFO.

As futuristic as the Silver Fern might appear, it allowed itself one indulgence from the days when trains and railcars were grubby railway red. It stopped at Taihape for lunch. Admittedly there was no mad dash to the Taihape refreshment rooms, nor wanton attacks on the thin green line of refreshment room ladies, with their armoury of huge, dented tea-pots. But there was a sense of urgency and stomach pangs for those who chose the lunch option in the revamped Taihape dining rooms, given that the meal was served at 3pm.

Image 66

The railway station at National Park, the highest point on the main trunk line.

In between times we had crossed the famous viaducts beginning with the Waitete, just south of Te Kuiti. The Makatote, Makohine and Mangaweka viaducts were enough to take your breath away. The Mangaweka was the longest on the main trunk, at 288m, then there were the Hapawhenua and Toi Toi viaducts. At one stage we seemed to be flying and the Silver Fern could have been an aircraft.

South of Taihape we began descending onto the plains. We stopped at Marton Junction and

Feilding before making a longer stop at Palmerston North, the first city on the line since Hamilton.

Image 67

From the cab of the Silver Fern going south over the new Hapuawhenua viaduct.

We'd appreciated some of the scenic bounty of the Kapiti Coast when the Auckland to Wellington express was travelling in summer and dawn had broken, but to be able to see the stormy Tasman crashing near commuter roads and the occasional seal on the rocks were rich experiences the Silver Fern made available to us, as the railcar sped down country through the Tawa Deviation tunnels and into Wellington Station.

All the Waimihas – some ramshackle dust heaps, others soldiering on and one or two showing a brave face to the world and evidence of survival and prosperity – drew back into the folds of the land. And into the recesses of the mind. Elsewhere the service towns of South Auckland, Waikato, King Country, the central regions, and Manawatu continued serving and cities like Hamilton and Palmerston North burgeoned.

Image 68

The new Silver Fern on the Waitete Viaduct. For a moment the airliner analogy returned: we seemed to be flying.

The main trunk had exposed success and failure and something in between. The Silver Fern railcar itself would go on to become New Zealand's most successful railcar, surviving for 40 years, in a variety of guises. It developed an aura of its own, with many requests from passengers wanting to ride up front with the driver.

Dave Simpson, a Silver Fern driver, remembers one in particular.

Departing National Park on one occasion, the guard came up to the cab with a request from a passenger who was a scientist from NASA in Florida. He said he wanted to ride in the 'cockpit', which was amusing enough, but then he began regaling me with the wonders of trains in the US and how fast they travelled. I couldn't get a word in but then we started the fast run down towards Horopito. The scientist looked at the speedo which read 120kph.

'Is that how fast we're going?' he asked with a start.

'Yep,' was my reply. The scientist rapidly left the 'cockpit' and on returning to his travelling companions was aghast that the railcar was travelling at 120mph. I had conveniently forgotten to tell him our speedos read in kilometres per hour, not miles.

Dave Simpson recalls further adventures with the Silver Fern when it was waiting at Ohakune station. The cab was accidently locked by a couple of inquisitive passengers, with Dave's keys and work gear inside. You couldn't smash the glass in the door because it was armour plated. The only way into the cab was to remove the glass pane in the door and to do that you needed a PK screwdriver to remove 24-odd screws.

My tool kit was in my workbag which was locked in the cab. I was now joined by Peter, a crew member and we noticed some workmen in one of the houses opposite the station. We figured they may have a PK screwdriver. I asked Peter to hop over the fence to investigate. He returned with a smile and a PK screwdriver. We set to work removing the glass, I unlocked the door and the journey recommenced. As we headed up the hill towards Horopito, Peter replaced the glass in the door. Then we realised we still had the screwdriver. Not to worry. I'm on the same job in a couple of days and I'll return it then, I thought.

I never did see the workman, but was always reminded of that day when working on that particular Silver Fern. The door glass we had unscrewed and replaced was put back the opposite way round and upside down, making its Please do not converse with the driver inscription basically indecipherable.

In 1990 the Silver Ferns stopped running on the main trunk and transferred to the Bay of Plenty lines, where they operated as two new services: the Geyserland Express between Auckland and Rotorua, and the Kaimai Express between Auckland and Tauranga. When we travelled on both services in 1997 it was like catching up with old friends. The Silver Ferns were looking well. In fact they still looked futuristic – like beacons in the landscape.

It was interesting, nonetheless, to hear of the Silver Fern going unnoticed on consecutive days. In 1976 the bright silver object hit a prison truck near Waikune Prison at Erua and the next day, nearby, the UFO-like apparition hit a car at a Rata level crossing. Perhaps they were too bedazzling.

However, this factor doesn't explain the situation when a Silver Fern driver had to slam on all anchors after rounding a corner and coming across a woman toting shopping bags, walking away down the middle of the track. The railcar was able to pull up – just, while the woman simply kept walking. Down the middle of the track.

After climbing down and approaching the woman, the driver was able, at length, to convince her that her best interests were not being served.

'I'm just walking home,' she pleaded. 'I live around the next corner.'

She claimed she didn't hear the Silver Fern. It was reputedly a stealthy mover. After reading the riot act to the woman about how dangerous and illegal her actions had been, the driver remounted his railcar, the woman stepped aside and the Silver Fern continued on its way.

Image 69

Before daylight passenger services like the Silver Fern were introduced, engine crews of goods trains like this one were among the few to see the Raurimu Spiral by day.

When the driver turned the next corner he was able to look back to see the woman continuing her long trudge – down the middle of the tracks.

Years later, when appraising my first journey on the Silver Fern, it was natural enough to highlight the viaducts, the Raurimu Spiral, the central volcanoes and plateau, the elevated escarpments of the Rangitikei River and the Kapiti Coast. But for some reason it's the off-the-wall, eccentric, sometimes gothic tableaux, usually randomly arrayed on the backblock belts of the Silver Fern's path, that return to remind me of my first daylight viewing of the North Island heartland.

These were the features not included in the official announcements. Not in the manner of 'if you look out to the left just beyond the next bridge you will see a hawk pecking at a cow carcass.' Similarly, attention was *not* drawn to the lack of uniformity applied to the naming of station toilets. Some featured 'Men' or 'Gentlemen', some both. 'Women' was less slavishly used. 'Ladies', harking back to earlier eras predominated. At one whistle stop the 'Ladies' sign was broken and 'Lads' presented a confusing message.

Travelling through the tidy dairy farms of the Waikato there were fewer examples of heartland gothic, but further south, when the land became rugged and far-flung, you'd see standalone objects that would do a conceptual artist proud. An old, abandoned homestead, now providing shelter for hay bales, had *Go the Rams* daubed in red paint on its peeling facade. A collection of whiteware gathered rust and dust somewhere near Ohakune. What looked like a Jerry-built shop stood in a rocky paddock above the line. Perhaps the vendor used to hawk produce to train travellers in earlier decades? Certainly there was an old embankment, which might have carried a loop line past the stop in the days of mixed trains. At Horopito hundreds of car wrecks created a graveyard, both sobering and horrifying. Not too many kilometres further on someone had used a lawn mower to etch the words 'Jesus Saves' into hillside grass.

Beyond the towns and stations, the landscape was bare of people. I do remember a man hitchhiking along a gravel road that shared a valley with the main trunk line. I waved out, probably in surprise. The man replied with a hitchhiking thumb gesture and an earnest look on his face. I don't think it was a whimsical touch. We were far from anywhere and rain clouds were banking. I remember there was nothing much of human habitation or activity for the next thirty kilometres. Just a couple of dead sheep, circling hawks and a tumbledown shed with 'Home Sweet Home' whitewashed on its side. It might have been near Waimiha.

10

Déjà Vu Express

The Endeavour, from Wellington to Napier

Image 70

The Endeavour Express threads its way back through the narrow Manawatu Gorge, on the return service to Wellington from Napier.

My grandfather had a photo of a K engine singlehandedly hauling the Wellington to Napier Express up and over the old Hutt Road, prior to entering the first of the long Tawa Deviation tunnels – and seeking freedom. This was taken in 1938, not long after the Deviation and its two serpentine tunnels had made redundant the original means of getting away from Wellington Station. This involved a long, exhausting haul up the original line, part of which still operates as the Johnsonville suburban branch. It was a backbreaking way to say goodbye to the city. At other times the train ran through the Hutt Valley and Wairarapa lines.

Now the Napier Express (number 612) could make a cleaner getaway, and such was my grandfather's thrill at seeing such a stirring sight he had the photo mounted and placed above his mantelpiece. Sometimes in winter when the open fire was burning, the wood flames and smoke looked as if they were coming directly out of the funnel of the K engine depicted in the photo. If you imagined hard enough.

It was this photo of the Napier Express which fired my desire to travel on the service when it came up on my roster of 'trains to travel' once I'd entered my rail odyssey years. By that stage of course, the Napier Express or Napier Mail had gone, and not just over the old Hutt Road. The curtain on the last steamhauled express was pulled down many years ago.

Publicity shots of a new train called the Endeavour Express, set to commence its term of duty in November 1972, didn't initially stir my soul the way number 612 used to – or at least as I imagined it did. In 1972 I still hadn't expanded my rail horizons to include the famous old route between Wellington and Napier, the one which made my grandfather chortle and blow out his cheeks, for all the world like a K engine.

But eventually the announcement of the new Endeavour service became enticing and before too long I found myself in Wellington, all set to travel to Napier.

Prior to taking on the new Endeavour Express I stayed with friends in Wellington. We had a lot in common: tastes in music; opinions on politics; theories on life and existence. Yet we never squared off over railways. To them trains were utilitarian, pedestrian, proletariat. Being Wellingtonians they were obliged to queue for the noisy, smelly things on cold mornings to take them into the corporate canyons. When the day was done they could be seen rushing like stampeding cattle to catch a homebound train, the wind tearing at their very beings.

To them, trains were a necessary evil and they looked down their noses at my rather romanticised perception of NZ Railways. They made me evaluate my passion for rail – but not for long. Besides, I have reason to believe I was exposed to rail influences beyond the norm, it wasn't just the all-pervading Te Kuiti railway environment. A grandparent at some stage made a passing reference to three little-known uncles who worked on the railways. They may have been up north, down south or out east. It couldn't be confirmed but if it was true there may have been trains in my blood – a predisposition to railway fascination.

The taxi driver pulled out all stops to get to Wellington Station after a late start in the morning, and after a sharp sprint to the relevant platform, I was surprised to find we still had twenty minutes up our sleeves. I threw open the carriage door and tossed my travel bag into a decidedly orderly Endeavour carriage.

In the old days, pre-departure would have included the chatter of passengers and well-wishers, the stentorian commands of rail officials, the thump and grind of luggage being loaded. Once I'd finished making my noise, the only sound was the steady whirring of air conditioning units. The carriage – teal blue and calming – was about half full and most passengers were reading. There was wall-to-wall carpet to contemplate and comfortable seats with several protrusions I will come to terms with once my racing heart has slowed down, and my dilated pupils have accustomed themselves to the unfamiliar interior.

Image 71

The imposing exterior of Wellington Station.

At precisely 7.55am the train pulled away from the platform and crossed the marshalling yards, through the hanging fog and swirling steam jets from beneath the carriage.

At the time, the Endeavour was a new train, introduced on 6 November 1972, to provide passenger services between Wellington and Napier and vice versa. Similar to the South Island's Southerner, it consisted of reconditioned steel carriages. Two were classified as smoking cars where liquor was available and two were non-smoking. Making up the train was a 20-seat dining car and a guard's van. Its official running times, for those who understood these things, saw it leave Wellington at 0755 and arrive at Napier at 1325. The return train departed Napier at 1405 and arrived back in the capital at 1937. It all sounded very official, but really meant we would arrive in Napier at 25 past one that afternoon.

A couple of gang members in patches looked menacing in their seat at the end of the carriage; however, perhaps in honour of the upgrading of the Endeavour, and the solicitousness of the train attendants, they proved to be model passengers.

Another group of young men, a motley long-haired bunch, harkened back to the old days of the overnight main trunk limiteds and expresses. Towards the end of their lives those trains were often like swilleries. Boisterous, sleepless pubs on wheels, where young men –

and older ones – bantered on through the night at the top of their voices and to hell with anyone else. What with guitars chunking, shearing gangs caterwauling and young men yelling, the second-class carriages often sounded like a public bar in downtown Palmerston North.

At this stage of the Endeavour's journey north, where it began to thread the cuttings and tunnels of the main trunk along the Kapiti Coast, all was quiet. Porirua, Plimmerton, Pukerua Bay, Paekakariki, Paraparaumu, all the P-towns (and by that I simply mean towns that begin with the letter P – nothing more sinister) flashed past as we gathered speed and the sun poked through. The train headed inland towards Waikanae and soon the Tararua Ranges claimed my attention now that we were clear of the coast.

The stretch along the Kapiti Coast has always been one of the most scenic maritime rail journeys and you marvelled at the precise engineering and construction feats of those who hewed the line out of the confined and the narrow cliff-face, opening on to the Tasman Sea. Normally, whether the train was heading north or south, this majestic stretch was hidden – unless of course we were travelling north by night train in summer, when the longer hours of daylight afforded a glimpse before the sun went down.

There was something distinctly sophisticated about seeing the beauty of the Kapiti Coast from a salubrious rail carriage which featured carpets on the floor and drinks served at your very seat.

The gentle undulations of the Tararua foothills were almost as beguiling as the Kapiti seascapes. Otaki, Levin and Shannon took the line further inland. The Endeavour ghosted along, not like the noisy steam-hauled expresses I was used to as a child. I guess the Endeavour made its presence felt to the outside world, but it was very quiet on the inside. This musing was prompted by the memory of our family staying at a Levin motel after a frustrating drive down the North Island, with the intention of making Wellington by nightfall. I was appalled at my father for not taking us by train – the tried and true method – simply because he had bought a Chrysler Valiant. A show-off car really, after he had been faithful to French Citroens for as long as I could recall. Dad spent so much time showing off his new American car by making many stops, that night had well and truly fallen by the time we made Levin. Mum put her foot down. Dad shut his mouth. We found a motel in the dark which backed onto the main trunk.

Image 72

The view across to Kapiti Island from the coastal railway line.

From the Endeavour, I swore I saw that line-side motel in the heart of Levin. It brought back memories of a long, sleepless night as trains of all shapes, sizes and lengths rumbled past, making a terrible din. There seemed to be a train every five minutes. If nothing else it opened my eyes to the sheer presence of New Zealand railways at a time when cars like the Chrysler Valiant were expected to render trains in general redundant.

Furthermore, here we were, at least a dozen years later, travelling on the sophisticated, made-over Endeavour, all the way to Napier. Palmerston North was in our sights now. Dad told the story of travelling through the heart of Palmerston North in the days when the main trunk still took a direct route through what would now be called the CBD. In those wartime larrikin days, expresses and troop trains would disgorge their clientele, not just to partake of conventional refreshments, but also to make lightning visits to pubs located in the square, not far from the station.

Some didn't make it back to their train. Stories circulated of soldiers who became stranded in Palmerston North and made new lives for themselves in the Manawatu. Others were identified as deserters, who simply went to ground because the jugs of beer touched a nerve and reminded them of what they could lose – their lives. Luckily my generation didn't have to make such desperate decisions. We were too busy protesting the Vietnam War, being abused by the RSA generation, or having protest rallies thwarted by the long arm of the law.

In peacetime we were seeking out Palmerston North, tiptoeing through the back-door station to the west of the city. The opening of the long-awaited Milson Deviation meant the main trunk had an easier egress from the sprawling suburbs. And times had changed. As the Endeavour sat silently at the relatively new Palmerston North station, it was impossible to contemplate any of our current passengers wanting to desert the Endeavour in search of a better life.

I certainly wasn't about to go to ground. While I had travelled the main trunk between Wellington and Palmerston North many times, and had in 1967 gone beyond Woodville to Napier and Gisborne for the first time, I had yet to travel between Palmerston and Woodville. So when the main trunk just north of Palmerston arced left towards Bunnythorpe, and the Endeavour headed right to the northeast, I knew I was now on virgin track. The sensation wasn't unlike scoring a try while playing rugby. It was hard to suppress my delight and harder to explain to the hostess, who hovered above me with a cup of coffee, why travelling on tracks I'd never touched before was such a thrill.

Ashhurst, with its two hs, was the last settlement before the Endeavour took on the Manawatu Gorge. Someone said the Manawatu River flowed backwards. Uphill even. Its principal headwaters rise on the east of the dividing range, yet its waters flow to the sea in the west. I watched it closely and if it did it wasn't always obvious to the casual traveller. But then I'm no geologist. Perhaps if Russ, my mate, was along for the ride he may have explained it. He studied Geology 1 at Auckland University.

What I did come to terms with as the Endeavour snaked through the gorge, was the loss of Bill, an acquaintance from home-town days. On a Saturday night, Bill, who was studying at Massey University, had his return north interrupted by a wild skid into the flooded Manawatu River. I reckoned I'd just about identified Bill's immersion point, looking down from the Endeavour, into a west-flowing river emanating from east-flowing origins. They never found his body.

Such introversion and reflection continued as we approached Woodville just beyond the gorge. Not only was it an important junction – the Hawke's Bay and Wairarapa lines met here – but it took on some personal significance for me.

Back in the 1970s ancestry and family history were not the burgeoning passions they have now become. Back then I barely knew my father's birthplace. Often in the years immediately beyond the golden weather we were preoccupied with moving forward in the 'greatest little country in the world'. The war was over, we were comparatively prosperous, equality and egalitarianism were social cornerstones and the future glowed. The tragedies and unspoken details of World War II were largely suppressed. It was a way of moving forward towards that glowing future, which was in fact already dimming.

Image 73

The Endeavour at Opapa. The famous folding hills of Hawke's Bay stretch out to the horizon. Usually the colour of Weetbix, they bear a green tinge here from recent rain.

'It doesn't pay to dwell on the past,' my father used to say, and he would know, having come through the Great Depression and active service in World War II. Yet some information seeped out, a fragment, a half-truth relating to my family's past. I had always sensed my father's family had a lot to do with the town of Woodville. When the Endeavour stopped at Woodville after we'd cleared the Manawatu Gorge, I was almost overtaken by the feeling I had been here before. But this was my first trip to Woodville – yet a sense of déjà vu hovered. I figured my blood sugar might be a bit low and a snack from the Endeavour's stockpiles might do the trick.

Years passed. The odd experience in Woodville was deleted from my immediate consciousness. Then much later – in 2010 – I came across a family history involving Woodville and I learned that one of the original pioneers in Woodville – he may have even been the first – was James Hutchins, my great-grandfather. In 1876 there were only two women in Woodville – Mrs J. Murphy, the publican's wife, and James Hutchins' wife, Elizabeth. The Murphys' two kids and James and Elizabeth's daughter were the first children in Woodville.

Back in 1972, on the Endeavour, I shook off my déjà vu like so many flu symptoms. I was still reeling from the magnificent rail passage through the Manawatu Gorge and now, beyond Woodville, there was the splendour of scenic Hawke's Bay to contemplate on a train designed for comfort and sightseeing. Attacks of unsettling déjà vu and the ghostly recall of long-lost Bill were deflected by the friendliness of the Endeavour train staff and the wonder of new fixtures and creature comforts.

As sophisticated as the Endeavour appeared to be – clearly a step up in our travelling habits – the noisy boys at the head of the carriage could have been transplanted from the first carriage behind the engine of the old, shambolic night express between Auckland and Wellington. Initially anyway.

Beer cans were now being punctured with pocket knives although the hostess had gone to the trouble of opening them in the conventional manner. At this point all four youths began talking at once, generally deriding their country of birth and threatening to do something about their perceived lack of status in an apparently egalitarian democracy. You'd imagine that in the old express they'd be telling blue jokes and chortling about this and that, but now, exposed by daylight and wall-to-wall carpet, they became quieter – strangely defensive and negative. Change doesn't take everyone along for the ride.

'The pigs will get ya, even if you're just standing there,' one youth with very long hair reckoned.

'Yeah, but what if you were standing on that fella's head?' replied a deep voice attached to another slumped in his seat with his back to me. 'That's different.'

By now the Endeavour was threading its way through classic Hawke's Bay hill country that had proved so alluring when I first encountered it back in 1967, on the Gisborne railcar. The contour of the land was easy on the eye. The multicoloured hills folded back on one another, concealing settlements in the folds. The light browns and greens and muted yellows produced an interesting tapestry. I felt so absorbed by the rustic beauty I wanted the train to go on forever.

The noisy boys weren't so absorbed. Beyond Dannevirke their conversation became a bit louder, yet strangely compelling.

'We feel like outsiders because conservative elements, and that means most New Zealanders, see us as not equal enough. Some Kiwis are more equal than others and they'll dictate the evolution of a new underclass.'

Thoughtful stuff indeed, as we curved on to the Ormondville Viaduct and ghosted through Kopua heading for Takapau. The Endeavour seemed to be coasting downhill. There were few engine sounds. Only the whirring of air conditioning, the purr of the train hostess and the continuing tirade from the noisy boys' enclosure.

'The trouble with you is that you allow losers to dictate your effing every movement. Destiny is not disposable. It's as effing tangible as a train on a predetermined track...'

Normally, as the cans of beer mounted, you'd expect such a noisy cabal to impose themselves on outsiders. You figured train staff and fellow passengers would be hectored and harried, but even the hostess who kept up the supply of beer cans was treated with respect.

The Endeavour created a mellow mood as the morning passed imperceptibly. Kids, old ladies, fellow long-hairs of indeterminate persuasion, even miniskirted young women were allowed to pass the noisy boys' enclosure with impunity. Finally the time came for me to use the toilet, which meant I had to walk past the gabbling phalanx. I fully expected some demeaning diatribe about my longish red hair. Something like, 'Get a haircut, carrot top.' Instead, as I passed I picked up the following:

'Of course, as Aristotle said – or was it Plato – a stitch in time saves ten.'

'I didn't know Aristotle was a seamstress.'

'Oh indeed, and he had long ginger hair...'

It was at this stage that I pondered the joint fascinations of long-distance train travel – the scenic delights, particularly if they were being seen for the first time, and the train's internal life, where fellow travellers provide a tableau of fascinating tirades and verbal jousting, or something simply intellectually stimulating.

To get the balance right. That was the thing. It's all very well listening to Einstein or John Lennon extolling their worldview if they were sharing your carriage while the train was clanking through boring, over-familiar territory. If, however, Lennon was explaining how the words of 'I am the Walrus' came to the surface, it doesn't pay to be travelling through a shimmering landscape like the one provided by the Hawke's Bay hills. Luckily he wasn't.

Image 74

Hawke's Bay from the imposing presence of Te Mata Peak.

I was able to absorb the scenic grandeur, undiverted by brilliant conversation, at a time when I needed to concentrate on the great outdoors through the Endeavour's windows.

As the train devoured the distance the noisy boys' enclosure fell quiet. The sounds of the train – the swishing and occasional clacking of the wheels as loop line points were crossed, the even more occasional honk of the diesel engine, preceding level crossings – became more prominent. Gradually you became aware of a new noise emanating from the enclosure. Beyond Waipawa the boys had, almost on cue, collapsed into a comatose state. They were all sound asleep and they all seemed to be snorers. For a moment I thought I was on the old overnight express, fighting for sleep beyond Taihape. The snoring in those situations formed a syncopation with the chuffs from the steam engine as it sought pulling power away from stationary positions. There was no such chuffing on the Endeavour as its DA diesel engine effortlessly eased us towards touchdown at Napier.

Towards the end of our journey we seemed to be tumbling down towards the ocean. The hills surrendered to the plains. The old-world villas receded and the distinctive art-deco houses and buildings of Napier lay before us. The market gardens and concentrated cropping on the flats gave way to ocean views.

After curving around the seashore and ducking in behind the backyards of old houses, the Endeavour finally came to a halt. Napier Station was a sudden hive of activity. Many passengers transferred to and from the Gisborne railcar waiting at the adjoining platform. The noisy boys stopped snoring and awoke, only to find they had snored through their stop – Hastings – several kilometres back up the line.

'Bloody hell. That's all we need,' one of them wailed. 'We'll be stranded in Napier for a week.' As luck would have it, the Endeavour was scheduled to turn around and head back to Wellington, and it would be a simple matter of someone staying awake until Hastings was reached again. But there was no time to lose. Because the incoming Endeavour was twenty minutes late, the return train was prepared for departure in double-quick time, to ensure the

Wellington-bound service left Napier at its demanding departure time of 2.05pm. There was no time for the boys to sneak a pint in a downtown pub, and check out 'Flossie' the barman, a mutual friend. There was barely time to purchase tickets to Hastings.

Image 75

A typical turbulent scene at Napier Station as the Endeavour arrives and disassembles. The Gisborne railcar, connecting with the Endeavour, adds to the scramble.

'The station only comes alive at this time.' The station attendant appeared to be speaking to no one in particular. A kid skinned his knee after taking a tumble. A woman snapped off one of her high heels. I thought I was having another attack of déjà vu. Had a great-uncle been stationmaster at Napier away back in time? Then I realised I had been to Napier Station before – about five years earlier while travelling through on the Gisborne railcar. And if I'd been to Napier before by railcar I'd already been through Woodville, which took some of the sting out of the family history-déjà vu association.

I wandered away from the station chaos to find accommodation in downtown Napier. I wasn't scheduled to return to Wellington until the following day. The sun was shining and the art-deco glistened. The people seemed friendly. I read somewhere that déjà vu can strike when you're tired, but I felt invigorated. The Endeavour had been a slick, comfortable ride – completely entitled to be the only train at the time to sport a headboard at the front of the engine.

11

Trundling on the 542

By mixed train on the Stratford to Okahukura Line

Image 76

The equivalent of our mixed goods was still steam-hauled when this shot was taken of the train on the Okahukura bridge. We were grateful to catch the same train before it was withdrawn – though it was diesel-drawn by then.

We'd seen them often enough, the goods trains with a carriage tagged on, just in front of the trailing guard's van. Sometimes you'd see a handful of faces at the old carriage windows as the goods train went ambling past, across the level crossing and out of town.

There was always a lot of noise associated with such trains. Empty wagons banged as if a panel beater was trapped inside, livestock bleated in sheep wagons heading for the works and there was always a wagon with a wonky wheel and a protrusion dragging in the ballast, sending out sparks and the sound of metal on metal.

The slower the train went, the more noise it made. Or the greater the chance for observers to hear the clatter. A fast goods train, like the goods express, barely seemed to touch the rails as it sped through town. It didn't stop much and was able to maintain a fast clip.

In the steam era the 'goods train with a carriage' was more prevalent, but they were still running when DA diesels stepped up. We travelled on one the day we needed to get to Taumarunui to watch a rep rugby match. That was the 443 Te Kuiti to Taumarunui mixed train on the main trunk – a classic, apparently, of its genre.

'Mixed trains' were usually defined as 'goods with car,' sometimes there were also 'mixed goods' and our own 'goods train with a carriage' widened the definition base. There were many of them running between intermediate stops on most lines – and back in the day they were as common as dirt and as cheap as chips, but they got you where you wanted to go, beyond the orbit of long-distance expresses, limiteds and railcars. Once the latter had sped between larger towns and cities, leaving rural locals gasping, the 'mixed' would come along, do a bit of time-consuming shunting, wait interminably for opposing traffic to enter passing loops and carry heartland folk at a doddle to somewhere down the line.

From Te Kuiti you could get to Frankton by mixed train, as well as by the Taumarunui service, but the day someone suggested you could catch a mixed train from Taumarunui to Stratford along the Stratford to Okahukura branch line, we tended to disagree.

David Leitch wrote an excellent hardback called simply *Railways of New Zealand.* It was published in 1972, after we'd undertaken two rail odysseys in 1967 and 1971, and had come home flushed with an awareness we'd broken the back of the New Zealand Rail skeleton. Leitch alerted us to the fact there were other lines and passenger services still available to rail aficionados.

The Stratford to Okahukura line was one. It ran a backwater course from Taumarunui to Stratford and played host to the Auckland to New Plymouth railcar, goods trains – and the 542, a meandering daylight 'mixed' which took most of the day to get through the 24 tunnels along 143 kilometres of remote and rugged backblocks.

The third of our rail odysseys occurred in 1975–76, after I'd recovered from preoccupation with marriage, overseas travel and other diversions. Part of our honeymoon included travelling around Northland on those 'mixed' trains which were still running. We were able to thread the needle between Auckland Central and Helensville and travel between Maungaturoto, Whangarei and Opua, all by Northland 'mixed' trains. Someone had traced 'silver star' in the window dust of one of the trains, which pointed up a certain run-down, ironic aspect.

As interesting as those 'mixed' journeys were, one much closer to home was to become the jewel in the crown: the mixed train between Taumarunui and Stratford. On a hot summer's day in 1975, within cooee of its final foray, with its lone wooden carriage occupied by five intrepid travellers, four of whom hadn't previously known the train existed, number 542 was in its element. We had been only vaguely aware there was such a serpentine line spreading so far through a narrow neck of New Zealand that was also little known.

Image 77

A passenger train on the road-rail bridge at Okahukura Junction – solid evidence of the presence of an inland Taranaki line.

We'd always thought the railcar which passed through Te Kuiti at 4 o'clock in the afternoon was on its way to Wellington. Even when the major flood of 1958 forced several trains – including the New Plymouth to Auckland service – to cool their heels in Te Kuiti, it didn't occur to us that the train from New Plymouth could have made its way to our backyard along a branch that was closer to home.

Finally someone checked the New Zealand Atlas. Sure enough, just north of Taumarunui at a place called Okahukura Junction, a line branched off the main trunk, heading west. We may have already seen the branch line arcing over a roadrail bridge across the Ongarue River, while travelling on the main trunk 'mixed' between Te Kuiti and Taumarunui, but it probably looked like one of the bush tramways, common in the bush-clad hinterland. On the way back from Taumarunui, with the late afternoon sun shafting its light through the grimy carriage window, our vision was probably impaired. We were otherwise occupied, drinking our first-ever bottle of beer to celebrate King Country's rugby win. And any other excuse for a shared, frothy, teeth-clunking swig.

In those days, there wasn't the burning hunger to know where any off-shoot branch line went. Not initially. We were quite happy to trundle up and down the main trunk, because that was the line that went through Te Kuiti.

Even when my friend Russ rhapsodised about the Northland Line, the Opua Express and the Taneatua Express on the Bay of Plenty line, we figured he might have been making some of it up, even though it was common knowledge that Russ and his family took their summer holidays in the Bay of Islands and

Tauranga. And they went by train. At the time we had a certain landlocked mentality. Not even when Mike Walker from Ohura, a coal-mining town we knew was located in the backblocks way off the main highway and main trunk, said he came into Te Kuiti by railcar to visit his grandparents in the weekend, did we twig to the notion of another line out there somewhere. We had always assumed Mike went by bus to Taumarunui and utilised the main trunk.

But now David Leitch and the New Zealand Atlas had confirmed it – an inland Taumarunui to Stratford line, with passenger trains running along its course. One of them was the 4 o'clock Auckland–New Plymouth railcar. Without further ado I booked a seat.

Image 78

My first trip on the Stratford–Okahukura line (the SOL) was taken alone on the

Auckland–New Plymouth railcar, seen here at Mercer. It was a lonely, dark pilgrimage, and I was relieved to wake up in Taranaki.

Image 79

The Silver Fern railcar waits at the main trunk Taumarunui platform, while the railcar to New Plymouth (via the Stratford–Okahukura line) waits at the other. It took us a while to realise the existence of the latter route.

Winter fell suddenly at that time of year. Fog drift accompanied us, and by Taumarunui it was getting darker. Then the railcar returned back up the main trunk until, at Okahukura, it curved westwards across the Ongarue River and disappeared into a world of enveloping blackness on the Okahukura–Stratford line and on to New Plymouth.

It's a most unlikely railway line, in an unusual setting, which is why its existence wasn't well known. The region features no large towns, nor remarkable natural phenomena, such as exploding volcanoes or massive waterfalls. Large towns were supposed to burgeon because of the presence of the railway line, or small ones at least become sizeable agriculture service settlements once the railway had stimulated the growth of farms and the breaking in of the land. But the bush won out and settlers continued to leave the backblocks, even after the line was opened.

After my railcar trip on the branch line – one that was shrouded by night – I felt there was some urgency to take the last available day train, which was the mixed goods with a carriage, from Taumarunui to Stratford. Passenger services were being cut back in several regions and I couldn't help but feel that the SOL – the common vernacular for the Stratford–Okahukura Line – would also be affected.

Destiny was on our side the day a group of us travelled on train number 542, the 'mixed' service from Taumarunui to Stratford. From one backwater to another through a New Zealand rail wilderness. We had no way of knowing the urgency of the situation when we climbed aboard the mix-and-match service – humans travelled on the same train with sheep and cattle, although not in the same wagon. It all seemed perfectly laid back on a fine, breezy early November morning. No urgency there. The ticket seller at Taumarunui seemed hung-over and ham-fisted as he scrambled around for the appropriate ticket book for the SOL.

Our train sat throbbing patiently as the official departure time of 8.55am came and went. Obviously no urgency there either.

'Why 8.55am? Why not round it up to 9 o'clock?' Harry's comment seemed reasonable but it elicited no response from the ticket seller, who couldn't seem to get his ticket stamper to work. 'That's why they don't say 9 o'clock. The ticket man needs five minutes to fire up his stamper.' It seemed a reasonable comment.

The driver of DA diesel 1518 looked anything but urgent as he swung himself up on the cute little stairs at the front of the engine and accessed the protruding cabin with a pie between his teeth. At 9.10am. We thought we'd better swing aboard too, despite the laid-back nature of our departure.

Eight fifty-five indeed. Mind you, the ticket seller was so nonplussed by five humans wanting to travel on 542 you figured it could be up and gone before you knew it.

'How many passengers do you normally get?' Russ asked.

'We normally get nil, sir.'

'But there appears to be a human form, sitting in the carriage. That's one more than none.' Russ was right. There was a sullen outline of a young man's face peering from a carriage window.

'Well, if that's the case, he hasn't bothered to buy a ticket,' the ticket seller replied. 'Good luck to him, but the guard needs to punch something. If it's not a ticket it might be his lights. It's happened before.'

'You mean if he's got no ticket the guard will punch his lights out?'

'Barney has his own way of doing things.'

We broke into a bit of a jog as we sought out the carriage at the rear of the train, a bit more urgency creeping in. Didn't want to upset Barney by holding up the train. The carriage, AA 1071, was one of those old wooden jobs last seen on the main trunk express back in the '30s. It had an open-air platform at each end and was surprisingly spick and span for a service that was hardly ever used. The urgency died as we realised we had the carriage to ourselves. The sullen-faced young man had disappeared.

We all found window seats. Russ and Julia opted to sit facing each other and were able to facilitate such positioning by manhandling the stiff, rotatable red leather seats into a one-on-one situation. Russ remembered he didn't like travelling backwards. It made him disoriented and light-headed. So Julia stepped up and crossed over. Harry spent his pre-departure time adjusting light-levels and focusing his movie camera, to take into account the carriage murkiness. I applied a blast of antihistamine spray to keep my hay fever at bay.

Which brought us back to the urgency issue. Back in 1975 when seasons were more predictable, November was the time in early summer when the cruel irritants of seeding grasses, pine dust, privet and honeysuckle pollen filled the air and set half the nation sneezing. November was also the month we had planned the rail trip on one of the least known and certainly unsung rambles into the middle of nowhere. You had to be more than a rail buff to catch this train. It was almost a case of calling all social historians ... and perhaps the odd archaeologist.

We travelled in early November, 1975 and on 28 November of the same year the last train to Stratford ran. The mixed goods, number 542, was no more. That was where the urgency came into it. Another week or two and we would have missed out. Beyond 28 November the ticket seller might have still groped around for his ticket book and stamper, but there would be no ancient wooden carriage slung on as an afterthought next to the guard's van. And no passengers needing tickets.

It was several years before we realised the closeness of the call. Once we'd sneezed and breezed our way through the inland Taranaki route to Stratford, we moved on. Generally we began looking outward, which meant seeking out the newer trains – mainly main trunk developments – or heading overseas.

There were many memories associated with train 542 but the true character of the mixed train was also in evidence. One stark memory in the semi-dark summed up the indifference and confusion associated with mixed trains in their death throes. If the ticket seller at Taumarunui, Barney the guard, and the driver of DA 1518, who may still have that pie between his teeth, were throwbacks to a prehistoric time, they were laid back compared with the shunter at Maungaturoto when we travelled by mixed train through Northland.

Image 80

Crossing the New Plymouth–Taumarunui railcar somewhere along the line, as the hills and ramparts continue to close in. At this passing point there were probably more people than were clustered anywhere else along the line.

Apparently the mixed train from Maungaturoto to Wellsford was curtailed in 1967, yet as we climbed down at the end of the line for the Whangarei to Maungaturoto mixed in 1975, a local shunter with beer on his breath and a large flashlight, operated with a certain urgency.

'Hurry up folks, this carriage has to be back in Wellsford as soon as possible,' he yelled.

It was all a bit mysterious. If the Maungaturoto to Wellsford mixed no longer ran why did the carriage have to be back at Wellsford as soon as possible? It was a lingering memory, the sight of the shunt gathering speed in the Northland night, taillights glowing in the gathering gloom as the train bounced over the rough track. Such was the pace of the retreat you had to question the need for such speed. Perhaps urgency means different things in different corners of the country.

The diesel pulling the Taumarunui–Stratford train sounded urgent enough as it growled into action, sounding its horn several times to ensure the town was awake. It took a surprisingly long time to travel up the main trunk to the junction at Okahukura – one of those lonely, one-horse stops in the middle of nowhere. Waiotira Junction in Northland, where the Dargaville line branches off the main north line, is another. Often rail junctions develop into sizeable settlements, but Okahukura was never more than a station, perhaps a railway house or two and maybe a garage.

We waited for a main line goods to clear the points before heading out to the west, across the Okahukura road-rail bridge and into unseen territory. It's interesting to contemplate the historical notion of travelling by trains which could only go as far as the line extended at any given point in time. In 1926 trains started running from Okahukura to Ohura, because that was how far the line extended from the east. From the other end – the Stratford starting point – work on the line began in the early 1900s. In 1975, for some reason you half-expected the train to reach its terminus beyond the first tunnel and just around the next bend.

The trip from Taumarunui to Stratford was a step into the past. This was how Kiwi train travellers got around in days gone by. From town to country, general store to farm, community hall to the 'pictures,' accident site to hospital. They said the railways opened up the land. With the SOL that maxim prevailed to a certain extent, but much of the land remained isolated despite the rail.

As we passed Matiere the hills were already dominating the landscape. This was a frontier railway, New Zealand style. We felt like extras in a train robbery movie. In the movie Harry made of the trip we are all at some stage captured sauntering down the carriage aisle like Gary Cooper entering the Dry Gulch saloon. Everything seemed to play out in slow motion and '70s sepia.

The mixed goods was also like travelling on a time machine. This was part of our history and we had been offered a rare opportunity to taste the past. This was no vintage rail experience with all the bit-players dressed self-consciously in period costumes. This was the real thing. The guard was dressed up as a real guard. His uniform was traditional NZ rail sandpaper and trim. He was even good old-fashioned grumpy as he wandered through the carriage to check our tickets.

'Weren't there six of you?' he asked through lips that didn't move much.

'There may have been another guy, but he seems to have gone now. Perhaps he got off.' My reply went unchallenged as the train approached Ohura, a settlement which looked positively urban after all that rural wilderness. At Ohura the summer heat shimmered on the corrugated iron roofs. The sun, finding a gap in the hills and clouds, assaulted the skin. Long hair and beards served a purpose – they kept out the recently discovered suspect rays piercing through the hole in the ozone layer. The train waited. The engine throbbed. The shimmering heat from the diesel's exhaust matched that of the Ohura roofs.

Still the train waited. The guard ambled through the ballast, kicking vaguely at something beneath a couple of sheep wagons. Ours was a long train and it took the guard as long as it takes a guard to walk the length of a long train to get back to his van. He didn't look up in recognition of our presence. He just clumped in his sandpaper uniform through the time warp we had invaded.

Our carriage was a bit of an afterthought anyway. It was a dislocated vessel that didn't seem to be part of the train. If it derailed in Tangarakau Gorge and disappeared into the undergrowth no one would come looking for it for weeks. Perhaps that had already happened and fellow rare-as-hens'teeth passengers were probably adapting as we spoke to life in an abandoned wooden carriage. Living off the land, tickling trout in the Ohura River, trying to eke out an existence, aware the search parties weren't coming.

Somewhere along the line – it may have been at Mangaparo – a short distance on from Ohura, our train switched to the passing loop. Ten minutes later the New Plymouth to Taumarunui railcar crept past on the main line. The railcar was half full, the most people we had seen in one place all day. Most were dressed conservatively. Perhaps some were off to a wedding or a funeral. By comparison, we looked like a bunch of folk singers.

Travelling on 542 on the SOL was a pretty folksy thing to do. At a time when young, once-urban tribes took to the backroads, decrying the city, to find 'paradise' in rural communes, trains like 542 seemed to honour retreatist behaviour. Certainly we saw some interesting old homesteads and peeling villas, abandoned and standing sentinel on lonely hilltops, waiting to be salvaged. No one would hassle you there. No city fathers, worried mothers, short-haired rednecks or trilling Presbyterian sisters. And 542 – Old Faithful – would remind you of the outside world and provide transport to town if you needed new guitar strings and other provisions.

We felt as if we were acting in New Zealand's equivalent of 'Easy Rider', with a mixed train substituting for Harley Davidsons. There was definitely something funky and alternative about our modus operandi and mode of transport as we continued to retreat.

Mind you, anyone could dream back then. I may have called it funky, but others called the service run-down. In the modern era 542 may not have been grand, but it remained redolent of something sacred: a transport hub which helped create the New Zealand we know. A museum on wheels, if you will.

Meanwhile the motor car had taken over. Not only did it kill, it hastened the isolation of Kiwi from Kiwi, with the kids in the back and Nana in the boot. In the days when trains ruled the transport roost people mingled – in carriages, on station platforms, in refreshment rooms. Mind you, the sullen-faced young man – the sixth passenger – hadn't mingled. At Tokirima he snuck out of the toilet, swung down into the long grass and disappeared from sight.

Talk is cheap. As the train continued to be delayed at Tokirima youthful self-expression did the rounds. Someone reckoned 542 was the drop-out express. And New Zealand railways of the '60s and '70s had become part of the anti-establishment expression. While many other young Kiwis adopted the rule of thumb, hitchhiking to freedom-come, or invested in battered panel vans fit for 20 drop-outs, or purchased strange, cheap brands of car like ancient Jaguars, Citroens, Rovers or Vanguards, we expressed our individuality by travelling on as many trains as we could find. The sense of adventure and freedom was profound, as was the ability of trains to throw up companions amongst fellow travellers. Besides, trains often went where roads didn't.

It was a time to dream but as the train went through the Tangarakau Gorge, a ruggedly beautiful stretch, it was appropriate to remember the hard times when the line was constructed. The construction camp of

Tangarakau was the only one in New Zealand that wasn't closed down during the Great Depression. Perhaps the bureaucrats forgot about the hard workers, beavering away at the rugged ramparts in the misty backblocks.

Others – dreamers – liked to think there was something mystical and intangible about the line. Something else was guiding its progress, but in reality it was probably the fact that there were fewer than 32 kilometres to go, to link the western line with the eastern equivalent, that saved the Tangarakau work camp. But for that timely connection, the line may have petered out into two branch lines, and then died altogether.

My hay fever was relentless as the line headed for Whangamomona. Honeysuckle, privet and diesel fumes impacted while the train was in the 24 tunnels and my plight called for another antihistamine.

Whangamomona. The very name captured the imagination. The town was nestled in a narrow valley. An old green weatherboard hotel stood vigil over a couple of grimy garages, a garish general store and a shoe-box post office. A deep stream surged out of the dense native bush and skirted the collection of railway houses where washing drooped from improvised clotheslines. A mechanic in overalls disregarded the train as he wandered over the road towards the pub. He appeared to be Whangamomona's sole occupant.

I knew of a guy who lived in the back of Whangamomona. I didn't know him that well. Besides, how could anyone live in the back of Whangamomona? This *was* the back. Surely the universe came to a clanking halt against its valley walls?

My travelling companions were interested in the guy from the back of Whangamomona. Did he have two heads? They bet he had facial hair to sink a ship. He was probably decked out in lightly-cured animal-skin garments made from bush varmints, that gave off pungent odours to signal his emergence from the dense undergrowth at the edge of the world. After all, the further you travelled into inland Taranaki – New Zealand's 'Deliverance' backwater, the more likely you were to stumble upon folk who acted out the roles of Ronald Hugh Morrieson characters. Where the bush was as dense as Satan's beard, folks had supped too long at an ever-shallowing gene pool and outsiders had better be wary.

Image 81

The Republic of Whangamomona celebration day, 2001. The back of beyond it may have been, but at least they could say they had a railway. Engines DC 4317 and 4006 bide their time as the visitors swell the hamlet's population for a few hours.

Yet Ben McDonald, the guy I knew slightly and played rugby against, was as clean-cut as Vic Damone or Paul McCartney after a trip to the barber. Open-faced and more friendly than most country boys. That seemed to be a relief to some as 542 finally headed towards Stratford. It wouldn't do to have hippy drop-outs sharing the wilderness with rednecks.

Late afternoon. No more sneezing. More snoozing, if anything. Coming out of the 'wops', down from the hills. Te Wera, Huiroa, Douglas, Toko. We're on the dairy flats now and Egmont is dominating the skyline. Finally 542 from Taumarunui clatters into Stratford yard, people uncoil and I start sneezing again.

The train stops with several lurches, followed by a loud crash, as all the energy from the domino effect between the wagons concentrates on the rear vehicles. If it's bad for us it must be worse for the guard in the van behind.

We all experienced a weird feeling of triumph as we climbed down from the train when it finally came to a rest on a Stratford shunting line, about four adrift from the platform. This wasn't like swaggering into Auckland Station at the end of an express run. There wasn't a soul around. The guard had gone. Had he already been made surplus to requirements? The need for guard's vans – and guards – was already being discussed. The engine still throbbed but the driver and fireman had scarpered. Then the engine began making irregular, coughing sounds. Did it have hay fever too?

It was an eerie, if triumphant setting. We had conquered a unique Kiwi train journey through a territory of which many would be unaware. Certainly not those of our cohort who had gone fishing for birds and spent the day trying to look very important on some Bay of Plenty beach with very few clothes, and now retreated to holiday tents with blistered backs, throbbing temples and empty sleeping bags.

And if the birds weren't biting, the mozzies soon were.

Our triumphant feeling was tempered by the pain of stepping on flint-hard ballast stones, which defied our flapping jandals. We had to scramble over four heaps before we were able to clamber up onto the Stratford Station platform.

My sister and her husband picked us up. They lived at New Plymouth and had to go out of their way to meet this odd train coming out of inland Taranaki, for no other purpose than to transport a few head of sheep – and humans – a bit of timber, a little lime, some empty LC wagons, a tractor tethered to an LA, a grumpy guard, a fireman and a DA driver with a perpetual pie between his teeth, to a rendezvous with the main Taranaki line.

'Why didn't it go all the way through to New Plymouth?' my brother-in-law asked.

'I think some of the timber had to go south,' I replied. 'No point taking it north and then turning it around to go back over the same tracks.'

'Yeah, but if it was a passenger train wouldn't it make sense to run through to the biggest place, New Plymouth?'

'It doesn't normally have passengers.'

'But it had a carriage – and you bludgers.'

'True.'

My brother-in-law, an Australian, shook his head, realising New Zealanders did things differently, probably because we lacked a sense of urgency.

As we bunked down at my sister's place and tucked into industrial-strength baked beans from catering-sized cans and fillets of a good-sized snapper caught off the rocks that day, no one spoke much about the day's rail adventure. Not because it wasn't momentous or memorable, a blast from the past, a slice of true Kiwiana ... but because we were all in.

The journey from Taumarunui to Stratford wasn't like a casual one-way fare from Te Kuiti to Auckland on the express or railcar. For a start it passed through territory we'd never seen before. Certainly not from the railway's perspective. All our senses were on high, and I had my hay fever to contend with. Antihistamines can wear you out. Apparently I sneezed 129 times between Te Wera and Douglas, before the medication kicked in.

As I drifted off at 9pm the images from a remarkable train ride washed over my subconscious: 24 tunnels bisecting green razorbacks; scrubby foothills; barely a town of any size. Hardly a fellow human. The *24* tunnels. You'd barely get a tunnel on our usual rail drag between Te Kuiti and Auckland. The Purewa Tunnel perhaps, or the Parnell if you were routed the other way. Honeysuckle vines dangling over the train, releasing their hay fever-inciting pollen. Standing for hours on the outside carriage platform, watching the lengths of timber swaying in the next wagon and allowing the rush of air to keep you cool. How cool was that? I thought we looked extremely cool, more so than our long-haired contemporaries sweating it out at a rock concert or twisting and shouting around a driftwood fire at the Mount, or some similar beach populated by those with a strong herding instinct.

Image 82

Mt Taranaki at sunset. The mountain is an inescapable focus for both locals and visitors.

After travelling on the SOL it was hard not to feel a bit smug about not only discovering the obscure route (the accompanying road is known these days as the Forgotten Highway), but actually travelling down it on one of the last mixed trains. A priceless link with the past was severed, but not before we'd savoured it. How many others could say they'd even heard of the inland Taranaki passage, let alone travelled on it?

My mother-in-law was someone who could lay claim to both. An infrequent train traveller, she'd taken the Taneatua Express a number of times, caught the overnight express from Hamilton to Wellington once – and on another occasion when she was invited to a 21st birthday party at Huiroa, she ended up travelling on the SOL. Huiroa is a few kilometres inland from Stratford and is located right on the line, in an area, between Te Wera and Douglas, where the highway and railway line part company. To get there from her home in Whakatane she utilised the Taneatua Express from Whakatane West all the way to Frankton Junction on the main trunk, where she had a long wait until the Auckland to New Plymouth night express arrived at 10.16pm. After transferring to the SOL at some ungodly hour, her train would have pulled into Huiroa a little before six in the morning.

She'd stolen my thunder.

Everyone's thunder was stolen in terms of train 542 and its sister ship going the other way, 529, when the passenger accommodation was taken off. Typically there were no passengers to commemorate the occasion, not even a sullen-faced youth or two. Slogans had been chalked on the side of the carriage. At least someone was aware of history receding down the line. 'The last farewell' festooned the final carriage – A1563 for the purists. The two DA locomotives used in tandem both ways were numbers 1505 and 1508.

We'd snuck in, but only just, and travelled on a New Zealand classic to which even my mother-in-law couldn't lay claim.

Postscript

In more recent years someone else discovered the SOL – and Whangamomona. Well-patronised trains descended on the town from both the eastern and western approaches, to help the locals (both of them someone reckoned) celebrate the Republic of Whangamomona Day. For several years the tiny hamlet was engorged by train lovers, country and western singers and fans, general friends of the back of beyond, rootin' tootin' shootin' types, and those who liked to say they'd been somewhere they'd never been before.

What happened on some of the homeward-bound trains has become part of New Zealand railways folklore.

12

In the wake of the Taneatua Express

Hamilton to Mount Maunganui by excursion train

Image 83

The Gorges Special negotiating the second of the gorges, Athenree. The train may have looked like an old-fashioned provincial express,

despite the Di engine's lack of grooming, but it felt like an excursion train.

In 1976, when the newly introduced Northerner overnight train pulled into the main line platform at Hamilton's modern station, it was a first in as much as the adjacent platform for the Bay of Plenty line was occupied by the Gorges Special excursion train. Specifically it was the first time the new station housed two passenger trains on separate platforms.

That's the kind of 'first' rail excursionists hanker after, along with a good day out trundling down branch lines not usually visited by passenger services. Running to timetables has its place but delays are all part of the fun. After all, these are usually train enthusiasts and to them the longer spent on board, the more value for money they feel they're getting. When the Gorges Special arrived back at its Auckland home base at 12.25am, instead of the programmed 10.57pm, there were few complaints, just congratulations for the tour organisers.

On 15 February 1976 the Railway Enthusiasts Society, based in Auckland, announced the excursion train. It would run from Auckland to the Bay of Plenty, via Hamilton, and traverse much of the old route of the Taneatua Express and the Te Puke railcar, before coming to rest at Mount Maunganui.

It was a very popular train and by the time it got away a bit late and said goodbye to the outer suburbs of Auckland, it carried over 400 enthusiasts. Some just enjoyed travelling by train – the steady rock and sway lulling them into a reflective state where they could gaze down with superior demeanour at the clustered motorists on the motorway or state highway. The latter had to keep their hands on the wheel and their eyes on the road. Those in the train could free up their extremities and have their eyes wander 360 degrees in the interests of taking in the scenery. And what the young couple further down the carriage were up to so early in the morning.

Admittedly, the 8.05am departure time had been compromised by brake examinations but it was still too early in the day for the pecking and necking that had the older couples, of whom there were a few, in a bit of a flap. Who did they think they were, the youth of today? Where in fact did they think they were? This was not the Auckland to Wellington Express, where such canoodling could occur at any time of the day or night. This was a family outing on an admittedly 'fun train', but obviously one man's fun was another man's (or woman's) private debauchery.

Thankfully morning tea was served on the train from Mercer south and as more passengers mingled, the young couple realised their groping belonged to the night. Despite lipstick smears and heavy breathing they realigned themselves and had a nerve-settling cup of tea.

The Gorges Special was never going to utilise traditional railway refreshment rooms. Most of them had gone the way of the railways cups and saucers – out the window. When I heard that tea was served on the excursion from Mercer south, I did a double take. I knew the old, angular Mercer refreshment rooms had long gone. They had been on such a lean that it wouldn't have surprised me to learn that, following one last battering from an express-worth of stampeders, the whole box and dice had disappeared beneath the unstable land and was last seen buffeting down the adjacent Waikato River, with customers hanging on for dear life with one hand, while the other, in best NZR tradition, was still balancing a pie and a cuppa.

As my wife Jenny and I continued to wait for the Gorges Special, the mind wandered. A young man with a walkie-talkie – the high technology of the day – kept us posted on the progress of our train.

'It's left Auckland,' he informed us, an hour after it had done so. 'They've reached Mercer.

They're serving tea,' he announced. 'Hold on. It's cracking up. Must be the Whangamarino Swamp. No – they're not serving tea. It's coffee.'

Trevor introduced himself and his technology. He treated the train, all trains, as technological capsules – little removed from Apollo 13 – integrated units, which through the miracle of machine and manipulation, travelled vast distances over steel carriageways, combining thrust, bearing and controlled propulsion. I think that's what he conveyed to us, as a DA-hauled goods train thundered through on the main trunk.

Trevor's vision lacked the human component. Apart from the train's driver – and even he could lose his role eventually – human beings and trains were a contradiction in terms. So why was Trevor travelling by train if he felt such a contradiction? Study purposes, he maintained, as many passengers waiting for the Gorges Special – and getting testy at the delay – followed the course of the main trunk goods as its wheels squealed on the curved platform line and showed no sign of stopping.

'Trains are about people.' Jenny directed her statement pointedly at Trevor, who wantonly returned his concentration to his walkie-talkie. His people-less corner of the world.

By now the excursion train was very late. Even Trevor couldn't explain its movements south of Mercer.

A good friend of mine, who left school suddenly to work at the local railway station, was transferred away to another provincial station. He was at Waipukurau for a while. Then one day when we were travelling on the afternoon's express south, and completely unaware of where Pete my friend had been transferred to next, we came across him as he wandered out to flag the express through the new concrete Mercer station.

Apparently part of the old subsiding Mercer Station had been transported to a sports field where it functioned as changing sheds. *How appropriate* I thought, as Pete and I had both been members of the school's first XV, and therefore bonded forever. Life flits past fast on the train. I wanted to stop the express so I could meet up with my old mate. Technically I could have pulled the stop cord but the penalties were severe. And what would I say to Pete anyway? Our paths had parted. He left school and the town, I stayed on. Then I did as I was told and went to Auckland.

Image 84

The legendary Taneatua Express crossing the old Claudelands bridge over the Waikato River, as the new one rises from its watery base. We hankered to be on that train, a hallowed rite of passage, but we were years too late.

As the Gorges Special pulled into Hamilton station, it made an impressive sight. There were those who knew little about such excursions, and probably thought a 'fun train' consisted of a string of connected jiggers, full-stopped by a guard's van. Or an ancient F steam engine, once a static exhibit covered in icecream stains and pigeon poo, doing its best to fire up and chug down the line, pulling a flat-deck wagon on which passengers had arranged deck chairs, beer kegs and tables suitable for laying out cucumber sandwiches and asparagus rolls.

The Gorges Special was certainly a 'fun train', but looked like an express. DA 1464, the sort that now fronted main trunk expresses, had in tow eight streamlined carriages and a van at the back. This was no mother duck DA and her jigger ducklings following faithfully behind.

As we climbed aboard the Gorges Special, DA 1464 disappeared to be replaced by a dirty, homeless-looking Di 1101. Jenny was disappointed as I explained the larger DA wasn't permitted access to the east of Hamilton. She was concerned about the Di's grungy aspect.

'It won't slow it down,' I reassured. But then what would I know? Just like the build-up of ice on an aircraft's wing, a layer of grime on the engine might slow it down. 'In fact it's a bit special. It's number 1101, which makes it leader of the fleet, leader of the pack.' Jenny still cursed the maintenance men who could have applied a damn good dusting. There were cobwebs in the cabin door corners and where there are cobwebs there are spiders. Jenny didn't like spiders. She did appreciate the trouble taken in affixing the placard at the head of the engine advertising the train's name. We didn't even mind that the organisers had included an unnecessary apostrophe. Gorge's Special it read, but these were the pre-PC years and the Apostrophe Wars hadn't broken out yet.

Part of the appeal of catching the Gorges Special at Hamilton was the fact that Hamilton Station was a new development. The focus of Hamilton rail travel had moved from the old, traditional Frankton Junction building to a position further south, where the sharply delineated junction to the Bay of Plenty was clearly obvious. In the old days, with trains arriving en masse at Frankton Junction Station, and hordes hoofing it to the refreshment rooms down the narrow platform, and people yelling and engines blaring, it was impossible to know who had arrived from where. Junction lines radiated out well beyond the cattle-yard of Frankton Station and it was just a matter of focusing on your pie and cuppa and shuffling back to what you hoped was your train.

In 1976 you can rest assured that it's the Gorges Special that's about to head east, despite the distraction created by the glare of the midmorning sun and the bewitching twitching of a couple of crazy-hatted rail enthusiasts who have been waiting since the Auckland departure for the chance to dance on the new Hamilton platform. Some form of initiation ritual apparently. Meanwhile grubby diesel Di 1101 slams none too gently while connecting with the carriages, and DA 1464 rejoins the main line muster.

Someone erects a trestle or two and filled rolls and sweet railway tea trickles. Tea does taste better by train. Perhaps someone has put something in it. I'm not usually a tea fan. Coffee is also available, but the cup of tea on Hamilton Station sets me up for a full day. The engine grapples and jerks with the long load as we gaze nervously out the window. The thought of a puny motive force is too much to absorb after all the expense, false promises, delays and expectations. Di 1101 sounds grunty enough.

The Gorges Special looks and feels like an old-fashioned provincial express as it finally gets some rhythm in its wheels. It prompted thoughts of expresses of old and the part Frankton Junction played in their distribution north, south and east.

There used to be expresses aplenty coming out of the Bay of Plenty. The Taneatua Express used to run all the way from the eastern reaches near Whakatane. If the authorities had been true to their word many years ago, an express from Gisborne via Moutohora and over the link line with Taneatua that was never built, could also have come out at the main trunk in Hamilton's Frankton. The Taneatua Express ran for more than thirty years and yet I had been largely oblivious to its existence – despite the fact that it actually covered more territory than the Christchurch to Dunedin trains.

Prior to the Taneatua, the Thames Express, its predecessor, ran a shorter distance for ten years fewer. Once the line through to Tauranga and beyond was completed in 1928, the Taneatua soon made the Thames Express redundant. Then of course there had been the famous Rotorua Express, or Limited, as it was once called, in 1894 the first express train in the Auckland province. It had a proud history. It therefore seemed a bit underhanded that these Bay of Plenty expresses had been sneaking onto the main trunk and heading for Auckland, unbeknown to us rail buffs, just a few kilometres south in Te Kuiti.

When we started expanding our inward-looking tunnel vision in the mid-1960s the expresses had gone – for good. In 1959 a railcar had taken over from the Taneatua Express but it only went as far as Te Puke. Still, beggars can't be choosers and after our first southern pilgrimage we sought a seat on the Te Puke railcar. Too late. It was withdrawn in September 1967 and we hadn't gone looking for it until December of the same year.

In 1968, in the time it took us to lick our wounds, the Rotorua railcar which took over from the Rotorua Express in 1959, was also withdrawn. We could have been a bit more proactive but we all seemed to visit Rotorua by car every second weekend at that time, and our sense of urgency dissipated.

That's why the announcement of the running of the Gorges Special was indeed special. So much rail action to the east of the northern main trunk, barely 80 kilometres from our home, had passed us by and this 1976 excursion train might be our last opportunity to travel over the old line before the Kaimai Tunnel deviation made the most interesting part defunct and derelict.

The new tunnel would chomp straight through the Kaimai Ranges and come out not far to the north of Tauranga. The old line meandered up through Te Aroha and Paeroa, then through the Karangahake and Athenree Gorges before encountering Tauranga Harbour south of Waihi. That's why they called it the Gorges Special. It was a fitting tribute to the incredible engineering and construction feat which enabled the line to thread the needle through the narrow gap in the ranges. But that was some way off, on the eastern side of the Waikato and Hauraki Plains.

Someone reckoned travelling from Hamilton to the actual gorges was the boring part of the trip. The initial plunge underground at the rim of the Hamilton City CBD, was interesting enough. It's not in the nature of Waikato trains to make like a metroliner, but here we were diving beneath the commercial streets, with all lights blazing, roaring past the 'white elephant' underground Hamilton Central before roaring out over the Claudelands Bridge, with the wide, muddy Waikato edging past like a stealthy beast stalking its prey.

We moaned about lost opportunities; how the Hamilton underground could have been utilised to carry passengers right into the heart of town. It would have been good for business and easier on the roads. A young Morrinsville commuter could have left her car in the garage before catching the Morrinsville–Hamilton Central–Frankton suburban train to her job in an office block. However, the car didn't stay in the garage. Locals suggested they wouldn't get out of their cars and catch trains that existed only as ideas. When actual trains were put in place to test the waters for Hamilton–Auckland commuter services, they didn't last very long. Hamiltonians like Aucklanders, developed a fetish for cars.

So the suburban and commuter train ideas, centred on the Hamilton underground, languished. The station closed in 1994. Someone turned the lights out, complaining that vandals were wrecking the place anyway and everyone went back to their cars for the purposes of personal convenience and arterial road clogging.

It was a surreal, short sojourn going through the Hamilton Underground station, for many years the only one of its kind in New Zealand. It was like going from 'cowtown' to a futuristic city in the space of five minutes, beneath an NZR Road Services bus depot and locals who figured an earthquake was visiting. The motives for the station's construction could have been mixed. Many considered it a futuristic move and step towards a more integrated inner-city train system. Others, aware of the dreadful congestion created by four major level crossings in the CBD, saw the underground option as a means of improving traffic flow above ground. Nothing more.

Some Aucklanders had never travelled this way before and one woman considered it the highlight of the trip. 'Pity we couldn't have stopped and had a look around,' she said to her husband.

'You'd get mugged for sure,' her husband replied. 'Half the homeless of Hamilton lurk down there and at this time of day they'd be stirring and feeling hungry.' The same husband reckoned thousands of old railway cups lay on the bottom of the Waikato River, having been tossed from the windows of all those express trains and railcars over the years. When the river is running low you can see them, he reckoned, particularly the saucers, lying on the river bed like scallop shells.

So far, contrary to what we'd been told, things had been anything but boring. By now we were picking up speed through the backyards of Hamilton homes in Claudelands, Ruakura and other eastern suburbs. It was a fine day and many home gardeners were out weeding and fossicking and were more than happy to drop their trowels and wave at the train.

In 1976 such a train, containing actual people, would have been an oddity along this stretch of the Bay of Plenty line, which last saw regular passenger service with the Te Puke and Rotorua railcars. And the occasional sister excursion trips which came along once in a blue moon, unannounced.

After passing the suitably formal looking Ruakura Agricultural Research Centre, the city thinned out and the trip *did* become boring. A flat stretch of broken, peat-pocked paddocks was bisected by the line in a monotonous, unbending way. The engine at this stage too, found it necessary to crawl across the desolate plain. Perhaps there had been some maintenance along the track. Maybe the train dropped anchors in response to line-side signals.

It was knitting and nattering time. As we edged along, the throb of the diesel was accompanied by several knitting nanas clacking up a storm, and a quartet of middle-aged enthusiasts nattering about the tractive efforts of the Di engine, its HP rating (1012 apparently) and the maximum tractive effort of 33,600 (I might have misheard this figure). When they began talking about diesel-vigilance devices, brake flow indicators and the Detroit hydrostatic lubricator, I figured it was time to seek out the company of a portly young man who was talking about the day the Cambridge branch was in its element. We had recently passed the junction serving the Cambridge branch so it was topical. In 1952 – the year the Commonwealth Games rowing events were held at Karapiro – several laden passenger trains had utilised the Cambridge branch to get closer to the action, according to the portly young man.

There's one in every carriage, it seems. A know-it-all.

'Excuse me, that was in 1950, sir,' announced a tall, silver-haired older man. 'And there were three special trains, operating at twenty-minute intervals and hauled by Ks as far as Frankton and ABs to Cambridge.'

'Did they use the underground railway under Hamilton?' I asked mischievously, knowing full well the subterranean line wasn't opened until 1964.

'If they did sir, there would have been one hell of a pile up. The trains would still be down there.'

Finally we picked up speed. Everyone sighed. The knitters and natterers ceased their knitting and nattering. Soon we pulled into Morrinsville, another junction where the Rotorua and Kinleith trains angle away. Not much angling away today on those branches and yet I remember my father showing us a photo of Morrinsville junction in which the Rotorua Express occupied one platform and the Taneatua Express the other, while on a siding a mixed train heading west added to the general clutter.

The monotony was relieved beyond Morrinsville when Te Aroha Mountain loomed large and the train swept northwest through the quaint old town of Te Aroha. The train continued to lose time because of the crossings necessitated by the approach of long goods trains pulled by double-headed Dis and Dbs. Not that many passengers were particularly restive at such times. The crossings enabled Trevor to describe wagon types, destination points and bulk loading figures on the other trains, which kept us on our toes.

Image 85

A DB-drawn goods train about to cross the bridge leading to the Karangahake Tunnel. The latter – the 'Rat Hole' – was not for the fainthearted engine driver.

In the old days the approach to Paeroa and the negotiating of different lines was problematical. Trains scheduled to pass through the Karangahake Gorge had to reverse out of the old Paeroa station, where the lines from Auckland and the Bay of Plenty came together at Paeroa Junction to form an inverted V. Prior to 1959, the Gorges Special would have been forced to travel backwards beyond Paeroa, with the carriage seats flipped over and the engine shuffled to the new head of the train, that used to be the tail. Kids in particular enjoyed the business of flipping the seats over so passengers could follow the forward path through the gorge.

However, that situation was purely academic. In 1959 Paeroa South Station had a direct line built, connecting the Waikato tracks with the Bay of Plenty spur through to the Karangahake. It meant bypassing much of the town, and the age-old reversing procedure was no longer an issue.

Now we were heading southeastward into the seemingly closing gap in the ranges that was the Karangahake Gorge. Almost as soon as we entered the Gorge, Trevor engaged us in conversation again. How the reverse thrust on the Di was only as powerful as that dictated by forward propulsion. Except when going downhill. Or when the draw bar limit was exceeded and bolts loosened, or something. 'Tighter nuts would help,' said Jenny.

The Karangahake Gorge was a dreamscape – soon be a distant one for train travellers. The hot summer sun was shut out by the towering ramparts and cliffs. The waters of the Ohinemuri River gurgled over rocks and around family groups cooling off. They were so engrossed they didn't even wave at the train. Had this been the South Island they would have taken the time. That was the basic difference between inhabitants of the two islands. North Islanders, even at leisure, seemed to have less time for the niceties. You could imagine some North Island time-and-motion men tabulating the time wasted waving at trains.

The Gorge is remarkable for its ability to accommodate road, rail and river. It's a tight squeeze admittedly, and quite complex in places. The train crosses the highway, enters a tunnel, then emerges at an angle and crosses the highway again – and the river. At least that's how we interpreted it.

You look at things superficially as an excursionist. To us, the Karangahake Gorge was a pleasant idyll and the impending closure of this stretch of track was seen by many as merely the loss of a scenic highlight. To train drivers it was something else.

The 'tight squeeze' of the gorge was only relieved by the 1006-metre-long Karangahake Tunnel known disparagingly by train drivers as the 'Rat Hole'. The tunnel, on a gradient of 1 in 50, presented many anxious moments to enginemen, particularly in the days of steam. To Dave Simpson, a former engine driver from Hamilton, the tunnel was the nearest thing to hell he could imagine:

The locomotive headlight now picks up the entrance to the tunnel. We glance at the boiler pressure gauge, now showing just short of 200lbs, water level showing ¾ of a glass. My mate opens the regulator fully and we hit the tunnel mouth at 25mph and slam the cab windows shut as we enter the narrow bore. The sound of the locomotive changes to a muffled roar, the cab begins to fill with exhaust steam. As we glance at the firebox doors we see the fire glowing orange through the swirling steam and the cacophony of sound, and we think is this what the entrance to hell is like?

The steam in the cab turns to condensation and starts to drip droplets from the cab roof and surrounds, as the heat builds up and begins to feel like a sauna. You can taste the oil in the rag that you are using to cover your mouth to keep the fumes out. After what seems like an eternity we burst out of the tunnel and open our cab windows. The gulps of fresh air are like nectar from the Gods.

Things didn't change much with the use of diesel electric locomotives in the tunnel. Engines heated, low oil pressure lights flickered and exhaust fumes started to roll back over you until all you could see was a blue haze.

Back here in the lazy afternoon carriage we figured we were entering heaven not hell, and the midsummer blue skies wanted no part of the diesel's underground blue haze.

'You know, the inverse ratio of the wheel flange pressure of the Di to the overall tractive effort is less than you might imagine.' Trevor's words seemed to emerge from a robotic mouth, somewhere between the engine drivers' reality and vague excursionist's dreamscape.

Pine trees stuck out of the rock like stubble on Trevor's chin. From Paeroa South we'd been travelling southeast before easing around to head northeasterly. For us we could have been going straight up in the air, such were the twists and turns and tunnels and bridges. After the somewhat banal throb across the Waikato Plains with the Di engine coughing to make up time, the eye-of-the-needle traverse through the Karangahake Gorge was as absorbing a stretch as we had seen. And with every glimpse of the old miners' settlements and cottages the past came roaring back like a goods train picking up speed on a passing loop.

'The Di's tractive effort, when multiplied by the tractive effort of the thrust bearings, equals the thrust effort of the internal differential divided by the tractive effort...' As the train roared into another tunnel Trevor's words became a mélange of technobabble. We weren't listening. Diesel fumes infiltrated through an open window. We hoped Trevor might have received a silencing dose.

Other passengers were unfazed by the grandeur of Karangahake. One bloke in silly purple shorts read a book between Paeroa and Tauranga, arguably the best bit. The couple in front of us crashed the *NZ Herald* around at random junctures and junctions. They'd obviously been this way before by train, perhaps on the Te Puke railcar or even the old Taneatua Express.

'No. Never been on this line before,' the man assured us.

Obviously the spectacular scenery hadn't struck a chord.

'Scenery's neither here nor there for us. We enjoy getting out of the home, away from the grandkids. Out of the city, more than anything.'

The Gorges Special edged past the tiny hamlet of Waikino with its pub, butcher's shop and sundry stores.

Cleaving the Karangahake was the highlight for us. On a hot day the shadowy gorge and stiff breeze kept temperatures pleasant in the crowded carriages. Mind you, there was often so little room to move as passengers wandered through or took up fixed positions in the aisle to get superior snaps, that oxygen supplies were becoming depleted. A bit of old-fashioned jostling set in.

Beyond the tight squeeze the train stopped, enabling photo opportunities and a chance to take the keen breeze first-hand, stretch the legs and catch a glimpse of the amorous pair from earlier in the day attempting to prise their lips off each other's faces.

We had been thoroughly charmed by the quiet, slow trek through the Karangahake Gorge. We have always found it a reflective setting, as the late sun peeping through a cleft in the rock wall reflected off a pool in the Ohinemuri River. Even today, passing through the village of Waikino and the station/café of the Goldfields Railway, it's easy to reflect on the passage of the Gorges Special on the first and last occasion we'd had to soak up the ambience passengers on the old Taneatua Express and Te Puke railcar would have experienced.

In 1976 Waikino was a bustling hamlet, until horrific floods in 1985 wiped out a good part of it. These days the Goldfields Railway glistens as a remnant of a special place which used to reverberate with the anguished hollers of steam engines and in our case the blunt bark of the Di diesel. It's a faithfully restored reminder of a line that dried up too many years ago, as its blue diesel hauls a green car-van carriage the six kilometres between Waikino Station and the equally ornate Waihi Station. The past is there for all to see.

South of Waihi the Gorges Special picked up speed. Beyond Waimata the waters of

Tauranga Harbour appeared. The second of the gorges, Athenree, came and went, a far more humble affair. Just beyond the gorge there had been a derailment and our train lost further ground as the maintenance crew were given free rein to clear the track.

For the first time in my life I realised the entirety of Matakana Island formed the ocean-facing barrier to the Pacific – and made a large part of Tauranga Harbour a harbour. Most fellow travellers seemed to know that already and I began wondering where I was the day they taught us stuff about Tauranga Harbour at school. The harbour continued to open its bays and vistas to us as we passed through Katikati. At Apata some preliminary work had been done on the approaches to what would be the Kaimai Tunnel. Having passed south of Apata I realised we had just completed our travels on the old line. Then someone reminded me we would be returning this way in an hour or two on the return Gorges Special and I didn't feel so bad.

Image 86

Preserving the past, today's Goldfields Railway has turned the old Waihi Station into a virtual work of art.

Omokoroa. We were really close to the harbour now and before too long the city was upon us. Just when we were itching to get to Mount Maunganui in order to avail ourselves of what was now a tight time schedule, our train was delayed at Tauranga. A slow goods train was given precedence and it was dispatched first.

Eventually we passed the Tauranga waterfront with its distinctive old hotels and guesthouses facing the harbour. Strand Station, very much a seaside stop, straddled the lapping waters. It reminded me of Key West in the deep south of the United States, and it remains one of the most distinctive New Zealand railway stations. Before we had a chance to soak up the atmosphere, we were rattling out across the harbour bridge towards Matapihi on the Mount Maunganui side of the water. It was the longest harbour bridge in the old Auckland province, as it curved across the harbour. I certainly didn't expect such a novelty at the very end of our journey. I figured the line would cross some workman-like causeway, like the highways, and reach Mount Maunganui that way.

We clambered down in the Mount Maunganui rail yards and set about doing what most visitors to the seaside do. Caught a wave at Mount Maunganui Beach and had a beer at a nearby pub. A sightseeing launch and bus tour were also factored in, but the latter was eventually truncated given our late arrival.

Before long we were retracing our steps back up around the harbour, defying the glare of the late afternoon sun. Our new engine crew were pulling out all the stops to make up time, but we managed to fit in a quick photoshoot at the new rail points near Apata, designed to lead into the Kaimai Tunnel.

Image 87

Homeward bound at Hemopo. In the late sun the engine looks even grubbier, but it's been a good day – and return journeys always seem shorter.

I don't know what the phenomenon is called, if indeed it has a name, but return journeys always seem to take less time than outward-bound ones. Familiarity of scenery can lead to passengers being lulled to sleep, which in turn speeds the train along. Then there's the business of a greater commitment to speed by the train crew, now the pleasantries of the outward journey have been done with and, having seen it all before, everyone is keen to make it back home.

We arrived back at Hamilton Station sometime in the dark of early evening. We bade farewell to our one-day friends and headed back to the northern King Country. We could have connected with the Northerner, the new overnight train heading south, but what would we have done with our car?

So we motored sedately back home, replete with railway experiences and, in my case, feeling I had touched base with a good proportion of the lines radiating out to the east of Hamilton. It had been gratifying travelling on the line which meandered through the scenic Karangahake Gorge. That chance has gone forever now, unless you count the 6.5km of the Goldfields Railway, which was set up in the wake of the opening of the Kaimai Tunnel deviation – and the closure of the Karangahake route.

The Goldfields Railway is a timely, if truncated reminder of what the old line was like. Waihi Station at the eastern end is beautifully preserved. It and the Waikino terminus located in the gorge itself are stark reminders of rail travel from a forgotten era. The Goldfields Railway also boasts the only preserved railway bridge in New Zealand to cross an official state highway.

Of course, the heyday of the Goldfields Railway was still in the future. Back in 1976 we were happy to have travelled on the Gorges Special, crossed a few Ts so to speak, and returned to tell the story of old routes which would soon disappear into the mists of time. We missed out on some, never making it to Thames by train. Even when the Kaimai Tunnel route was opened it seemed likely we would miss out there too, as regular passenger services weren't scheduled. In 1988, when Tranz Scenic introduced a service called the Kaimai Express running from Auckland to Tauranga via the Kaimai Tunnel, I was finally able to cross that T.

Image 88

The Goldfields Railway train meanders through a countryside that used to reverberate with the sound of heavy industry and a busy railway.

My wife Jenny has always had it over me that she had travelled on a particular scheduled passenger service – the railcar from Tauranga to Te Puke – along the stretch of the Bay of Plenty line which no longer features regular services. For some reason she wasn't with me when I took the Kaimai Express and when that scheduled service was withdrawn a few years later, we figured we were equal.

A few days after motoring sedately home, leaving the Gorges Special to its fate, we received a newsletter from the excursion organisers. 'The committee wishes to apologise for the amount of delay experienced on the recent Tauranga trip.'

The apology was unnecessary. For most excursionists, including us, the longer spent on the train the better. We weren't in a hurry. We didn't have a train to catch.

13

Twenty-first Century Limited

The Northern Explorer

Image 89

New train on the block, the Northern Explorer, leaving Hamilton. The DFB engine might look a bit clunky but the rest of the train has a coordinated and contemporary presence.

The Northern Explorer sounded a bit like one of those old paddle steamers Humphrey Bogart might have steered up the Congo in best *African Queen* tradition. It also sounded like the name of a new main trunk train plying the principal route of the North Island, New Zealand. A name with connotations of the Northerner and Overlander, two recent long-distance trains connecting Auckland with Wellington – one by day, the other by night.

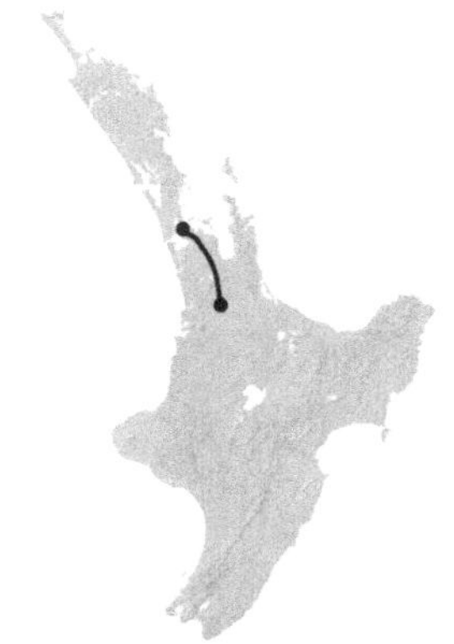

The Northerner completed its tour of duty in 2004. There were no more night trains after that. The Overlander was lucky to survive as long as it did. Perhaps that was why there was little kerfuffle when the final demise of the Overlander was announced. Supporters were weary of the fight and besides, there was a brand new, diamond-bright replacement to step into the breach: The Northern Explorer. It came into service in June, 2012.

It was the first new train – well it had a new name anyway – to grace our tracks since the coining of services such as the Geyserland Express, Kaimai Express and Bay Express back in the 1990s. Others like the Waikato Connection and the Helensville Express had come and gone in the interim but their fleetingness hardly classified them as household names.

My wife Jenny and I were genuinely excited by the new arrival. Would the Northern Explorer presage another rail renaissance, as the significant developments of the Auckland suburban network had – and we conjectured about a completely new loop line disappearing beneath the streets of the CBD and turning Auckland into a real city. We planned to spend a day in the Queen City, checking out the rail upgrades after travelling on the Northern Explorer before returning home.

It was still the same old scruffy Hamilton railway station. The Britomart influence hadn't extended south down the main trunk. It was funny to think the two cities under discussion, Auckland and Hamilton, both had had flirtations with underground railway stations. Britomart has a look of permanence about it, but they also said the same about the Hamilton Central underground station. Not in so many words perhaps, but dignitaries on opening day pontificated about 'one small step for mankind' and left it at that. Toasts were offered, ribbons cut and everyone nodded solemnly.

It seemed to be of some moment that the Hamilton Underground Station didn't come to a blank-walled halt. Not like Britomart, as it now stands. The underground line carried on through Hamilton, up into the light and off across the Waikato River. Recent developments point the way to Britomart becoming part of the inner-city line. Its range beyond the blank-walled halt seems assured, while the fate of the Hamilton underground station remains the domain of soothsayers.

Back at the still scruffy Hamilton railway station – the one above ground – soothsayers were thin on the ground. There were a couple of railway employees manning the place; in what capacity, was never really established. We had no luggage to check in. Hand luggage was suitable for our needs. The station was just somewhere to sit and wait, but for how long, that was the thing.

'Is the train on time?' Jenny asked the elderly guy behind the counter, who seemed to be assembling magazines on the counter top.

'Just left Otorohanga, ma'am,' was the reply.

'Te Awamutu wasn't it?' the other worker in hard hat and high-viz bright yellow chipped in.

'Could have been.'

Silence then reigned, until disturbed as a south-bound freight gathered pace in the distance. Even after the goods train had veered east towards the centre of town and beyond to the Bay of Plenty and silence returned, the issue of the Northern Explorer being on time remained unresolved. It wasn't even revisited as the elderly guy and High Viz thumbed through *North and South* and *New Zealand Rail Fan* magazines.

Image 90

The DC engine looks the part as the Northern Explorer hits its straps south of Horotiu, north of Hamilton. We swore we saw more of the countryside from the huge new windows.

'That's a good one,' High Viz said to the elderly guy.
'What? *North and South?*'
'Nah.'

The Northern Explorer was on time. God knows what had just left Otorohanga. Or Te Awamutu. You could tell it was the Northern Explorer because it was like a new pin. At least the carriages were. The motive force was an old DC diesel, admittedly freshly painted, in grey, orange and mainly yellow. The carriages were a striking off-white and the most telling feature on first appearance was the size of the windows. There'd be no excuse for missing anything that passed by those beauties. As the brand new Northern Explorer tiptoed shyly around the curved platform at Hamilton, its make up became apparent. It had a rebuilt guard's van as a luggage car which followed faithfully behind the engine and, in no particular order, three carriages capable of accommodating 189 passengers, a café car and an open-air viewing van which was also a rebuilt guard's van.

As we waited on the platform for the train to clear of alighting passengers, a jovial guy in a brown denim jacket and cowboy hat jumped down. 'Is this here, Hamilton, New Zealand?' he asked of a slightly built young man, in a North American accent.

The latter, with puckish features and a twinkle in his eye took up the challenge. He seemed to have a sense of humour. 'No siree. This here is Hamilton, Ontario, unless I'm very much mistaken.'

The jovial guy in the cowboy hat thumped the puckish traveller's back sending him teetering towards the edge of the platform. 'Hamilton, Ontario's my home town, boy, but thanks for pulling the other one. Ain't that what you say in New Zealand when you're having someone on? You're said to be pulling their leg?'

'I guess so.' The young man now just wanted to get on the train.

'And when you're really having them on you're pulling the other one, huh?'

The young man said nothing.

'So what are we talking about son? What are we pulling, huh? Legs or something else? Know what I mean?'

While this strange encounter unfolded, train and station staff hurried along, dealing with matters of luggage, tickets and general guidance. High Viz guy was just a yellow blur as he undertook a plethora of duties, none of which seemed entirely constructive.

As we climbed on board the concept of space was overwhelming. It may have been accentuated by the rucks and ruckus on the platform. Tall people used to stoop on cue climbing into most New Zealand carriage trains, but the Northern Explorer had a profound sense of roominess. The vestibule itself, unlike vestibules of old, presaged the general sense of space. It was hard to believe all of this came with the compliments of a 3 foot, 6 inch rail gauge. If you'd been out of the loop and didn't know, you'd swear the standard New Zealand gauge had been widened.

Automatic sliding doors meant there were none of those awkward arm wrestles with hard-to-budge, below-the-waist knobbly handles.

'Everything seems bigger,' Jenny declared. She was referring to higher ceilings, wider walls, certainly bigger windows. There might have been some cunning optical illusions applied by railway construction teams, but good on them anyway.

Image 91

Graham Hutchins in the observation section of the now withdrawn Overlander.

We found our seats – 4D and 4C – and a man and a woman occupying them.

'There are plenty of spare seats back there,' the woman gesticulated with a sweep of her hand.

There indeed were, but that wasn't the point. There was something about the set to the woman's mouth that was unsettling. No one was denying 4D and 4C weren't our seats, not even the woman, who continued talking to her male companion who looked about as set upon as we began to feel.

'We can each have a window seat back there,' Jenny said, unwilling to be drawn into a situation which would besmirch this singularly fine railway experience. Principles were abandoned. Points of order overlooked.

The train manager was laid back about the issue. 'Sit where you like folks. Half the passengers in this carriage got off at Hamilton.'

Regimented the operation wasn't. Even during the reign of the Overlander you were often obliged to sit in your allocated seats, even if it meant ten passengers clustered in a congealed blob in one corner, while the rest of the carriage looked like the single carriage tagged on the end of the Taumarunui to Stratford daily. Empty. Bereft of humankind.

Besides, who would want to sit too close to the woman with the certain set to her mouth? It wasn't a quiet conversation she was having with her male companion. And it was full of invective.

'It's time Beth realised that bloody inheritance doesn't grow on trees,' the woman trumpeted. 'Seven of those rental properties are earmarked for Guy, you know. Beth thinks she should be getting all seventeen.'

The male companion didn't say a thing. He just sat there with a certain set to his teeth. This was New Zealand in 2012 – a different country. An ossified place where the rich have become super rich – and don't care if they're sitting in your seat. They probably own all the seats anyway.

Towards the front of the carriage a real Kiwi battler was totally preoccupied looking after his toddler daughter and a baby in a carrycot. The battler was a young father, and he had taken it upon himself to shepherd his flock on the Northern Explorer, all the way from Wellington to Auckland. The baby was restless, the toddler unreasonable. During the passage from Hamilton to Auckland, he was rushed off his feet.

A kindly middle-aged woman had taken it upon herself to watch over the little girl, while the father did his best to settle the baby in the carrycot, by carrying it up and down the aisle, hoping the increased motion would send the baby to sleep.

'Anyone would think this was a crèche on wheels,' the hard-mouthed woman declared, raising her voice. 'Where's the bloody mother anyway? I suppose he's going to breastfeed it next.'

A well-known TV chef walked past, heading for the café car – where else? He looked so familiar neither of us could remember his name. Then came a columnist for one of the Sunday papers and when we couldn't remember his name either we figured it was time for coffee and a bite to eat.

Moving around the train was a breeze, compared with the old days when crossing from carriage to carriage on crashing, swivelling steel plates, always seemed less safe than it could have been. It was one of the unspoken realities of train travel and one of the reasons that passengers tended to stay in their own carriages.

I remembered the time on the Overlander when I stumbled upon a frail old woman in a state of panic, stranded on the steel plate between carriages.

'Don't try to save me, sir. I'm done for,' she yelled above the roar of steel on steel as the Overlander increased speed, making up time. The situation was a bit dire. I thanked the Lord she wasn't on a mobility scooter or wheelchair or Zimmer frame, which on second thoughts might have been preferable, given that she seemed on the verge of collapse. God knows how long she'd been stranded, clinging grimly to the guide ropes as she sagged at the knees.

'Don't move, madam,' I yelled back.

'There's no chance of that, sir,' she yelled. I considered activating the device that would stop and train and incur a penalty of $100, payable by me. In a panic-stricken fog myself, I looked around for the small hatchet I imagined used to occupy a glass case on the vestibule wall. The idea, as I remembered it, was to use the hatchet to smash open life-saving equipment – perhaps fire hoses and the like – but I wasn't thinking rationally. Was the hatchet to put a stranded passenger out of their misery as they waited, dangling, to meet a grisly fate beneath the train's wheels? Suddenly the Overlander lost its pace and pulled into Hamilton Station.

Perfect. The solution to the problem. The colour returned to the woman's face and she cleared the now still no-man's land between carriage and buffet car with a sprightly gesture. 'Bloody men,' she directed up at me. 'They build these things.' I considered this to be valid venting given the previous situation.

In 2012 on the Northern Explorer I felt more justified than most in celebrating the fact that the navigation between carriages was a piece of cake. In fact a piece of cake to go with the coffee sounded inviting. I began talking to a guy waiting for coffee at the café bar. Or rather he began talking to me. 'It's a nicely appointed train but it's the same old scenery out there,' he said while waving his free hand towards the great outdoors. By now we had cleared Hamilton and its light industrial zone of Te Rapa, and were making good speed through the rural pockets this side of Ngaruawahia.

'Yes. I guess we've seen it a thousand times before,' I agreed. 'Mind you, we get to see more of it through windows like that.' I waved my free hand (the other cupped a container of potato gratin), towards the expansive café-car windows.

North of Ngaruawahia we kept an eye out for a tourist attraction set on a high hill, like something out of the Hobbit movies. If the Northern Explorer was a twenty-first century train, the hotel on the hill was also very contemporary. The old landmarks like the Waikato River, the Whangamarino Wetlands and all that came in between, were still beguiling. As the sun disappeared into the west, casting dazzling light into the carriage, the ancient presence of the Waikato River seemed as permanent as the sacred Taupiri Mountain and the old hills to the east.

Image 92

DC 4594 hauls the former Overlander at Hangatiki in 1981. There's evidence of recent rain and my old home town, Te Kuiti, is near at hand.

Then we saw it, the hill-top hotel accessible by a deeply rutted road that shook dentures and tested car suspension as you drove into the hills above the Waikato River and the North Island main trunk. During the course of our stay there we had been able to look down on the crowded State Highway after dark, with car lights cutting through the river fog hundreds of metres below. From the south, a train lit up like the fifth of November could be seen overtaking the gridlocked cars. It was the Overlander heading north, running late at a time in midsummer when the expansion of rail lines further south had reduced it to a snail's pace. Now, in the cool of early evening, it was pulling out all stops to get to Auckland at a respectable hour.

It was that experience which made us hanker after life on the main trunk line again. The Overlander, although we'd travelled on it many times, looked mighty inviting. In the nature of things, by the time we got around to booking seats, the Overlander had become the Northern Explorer.

Just this side of Huntly a fire alarm sounded. Or that's what I thought it was. So did a couple of other passengers, who had sprung to their feet. The commotion continued until a woman, after ransacking her handbag, was able to control the cacophony. It was her cellphone – one with a novelty ring.

'Hello Basil. You know I'm on the train.' The woman had a voice that was louder than the train's PA system.

'I'm not prepared to go back to you unless you show some appropriate action to convince me your fling with Casablanca was just that. Something that was inappropriate and not likely to happen again, because if you try that on again mate, there will be appropriate consequences and actions I won't be responsible for, if you know what I mean. And just because...'

Meanwhile, the PA system had come on to advise us the Waikato River was the longest in New Zealand. And other stuff we couldn't hear because the cellphone person was raising her voice – appropriately or otherwise. Amongst the other stuff was an update regarding the Northern Explorer's estimated arrival time at Britomart, bearing in mind that a bit of dawdling somewhere down the track meant we were twenty minutes late. We were informed of this when we arrived ten minutes late.

Meanwhile the cellphone person was sounding off on one side of the carriage and the PA announcements struggled through the intercom on the other.

'And just because I've got three cellphones doesn't mean you've got the right to listen to any of them, Basil...'

'...service will be arriving into Britomart Station at...'

'...not that it's any business of yours but I've got three cellphones because...'

'...apologises for the delay which has been caused...'

'...and the third one is the one I use for important stuff because I know you listen to the other two. What choice did I have? You made...'

'...and butter chicken is still available at the buffet car for the next...'

'...if you do that stuff again Basil, I can't be responsible for the appropriateness of my actions...'

'...and potato gratin...'

The train staff could have been advising us to brace for a crash-landing for all we knew.

Who needed endlessly awesome and unfamiliar scenic delights when fellow passengers were providing an on-board slanging match?

The scenery along the Waikato River and through the Whangamarino swamp is always enticing, no matter how many times you see it. The mood and flow of our longest river, its colour and current always full of contrast. And travelling on the Northern Explorer, the new train built for scenery watching, affords you chances to see aspects of the countryside you've never seen before. Larger windows can open up new vistas.

Back at our seats the potato gratin was warm and tasty. Jenny's butter chicken and rice stood up well too, except when the plastic cutlery proved too puny. You never knew if you had total control over a forkful, especially when the train lurched. It has to be said that the Northern Explorer was a very stable train. Someone had put a good deal of effort into balancing the bogies.

It would have been much easier carrying a hot pie and cuppa back to your seat if the Northern Explorer had taken to its wheels in the 1960s. Mind you, back in the 1960s everyone would be doing the same thing at virtually the same time. It was an egalitarian exercise getting to and from the refreshment rooms back then. In 2012, on the Northern Explorer, you had a wider ranging clientele who free-ranged and grazed in their eating habits, and they weren't all Kiwis.

Even though times have changed, I've always treasured the train ride north to Auckland from either Te Kuiti or Hamilton, even when a good portion of it took place in darkness. For a start it was only two or three hours' worth of travel, either with the dawn breaking on an exciting day for us young bucks or the sun setting in later years along the northern reaches of the Waikato River. Three hours seemed like a goodly amount of time to spend on a speeding train. Beyond that boredom can set in and fellow passengers can become a bit too familiar.

The glistening Waikato heaved out of sight to the west beyond Mercer, and the sun sank in the August sky. Beyond Pokeno the main trunk parted company with the motorway and shifted north beyond Tuakau towards Pukekohe, after travelling due west for some time.

The train was making up time as we encountered the edges of the sprawling Auckland conurbation, where darkness continued to fall and lights were popping on in streets and houses. Just beyond Pukekohe we whistled through Paerata, junction point of the Mission Bush branch feeding the huge Pacific steelworks. It used to function as the suburban line to Waiuku until 1968, when the branch ceased operating. A fellow rail fan friend of mine once lived in a railway house with his family and he used to delight in recounting the hi-jinks young boys got up to on branch line trains. He also remembered hearing about some of the close calls that were associated with the morning train from Waiuku which ran down the branch and connected up with the Auckland suburban network at Pukekohe.

It always struck me as being a bit odd, having a branch line to Waiuku. The latter, even back then, seemed to be on the way to nowhere. If it went much further it would end up in the Tasman Sea. If the authorities had it in mind to extend the line south there was the small matter of the yawning Waikato River delta to bridge.

Image 93

The Glenbrook Vintage Railway, resurrecting a section of the old Waiuku branch. A step back in time – a step in the right direction, some would say – serves to show all generations the continuing appeal of passenger trains.

Image 94

Jenny enjoying the restored interior of a Glenbrook Railway carriage. This was a far cry from travelling on the Northern Explorer.

The business of politicians and railways entered the argument – and how branch lines could end up going in the darndest direction if a personage of prominence and influence had a property perched on some isolated promontory. Such wayward lines had little to do with providing social services for the majority, but, in the case of the Waiuku branch, served the selfish motives of the Reform Prime Minister, William Ferguson Massey, through whose Franklin electorate the Waiuku branch was built.

In recent times we could say we'd been on a section of the old Waiuku branch, reinvented as the Glenbrook Vintage Railway. The latter was a brilliantly restored and replicated heritage operation running from Glenbrook Station, near the steelworks to the very edge of Waiuku township. Any selfish motives displayed by Prime Minister Massey all those years ago were forgiven when we realised his playing political games led to a rail environment in which the Glenbrook Vintage Railway could play with their life-size toys, for the considerable enjoyment of train buffs like us. And for those younger generations who wanted to know what trains and railways were all about in a bygone era.

Back in 2012 I mentioned to Jenny that the Northern Explorer would provide a spectacular sight as it came into Britomart Station, heading along the waterfront, after deviating east beyond Westfield. She'd be able to see all the ships lit up.

There was quite a commotion on board now, for although the Northern Explorer carriages are noted for their smoothness and quietness, passengers and staff were making ready for quick getaways. Cupboards and cabinets were being slammed shut, hand luggage was dropping noisily from overhead racks, bottles and crockery were clinking. It was enough to wake a hundred babies, yet the baby from Wellington slept through it all. The father, after his child-minding marathon, did the same. The little girl was starstruck by the inner-city lights. Jenny had nodded off too.

I swear I always thought that trains arriving at Auckland at night approached Britomart along the waterfront route. Certainly the Overlander did the last time we travelled on it. But here we were heading up past Ellerslie, Greenlane and Newmarket before sneaking in the back way to Britomart.

'Did I miss much?' Jenny asked.

I could have said something about missing at least ten American cruise liners, all lit up like Christmas trees, and hundreds of ferries and other marine craft with their lights dancing and reflecting off the choppy Waitemata like glowworms. But even I could see, as we crept around the tight curve from the Newmarket line to the Britomart tunnel, that a heavy fog obliterated anything worth seeing along the waterfront.

It was my saving grace. There was no disappointment at the end of a remarkable train journey, although we declared the viewing van to be a bit sparse. Just a bit.

Postscript

We had a spare day in Auckland before returning home to Hamilton, so, in the interests of appreciating new developments in the Queen City (as well as it being the terminus and departure point for the new Northern Explorer) we took a look at the considerable improvements to the western line. We also took a run on the revamped Onehunga branch line, a route with a considerable history. Prior to the opening of the main trunk line, boat trains used to carry passengers scheduled to catch a steamer at Onehunga wharf, along the short branch. The steamers sailed to New Plymouth where the completed through line linked with Wellington.

Having reached Onehunga by train in 2012 at least we could say we had touched base with another virgin stretch of New Zealand line, albeit on the short side. The rail official at Onehunga station, an Indian, was on the short side too, but he was most determined to instruct us in the ways of the new automatic ticket dispenser, due to come on line in the next month or so.

I approached the machine with money at the ready. Obeying instructions I inserted what I considered to be the appropriate amount and pushed a button or two. Nothing happened, yet when it did, it seemed sluggish. I pushed a few more buttons.

'No, no, no,' yelled the rail official. 'Please be waiting for your money to descend. Then push, push, push your destination key.'

This I did.

'No, no, no. Don't be pushing it too soon. Wait, wait, wait for the yellow light. Go back to start and retrieve your money. Push retrieve but – no, no, no – not until the green light is flashing. Your money will not come out. Oh, oh, oh. No, no, no.'

'We simply want to travel from Onehunga to Waitakere. Perhaps if we just paid for it on the train. Presumably the guard has a ticket book.'

'Oh yes, yes, yes. But no, no, no, you must get acquainted with the new automatic ticket system. It will be introduced at the end of the year and you will be stranded if you don't come to grips with it.'

The official was clenching his fists as he dispensed this final advice and we were pleased to be on our way. We caught up with the Waitakere train at Newmarket.

On the service to Waitakere some dislocated voice reminded us to: 'Please beware of the gap between the carriage and the platform.'

Image 95

The futuristic Britomart Station, Auckland – a good place to begin a bit of suburban side-tracking while waiting for the return Northern Explorer.

Auckland, 2012, and it's hard not to notice the gaps. Mainly between the haves and the have-nots and across the generations. Auckland is suddenly a big city and that means a wide-ranging ethnic mix on your everyday feeder trains. Even a few tourists. At Kingsland Station a group of Americans off a visiting cruise liner climb aboard, all speaking at once. They are middle-aged and kind of prosperous looking. A bit over-fed too. They'd been visiting Eden Park, scene of New Zealand's Rugby World Cup win the previous year.

Image 96

The push-pull trains that provide much of Auckland's suburban services. This pair are poised at Papakura for the afternoon rush.

'The All Blacks beat All France, huh,' a friendly Texan announced. 'Eight goals to seven. One is always enough, I say. No point in overdoing it, eh? One hundred and eight to seven means the same thing, eh fella. It's only a game. Gridiron came first anyway.'

Whether I knew it or not the above pronouncement had been directed at me, although the jovial Texan appeared to be directing his diatribe to the whole carriage. At Mount Eden most of the passengers got off. A young mother with a pramful of twins, a younger couple of indeterminable race, furiously texting, probably to themselves. How could they be aware of the gap between the carriage and the platform? Wagging schoolkids wearing an unappealing uniform of green, blue and purple. An Asian guy with orange mohawk squeezing through the doors at the last minute because his cellphone, making the sound of a jazz musician playing out-of-tune vibes, summoned him at an awkward time.

More Americans off the *Pacific Princess* got on at Mount Eden. None of them were underweight. One of them introduced himself to his fellow Americans. He used to work on oil rigs and originally came from Detroit, when Detroit was OK. Detroit's derelict now, so I guess that was the point he was trying to make. He was OK because Detroit used to be OK – in the days of Motown music and prosperous car assembly lines. You can learn a lot about America while travelling in a New Zealand train.

There are certain things you don't want to learn about some New Zealanders. Jenny and I both sensed danger when a young man and woman climbed on board at Henderson. The young man sported a smirk that screamed self-absorption. His partner, bearing tattoos that were less ethnic than emblematic, shoulder-charged her way past an Asian girl who was i-Podding with one ear and listening to a cellphone with the other.

Some people sit demurely in train seats. Some slouch. Others sprawl with legs akimbo. But our Tarzan and Jane sat with a twitching swagger. Poised to strike if anyone should as much as turn a head towards the vicious conversation they unleashed as the train headed for Ranui.

It's amazing the scenic highlights fellow passengers are able to identify at such times, pretending to disregard the expletive-charged spat between the man and woman. Even the guard, a pleasant English woman, suddenly took an interest in us and asked if we were going all the way to Waitakere.

'You deleted my effing message,' interrupted our reply, as the man reared up after prodding a cellphone, and virtually spat at his partner.

'You deleted your own effing message,' the woman replied, as both got up and left the train at Ranui, trailing curses, violent hand gestures and plastic soft drink bottles.

'It's best to pretend they don't exist,' the English guard advised. 'If you so much as stare at them they'll challenge you. Sometimes I think they just fabricate a domestic argument and hope an innocent bystander takes the bait. It adds a bit of excitement to their pathetic day.'

A week later a news item announced that a 29-year-old male had been murdered in Ranui with a blunt instrument. We couldn't help but make the macabre association. Was that the result of another fabrication?

'They're all the same,' the guard had said so it was probably someone else. And yes we did make it all the way to Waitakere – just as the threatening skies exploded. Heavy, near horizontal rain dumped. The new automatic ticket dispenser, not entirely protected from the elements, saw us drenched and dumbfounded as we tried to put into practice the instructions given to us by the attendant at Onehunga Station. Had the rain been factored in to the setting up of the new ticket system? It was certainly getting in, but that was different.

Travelling on the Northern Explorer – a new train on the old line – and checking out the upgraded Auckland suburban services – newish trains on newish lines – gave us a glimpse into the future. The Northern Explorer was advertised as a tourist train. We were tourists I guess. We certainly didn't feel like commuters. We met Americans and travellers from Invercargill. Journalists, chefs. We also shared a carriage with privileged and underprivileged Wellingtonians. In between times we made like commuters in New Zealand's largest city. And still we met Americans. And a wretched breed of hometown underclass, turning feral.

We didn't quite make the new service to Manukau, but it'll keep. It was only 1.3km of new line, but it was brand new – that's the thing. Brand new lines will soon become common in Auckland as the city wakes up at last to the importance of rail.

But we were chuffed to make it on to the historic Central City to Onehunga branch, one that had finally been resurrected as a commuter line in 2010. We sat next to a pimply gentleman with wires protruding out of both ears, connecting to high-tech devices, the next best thing to a twenty-first century robot – and I couldn't resist calling up the past.

'Trains on this line used to carry passengers all the way to Wellington, via Onehunga wharf, steam ship and the train service from New Plymouth to the capital.' When the young man on the Onehunga train realised I was talking to him, he removed an electrode from an ear.

'What?' he said.

I repeated my comments whereupon the young man grinned and re-wired himself.

'Yeah, right,' he said.

Bibliography

Bromby, Robin, *Rails that Built a Nation,* Grantham House, Wellington, 2003.

Churchman, Geoffrey B. and Hurst, Tony, *South Island Main Trunk,* IPL Books, Wellington, 1992.

Churchman, Geoffrey and Hurst, Tony, *The Railways of New Zealand,* Transpress, Wellington, 2001.

Dangerfield, J.A. and Emerson, G.W., *Over the Garden Wall: The Story of the Otago Central Railway,* Otago Railway & Locomotive Society Inc., Dunedin, 1995.

Grainger, J.M., *On and Off the Rails: A Railwayman's Story,* Whitcombe & Tombs, Christchurch, 1964.

Leitch, D.B., *Engine Pass: New Zealand Railways,* AH & AW Reed, Wellington, 1967.

Leitch, David B., *Railways of New Zealand,* Leonard Fullerton, Auckland, 1972.

Leitch, David and Stott, Bob, *New Zealand Railways: The First 125 Years,* Heinemann Reed, Auckland, 1988.

Mahoney, J.D., *Kings of the Iron Road,* Dunmore Press, Palmerston North, 1982.

Miller, F.W.G., *The Story of the Kingston Flyer,* Whitcoulls, Auckland, 1975.

New Zealand Railfan Magazine (various editions), Triple M Publications, Wellington.

New Zealand Railway Observer Magazine (various editions), New Zealand Railway and Locomotive Society Inc., Wellington.

Sinclair, Roy, *Rail: The Great New Zealand Adventure,* Grantham House, Wellington, 1987.

Stewart, W.W., *Grand Old Days of Steam,* AH & AW Reed, Wellington, 1975.

Wood, Chris, *Steaming to the Sunrise,* IPL Books, Wellington, 1996.

Photo credits

The following people and organisations provided photographs for this book: Alexander Turnbull Library: Image 4 (ATL-23246609-PA COLL-5927-52), Image 10 (ATL-30655553-EP/1960/1190-F), Image 46 (ATL-22603373-APG-1704-1/2-G).

Terry Bishop: Image 63.

Tony Bridge/Exisle Publishing: Image 14, Image 28, Image 40, Image 45, Image 48, Image 49, Image 55, Image 56, Image 66, Image 82.

K.T. Cullen: Image C, Image 20, Image 21, Image 23, Image 33, Image 34, Image 59, Image 84.

J.D. Fitzgerald: Image 5, Image 6, Image 37, Image 53, Image 73, Image 75, Image 76, Image 83, Image 87.

Graham Hutchins: Image B, Image 2, Image 42, Image 50, Image 54, Image 86, Image 88, Image 91, Image 93-94.

C. King: Image 70.

NZR Publicity: Image 62.

D.R. Simpson: Image D, Image 3, Image 6, Image 7, Image 12, Image 19, Image 27, Image 35, Image 88, Image 57, Image 58, Image 61, Image 65, Image 67, Image 77, Image 80, Image 85, Image 90, Image 95, Image 96.

M. Smeaton: Image 26, Image 32, Image 43.

J.A.T. Terry: Image A, Image E, Image 1, Image 11, Image 24, Image 25, Image 44, Image 47, Image 50, Image 69, Image 78.

K.B. Ward: Image 8, Image 13, Image 15, Image 17, Image 22, Image 38, Image 60, Image 64, Image 68, Image 79, Image 81, Image 89, Image 92.

Shutterstock: Image 18 (1089900560), Image 31 (98329616), Image 36 (142902484), Image 71 (187562078), Image 72 (139729906), Image 74 (4069396).

Russell Young: Image F, Image 16, Image 29, Image 30, Image 39, Image 41.

Front Cover Flap

Graham Hutchins fell in love with trains at an early age. As a youngster growing up in the railway town of Te Kuiti, he would gaze on the steaming monsters as they thundered through the King Country. Before long, train travel became more than a pastime, more than a fascination: he was hooked. As he recounts in this book, he was just ten years old when he undertook a journey alone on the night train to Auckland. From then on he travelled as much as he could, and later as a young man searched out the smaller forgotten lines to experience what they had to offer.

Stop the Train! I want to get on describes his experiences travelling throughout New Zealand on regular passenger trains, railcars, goods trains and work trains. The routes he traverses include the Central Otago line, the Gisborne Railcar, the Southerner to Invercargill, a mixed train through rural Taranaki, a workers' train from Greymouth on the Rewanui Incline, the Endeavour to Hawke's Bay, the Silver Fern Railcar and more. Many services have now been axed, but he vividly recalls their delights, from the scenery outside to the often primitive conditions inside and the people he encounters along the way. He also tells many engaging tales about the history of the lines and what makes each so distinctive. Sometimes alone, on other occasions with his wife Jenny or his mate Russell, he conveys the unique experience and sheer pleasure of rail travel in every corner of New Zealand, from the 1950s to the present day.

Back Cover Flap

Graham Hutchins has been a train enthusiast all his life and has written several popular books on the subject, including *Great New Zealand Railway Journeys* and *Last Train to Paradise.* From his home base in the Waikato and King Country, he has travelled extensively on trains throughout New Zealand, Australia, the United States and elsewhere. He has also written on a range of other subjects, including rugby, cricket and popular music: his book about the Beatles' tour of New Zealand, *Eight Days a Week,* is available as an ebook. Married with two daughters and two grandsons, Graham is a full-time writer living in Hamilton.

Back Cover Material

'Some people take to the bottle, others go shopping. I jump on a train, if I can find one, and wait for the swish and sway to take me away. Away from the down times. For me the diversion comes as much from the rhythm as the passing landscapes from the train window.'

Graham Hutchins remembers the incredibly varied journeys he has taken by train throughout New Zealand. They have given him a lifetime of pleasure.

Night trains and The Northerner
The Midland Line: Christchurch to the West Coast
The Gisborne Railcar
The Central Otago Line: Alexandra to Dunedin
The Picton-Christchurch Railcar
The Silver Star: Auckland to Wellington
Greymouth to Rewanui and back

By mixed train on the Stratford to Okahukura Line
Hamilton to Mount Maunganui

The Silver Fern Railcar on the Main Trunk Line
The Endeavour: Wellington to Napier
The Southerner: Christchurch to Invercargill
The Northern Explorer

Lightning Source UK Ltd.
Milton Keynes UK
UKOW07f1807230315

248363UK00004B/136/P